'"Mr Naipaul is an 'East' Indian Trinidadian with an exquisite mastery of the English language which should put to shame his British contemporaries." Evelyn Waugh's welcome for *The Middle Passage* in 1962 was generous and perceptive and true. V. S. Naipaul had indeed been a wondrous arrival on the English literary scene, as his dazzling early novels had already demonstrated. Since then he has established himself as one of the finest writers of his age, perhaps the greatest living British writer; a worthy successor to Waugh as supreme novelist and master of limpid prose.'

Independent, August 2001

The Middle Passage

V. S. NAIPAUL was born in Trinidad in 1932. He went to England on a scholarship in 1950. After four years at University College, Oxford, he began to write, and since then has followed no other profession. He has published more than twenty books of fiction and non-fiction, including *Half a Life*, *A House for Mr Biswas*, *A Bend in the River* and most recently *The Masque of Africa*, and a collection of correspondence, *Letters Between a Father and Son*. In 2001 he was awarded the Nobel Prize in Literature.

ALSO BY V. S. NAIPAUL

FICTION

The Mystic Masseur
The Suffrage of Elvira
Miguel Street
A House for Mr Biswas
Mr Stone and the Knights Companion
The Mimic Men
A Flag on the Island
Guerrillas
A Bend in the River
The Enigma of Arrival
A Way in the World
Half a Life
Magic Seeds
In a Free State

NON-FICTION

An Area of Darkness
The Loss of El Dorado
The Overcrowded Barracoon
India: A Wounded Civilization
The Return of Eva Perón
Among the Believers: An Islamic Journey
Finding the Centre
A Turn in the South
India: A Million Mutinies Now
Beyond Belief
Letters Between a Father and Son
The Writer and the World: Essays
Literary Occasions
A Writer's People: Ways of Looking and Feeling
The Masque of Africa

V. S. NAIPAUL

The Middle Passage

Impressions of five colonial societies

PICADOR

First published 1962 by André Deutsch

First published by Picador 1996

First published in paperback in a corrected edition 2001 by Picador

This edition published 2011 by Picador
an imprint of Pan Macmillan, a division of Macmillan Publishers Limited
Pan Macmillan, 20 New Wharf Road, London N1 9RR
Basingstoke and Oxford
Associated companies throughout the world
www.panmacmillan.com

ISBN 978-0-330-52295-3

A CIP catalogue record for this book is available from
the British Library.

Typset by Intype London Ltd
Printed by in the UK by CPI Mackays, Chatham ME5 8TD

Preface

IN 1950, just before my eighteenth birthday, I left Trinidad, where I had been born, to go to England. It was my hope to make myself a writer in England. It was a long shot, but miraculously (in my own eyes) it happened. My first book was published in 1957. Three years later there came an unexpected invitation from the government of Trinidad to revisit the island at their expense, to refresh myself with the local view. There had been a little political turbulence in Trinidad. It was soon to become independent, under the Prime-ministership of Eric Williams.

Eric Williams, an academic, had become a name four years before, for the political-racial speeches he made at Woodford Square in central Port of Spain. Woodford Square was named after the first British governor of the island. He had been made governor when he was very young, in his twenties, and he was a reformer. He put an end to torture in the Port of Spain jail – until then a planter simply paid for his slaves to be flogged or maltreated in certain prescribed ways by the jailer (a Frenchman called Porto Rico or Bourrique) – and Woodford, to mark the change, had thick bronze letters (in the elegant Georgian style) manufactured in England, brought out to Trinidad, and placed over the entrance of the jail: *Pro Rege et Lege*, 'for King and Law'.

There was no link in people's minds between Woodford the reformer and Eric Williams the emancipator. When I went looking one day for the Georgian lettering above the main gate of the jail I could find nothing. Woodford's celebration of King and Law had been taken down because it was part of the colonial past. I hadn't been destroyed; it was hidden away somewhere, but no one knew precisely where.

In 1960 Eric Williams was the supreme ruler of the little island. It was he who would have been behind the invitation to me to return to Trinidad for a 'refresher'. The local nationalism Williams promoted was still at its romantic stage; it wished to stretch out to all elements of the multi-racial island. But in fact the idea of my refresher had been put to Eric Williams by C. L. R. James, widely known as a black Trotskyite, and less well known as a man of culture. I gathered, when I met James, that he had been following the monthly book reviews I did for the *New Statesman*. Williams wouldn't have known or cared about that.

In Trinidad now, on my refresher, I was invited to lunch by Eric Williams. This was an immense courtesy. Eric Williams was almost divine in the eyes of his admirers. He had published his doctoral thesis, *Capitalism and Slavery*, and this book, or the fact of its publication in the great United States, added to his myth; it was on the bookshelves of most educated people; even my father had bought a copy. It wasn't an easy book to read; and it was hard to imagine local people turning to it for pleasure. But word had got around that Eric Williams had downplayed the role of the abolitionists in the abolition of slavery; his idea was that slavery had been abolished because it had ceased to pay.

It was on topics like this that he lectured the Port of Spain crowd in Woodford Square, not shying away from difficulty, and so it came about that he was thought by his local admirers to be the second most int̶ ̶l̶igent or educated man in the world. He had power; he was ̶ ̶ ̶ ̶ly admired. Yet he lived simply. He was looked after by ̶ ̶ ̶black women; he felt safe with them; it was like an exten-
̶ ̶ ̶ life.

̶ ̶ ̶exercised and plump, with dark glasses. The
̶ ̶ ̶nd local, rice, fried fish, and fried plantains.
̶ ̶ ̶olonial regimes in the Caribbean area,
It was only later that I marvelled at

the way we had been educated in Trinidad, knowing more about the larger metropolitan world, and almost nothing of what lay around us.

It was during this lunch that Eric Williams put to me the idea of travelling in the region and doing a book about it. The travel would be paid for by the Trinidad government and I would be given a monthly stipend. It was all on a modest scale, nothing to frighten me (I would not be required to give accounts), and I was dazzled by the idea of the travel, with expenses paid.

So, in the most frivolous way, I stumbled into the idea of the non-fiction book, the travel book. I had hardly thought about this as a form, and I thought at the lunch that the travel Eric Williams was asking me to do would be like a version of the various two-week jaunts I had done on the continent of Europe: new roads and streets, new cafes and restaurants, new newspapers, new cigarettes: pure pleasure. Everything, I thought, would hit me in the face, and I would be like a surveyor among many treasures.

I decided to begin my Caribbean travel after Christmas and I decided to go to British Guiana first of all. I did so because at about this time I had met people who had been to British Guiana and were full of stories of the hospitality of the people.

The people were hospitable. The only trouble for me as a writer, with the heavy duty laid on him by Eric Williams, was that I couldn't see how to make a large narrative of this round of hospitality. These events made for bits and pieces of a journal. It seemed that to make a large story I might always be having to say, 'And then,' and then in the next paragraph saying it again. So very quickly I understood that to write this kind of book one had to be organized as a traveller. At its simplest, one had to make arrangements at the other end and – to make the bigger political or historical or social point – one had to travel as though travelling itself was a form of writing, one discovery leading to another. All the pleasant idle periods I had known so far in British Guiana I had to abandon as material – though those periods might in truth be thought of as part of the pleasure of travel.

The reader of the pages that follow will see that the structure of

the book I wrote was quite different from what I had imagined. I had
to make a larger narrative of the material. So I wrote first of all of the
journey out from England by steamship – and this enabled me to
make points about the migration from the Caribbean to England. I
had not intended to write about that difficult business at all. I found a
second large narrative in my own life in Trinidad; and I found a third
narrative in the politics of Cheddi and Janet Jagan in British Guiana:
the colonial background, the Marxist or Communist overlay, the
resulting mess. I could do no more in the way of large narrative after
that; the reader will see that after that the book becomes broken and
bitty at this stage.

There was nothing I could do about that. I had not yet mastered,
for the purposes of writing, the art of travel, the art which seems
effortlessly to lift people and events from life to the printed page.
I hadn't yet discovered that this kind of travel, however natural it
might appear, was in fact artificial; and the reader will understand why
during the writing of this book the art of fiction seemed to me much
more natural and rewarding.

With all its flaws, however, the book is suffused with the writer's
delight in travel, and this delight is responsible for such virtues as the
book has: the pace, the detail, the love of landscape, the people, the
comedy. Fifty years after the writing some of the shipboard dialogue
is still with me. And the still fresh memory of certain passages of
landscape is like a blessing, bringing back youth itself: the openness
of the savannah country of the Rupununi in Guyana, the cool streams
of the Highlands with neatly cracked boulders (displaced by giants,
as it seemed) that caused the mind (perhaps ignorantly) to play with
geological ages.

The book is also full of jokes, a young man's jokes. They lighten
the darker material that Eric Williams spoke to me about at lunch.
Perhaps the comedy was too unsuited for the book Eric Williams had
in mind. Perhaps Eric Williams, misunderstanding the nature of my
work, as much as I misunderstood the travel form (so that here as
elsewhere it might seem we met in a kind of mutual misunderstand-

ing), perhaps Eric Williams felt let down by the writer to whom he had extended his patronage. His government scrupulously paid the expenses he had undertaken to pay. But he sent me no word about the book. At about this time he also quarrelled with his former champion, C. L. R. James, and eventually put the old man under house arrest. Whatever the personal conflicts, the reason for his mood of rejection might be that he, Williams, out of the very fullness of his power, and his clear view over time of its limits, had become bored.

Contents

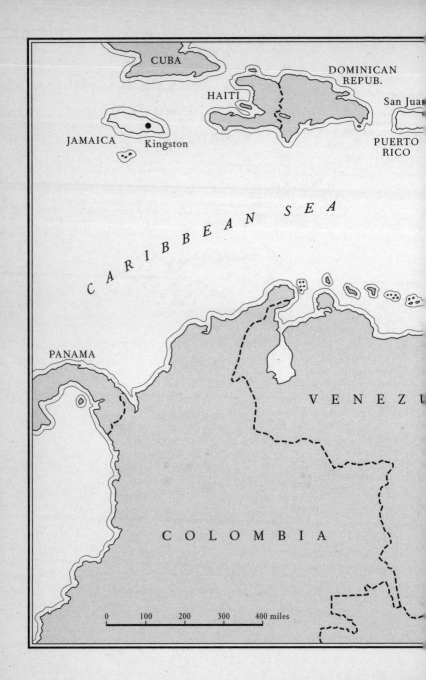

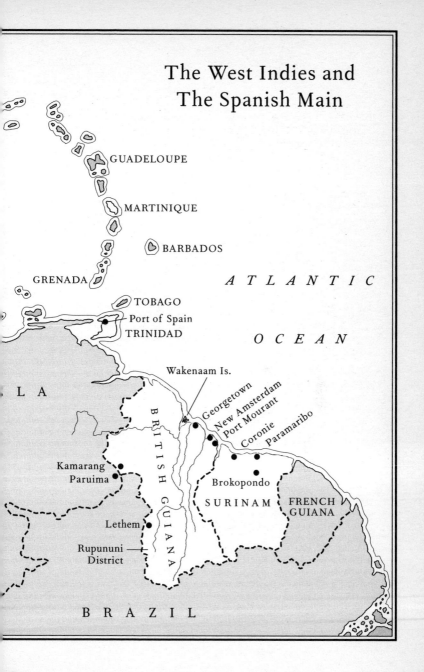

The West Indies and The Spanish Main

GUADELOUPE

MARTINIQUE

BARBADOS

GRENADA

ATLANTIC

TOBAGO

Port of Spain
TRINIDAD

OCEAN

Wakenaam Is.

Georgetown
New Amsterdam
Port Mourant
Coronie
Paramaribo

BRITISH GUIANA

Kamarang
Paruima

Brokopondo

SURINAM

FRENCH GUIANA

Lethem

Rupununi
District

BRAZIL

LA

Foreword to the 2001 Edition

In September 1960 I went back to Trinidad on a three-month scholarship granted by the government of Trinidad and Tobago. While I was in Trinidad the Premier, Dr Eric Williams, suggested that I should write a non-fiction book about the Caribbean. I hesitated. The novelist works towards conclusions of which he is often unaware; and it is better that he should. However, I decided to take the risk. The Trinidad Government paid for the travel.

They were valued only for the wealth which they yielded, and society there has never assumed any particularly noble aspect. There has been splendour and luxurious living, and there have been crimes and horrors, and revolts and massacres. There has been romance, but it has been the romance of pirates and outlaws. The natural graces of life do not show themselves under such conditions. There has been no saint in the West Indies since Las Casas, no hero unless philonegro enthusiasm can make one out of Toussaint. There are no people there in the true sense of the word, with a character and purpose of their own.

James Anthony Froude: *The English in the West Indies* (1887)

1. MIDDLE PASSAGE

In the carriage with me were several gentlemen; officers going out to join their regiments; planters who had been home on business; young sportsmen with rifles and cartridge cases who were hoping to shoot alligators, &c., all bound like myself for the West Indian mail steamer. The elders talked of sugar and of bounties, and of the financial ruin of the islands.

James Anthony Froude: *The English in the West Indies* (1887)

THERE WAS SUCH a crowd of immigrant-type West Indians on the boat-train platform at Waterloo that I was glad I was travelling first class to the West Indies. It wasn't an expensive first class. Ninety-four pounds, which might have bought cabin-class accommodation on one of the ships of the French Line, had got me a cabin to myself on the Spanish immigrant ship *Francisco Bobadilla*.

Most of the people on the platform and many of those in the train were not travelling down to Southampton. But the compartment I got into remained crowded. One man with a Nat King Cole hairstyle was dandling a fat bonneted baby that was gift-wrapped in ribbons and frills, with a rubber nipple stuck like a gag and a final flourish in its drooping, dripping mouth. Two ladies with felt hats and pink stockings sat slumped against the window. They wore gauze-like dresses over satin petticoats of a fiery pink. The powder on their faces had dissolved in patches, and they crumpled tiny embroidered handkerchiefs in large shining hands. They looked constrained and unhappy. There were baskets with food and baby-supplies on the rack and on the floor.

The man with the baby was talking to the man opposite him of the hardships of life in London.

'Is like that Stork on television,' he said. 'Three out of five can't tell the difference from butter. Three out of five don't care for you.'

He spoke in a slow, negligent way. The slumped women stared out of the window and said nothing. The baby, fat-cheeked, big-eyed, dribbled. London rolled away on either side of the railway canyon: the grimy backs of houses, the red tops of buses, the bright new advertisements, the signs on small shops, the men in white overalls on ladders: pictures that already felt like memories: the promised land from which we were already separated: the train just another of the morning noises.

'Eh! I tell you about the foreman?' He spoke easily; the train was not England. 'One day he say, "Blackie, come here a minute." I watch at him, and I say, "Good. I coming." I went up and hit him *baps!* Clean through a glass window.' He didn't gesticulate. He was dandling the baby on his knee.

In the baby's basket one saw the things of England, a few minutes ago commonplace, now the marks and souvenirs of the traveller: the bottle of Lucozade, the plastic baby bottle (in the West Indies it would have been a small rum bottle), the tin of baby powder.

'*Baps!* Clean through the glass window.'

The ticket collector, tall and elderly, slid the compartment door open. On this train he was a foreigner, but his manner was neutral; he might have been on the Brighton train.

'T'ank God, I didn't have the monkey-wrench in my hand. I wouldn't be sitting down in this train holding this baby on my lap today.'

The ticket collector examined and clipped, and slid the door shut.

From the next compartment a very tall and ill-made Negro stepped out into the corridor. The disproportionate length of his thighs was revealed by his thin baggy trousers. His shoulders were broad and so unnaturally square that they seemed hunched and gave him an appearance of fragility. His light grey jacket was as long and loose as a short topcoat; his yellow shirt was dirty and the frayed collar undone; his tie was slack and askew. He went to the window, opened the ventilation gap, pushed his face through, turned slightly to his left, and spat. His face was grotesque. It seemed to have been smashed in from one cheek. One eye had narrowed; the thick lips had bunched into a circular swollen protuberance; the enormous nose was twisted. When, slowly, he opened his mouth to spit, his face became even more distorted. He spat in slow, intermittent dribbles; and when he worked his face back in, his eyes caught mine.

I felt I had attracted his malevolence. And thereafter I couldn't avoid this Negro with the ruined face. I went to the lavatory. Our eyes met, twice. I went looking for a buffet car. I saw him. There was no buffet car. On the way back I saw him. Next to him sat a much smaller Negro, in a grey coat as well, with big blank eyes as lack-lustre as boiled eggs, long arms and long hands, clumsily clenched, resting on his knees. His trousers were too short and rose tightly inches above his socks, so that he looked like a boy who had outgrown his clothes. His mouth was open. In the same compartment there was another Negro with the physique of a wrestler, and two young white men, one fat, one thin, both bald, in new sports jackets and sharply-creased flannels.

In my own compartment the baby was being fed. Its nose ran; its mouth leaked; it slurped and squelched and was frequently winded.

' "So you want rent?" ' the baby-feeder was saying. ' "I tell you I ain't paying any more than what I was paying before." He say, "Blackie, I coming up to get my rent or to get you out of that room." I watch at him and I say, "Good. Come up, *bakra*." He come up. I give him one kick *bam*! He roll down the steps *bup-bup-bup*.

'I pass round there last week. He gave up a big sign in green paint. Please No Coloured. In green paint. I tell you, man, is like Stork.'

At Southampton there was a further thinning out of passengers. The man with the Nat King Cole hairstyle was only seeing off his wife and baby; he himself was remaining behind to face aggressive landlords and foremen and Please No Coloured signs.

We were directed to one of the ocean terminal's less luxurious waiting rooms, next to the railway sheds, in the gloomy recesses of which we could see the immigrants who had arrived that morning on the *Francisco Bobadilla*: a thick, multi-coloured mass herded behind wooden rails, and as silent as though they were behind glass. We stood at the doors and watched. No one stepped out of the travellers' waiting room into the immigrants' shed. There was interest, disapproval, pity and mockery in the gazes, the old hands sizing up the clothes of the new arrivals, clothes like those in which they had themselves landed some time before: thin white flannel trousers, sky-blue tropical suits, jackets with wide shoulders and long skirts, and those broad-brimmed felt hats, unknown in the West Indies yet *de rigueur* for the West Indian immigrant to Britain. Cheap cardboard suitcases were marked with complete addresses, all ending with ENGLAND in large letters. They stood motionless in the gloom; about them bustled dark-coated porters and railway officials; and there was silence.

The Negro with the ruined face stood, tall and totem-like, in the centre of the waiting room. Beside him was the stunted Negro with the short trousers, long arms and big eyes; from time to time he swivelled his head, his eyes never changing expression, his mouth open and collapsed, his large clumsy hands loosely clenched. The fat Englishman gave a cigarette to the man with the ruined face and lit it for him. There was much solicitude in this gesture, and I wondered about their relationship.

As yet we were subdued, as silent as the immigrants outside. But whispered rumours were beginning to circulate. Seven hundred, a thousand, twelve hundred immigrants had come on the *Francisco Bobadilla*. Two trains were taking them to London, from where they would make for those destinations written so proudly in those illiterate hands on their suitcases.

'You wouldn't want to travel with all them West Indians,' the man at the travel agency had said. 'Even the dockers are sick when they come off those ships. And it takes a lot to make a British docker sick.'

The *Francisco Bobadilla* was indeed in an appalling condition. The crew had not had time to clean up after the seven hundred immigrants. Paintwork was tarnished, metal rusting. In my first-class cabin, so cramped that I could open my suitcase only on my bunk, there was dust and fluff everywhere. The water carafe was hazy with dirt; the hot water didn't run; the lights didn't work. I rang for the steward; and many minutes later such an old, fatigued man appeared that I regretted disturbing him. I mentioned only the lights and the dust. He argued; I insisted; I mentioned the hot water.

'*Luego, luego,*' he said.

It was a more urgent word than *mañana*. When, some time later, I passed his cubby-hole, I saw him dozing on his chair.

But there was an advantage. On this outward journey there were few passengers, and most of those who lined the deck rails as we moved down the Solent were travelling tourist. When the dinner gong went they disappeared to their canteen below decks. There were only nine first-class passengers, and we sat at three tables in one corner of the large shabby dining room.

As he sat down, an elderly coloured man said, just to open the conversation, 'A lot of these black fellers in Tobago are damn intelligent, you know.'

We were in the West Indies. Black had a precise meaning; I was among people who had a nice eye for shades of black. And the elderly coloured man – a man, that is, of mixed European and African descent, with features and skin-colour closer to the European – was safe. There were no black men or women at the table. The coloured man's wife was, we were told, Spanish. Correia was a Portuguese from British Guiana. And Philip, who came from Trinidad, where he had 'a little business', could have been white or Portuguese or coloured or Jewish.

'A lot of those black fellers in B.G. ain't no fools either,' Correia said.

The intelligence of black fellers in Trinidad and Jamaica and Barbados was assessed; and then they started groping for common acquaintances. It turned out that Correia and Philip had some, in a football team that had toured the West Indies in the 1920s.

Correia was a small, bald man. He wore spectacles, had a sharp hooked nose and had lost his teeth. But he was once a goalkeeper. He had a booming voice.

'You remember Skippy?' he asked.

'I can't remember when last I see Skippy,' Philip said.

'Well, you not going to see him again. Son of a bitch catch a pleurisy and dead. Frankie and Bertie and Roy Williams. All of them dead like hell.'

The waiter, middle-aged and mournful, couldn't speak English.

'But look at this, nuh,' Correia boomed. 'And I got to spend fo'teen days on this ship. Look here, man, look here. I want some tomatoes. You got that? Tomatoes. Having a lil trouble with the stomach,' he explained to us. 'Tomatoes. You got that? Me. Wantee. Tomatee. Me wantee tomatee. I don't know where they pick up these people who can't speak English.'

The Spanish lady couldn't talk Spanish; Correia himself couldn't talk Portuguese. West Indians are English-speaking and when confronted with the foreigner display the language arrogance of all English-speaking people.

A young couple from Northern Ireland and an English librarian sat at the next table. The librarian was distressed. She had been under the impression that the *Francisco Bobadilla* was a cruise ship and had booked for the round trip. She had just learned that we were going to the West Indies to pick up another seven hundred immigrants.

When I went down I saw the old steward coming out of my cabin with brush and pan. He smiled and limped away. But the floor was still dusty; the balls of fluff were still under my bunk; the carafe was still dirty; the hot water didn't run. I couldn't complain, though: the lights were now working.

Early next morning I was awakened by Correia. He had the cabin across the corridor from mine. He came into my cabin naked except for a pair of pants. He was without his spectacles; his little face was haggard; his beard had begun to sprout; his thin hair was disarrayed; and he was hugging himself.

'Hi there, man. How you sleep? Lemme see a cigarette, nuh.' He took one of mine and lit it. 'You look as if you sleep well, you know. I had a hell of a night, boy. Didn't want to wake you up earlier. Thought you would be sleeping. But I can't open my suitcase. The one with pyjamas and soap and razor and Eno's and every blasted thing in. You want to try it?'

The canvas suitcase was bulging and taut; it was a wonder that Correia had managed to close it.

'I try those blasted keys all how,' he said, sitting on his bunk, while I tried.

Eventually we opened it, Correia jumping on the suitcase, I turning the key.

'Thanks, thanks, man. I hope I ain't catch a cold, boy. You ain't have a lil Eno's or Andrews with you? Stomach giving me hell, boy. Went three times already this morning. Not one blasted thing. Is this damn *mañana* food. First and last Spanish ship you catch *me* on.

And all that morning he padded up and down outside the lavatories, smoking, head bowed as if in meditation, tie slackened, spectacles half-way down his nose, hands in pockets. Whenever I went down he gave me a progress report.

'It coming, it coming. I feel it coming.'

By lunchtime, to add to his troubles, he was sea-sick.

I reported this to the table.

'He wake me up at five this morning asking for Eno's,' Philip said.

The coloured man, Mr Mackay, said, 'We have two madmen with us this trip. Black fellers. I was talking to their keepers this morning. White fellers. The British Government paying for them going out and coming back.'

'I see them walking up and down,' Philip said. 'Is a funny thing. But you could always tell people who make it their business to keep other people lock up. They have this walk. You ever notice?'

'You see how these black fellers going to England and stinking up the country,' Mr Mackay said. 'I mean, if a black feller want to get mad, he could stay home and get mad there.'

They spoke of the telephone strike in Trinidad, which had been going on for some time. Mr Mackay said that the strike was a racial one. He spoke of this with feeling. Quite suddenly he was identifying himself with the black fellers. He was an old man; he had never risen to the top; superiors had always been imported from England.

'Is these Potogees who cause the trouble, you know,' he said. 'They have their hands in the stinking salt-fish barrel and they are still the first to talk of nigger this and coolie that.'

'I believe the ship has a list,' Philip said. 'Go up on the sun deck and see.'

'I must say I don't care for the look of those lifeboats. If anything happens we drowning like hell. As soon as we get to the Azores I am going to try to insure Mrs Mackay and myself against accident. I suppose you could do that sort of thing in the Azores?'

'But you don't know the language, Daddy,' Mrs Mackay said.

'Why, what they talk there? A sort of Potogee *patois*?'

'Something like that,' Philip said. 'But I could help you with it.'

'What, you know Potogee?'

'We used to speak it at home,' Philip said.

So Philip was Portuguese.

Mr Mackay fell silent. He stared at his plateful of Spanish food and looked unwell.

Philip said briskly. 'This Trinidad coming like a little America. All these strikes. All these hold-ups. You hear about that man the police catch with eighty-three thousand dollars in notes stuff up in a chest-of-drawers?'

Mr Mackay spoke at length about getting insured at the Azores. And for the rest of the journey he was silent about Portuguese and others and spoke only of black fellers. It was a cramping of his style; but in the West Indies, as in the upper reaches of society, you must be absolutely sure of your company before you speak: you never know who is what or, more important, who is related to what.

It was warm. The tourist-class passengers, who had for a day or two been battened down, it seemed, on the lower decks, emerged singly and in pairs and sunned themselves. The two lunatics came out with their keepers. The young Baptist missionary from the North of England, off to the West Indies on his first posting and travelling tourist out of a sense of duty, read large theological works and made notes. A Negro woman of about eighty, wearing sensationally old clothes, wandered about with cheerful inquisitiveness. She had left St Kitts to look for work in England; the rumour went round that the British Government was paying for her passage back.

Because there were so few passengers the class divisions on the ship were ignored. An Indian butcher from British Guiana trotted round the first-class deck morning and afternoon. A tall handsome Negro, who spoke to no one, walked around the deck as well, for hours at a time, smoking a tiny pipe and holding a paperback called *The Ten Commandments*, the book of the film. This man, according to Mr Mackay, had had some mental trouble in England and was being sent back, at his own request, at the expense of the British Government.

We all rooted among the tourist-class passengers and brought back stories.

Miss Tull, the librarian, came back distressed. She had met a woman who had left England because she couldn't get a room for her baby and herself. 'The landlord just threw them out when the baby came,' Miss Tull said, 'and put up a big sign in green paint. No Coloured Please. Do you mean that in the whole of Britain they couldn't find room for one woman and her baby?'

'They've found room for quite a lot,' Mr Mackay said.

'I can't understand it. You West Indians don't seem to care at all.'

'All this talk about tolerance is all right,' Mr Mackay said. 'But a lot of you English people forget that there is a type of black man – like the Jamaican – who is an animal.'

'But this woman isn't Jamaican,' Miss Tull said, conceding the point.

'A lot of these black fellers provoke the English people,' Mr Mackay said, putting an end to the discussion. Like all good West Indians, he was unwilling to hear anything against England.

My own encounter had been with a fat brown-skinned Grenadian of thirty-three. He said he had ten children in Grenada, in various parishes and by various women. He had gone to England to get away from them all, but then had begun to feel that he should go back and face his responsibilities. He thought he might even get married. He hadn't yet decided who to, but it probably would be the mother of his last child. He loved this child; he didn't care for the others. I asked why, then, he had had so many. Didn't they have contraceptives in Grenada? He said with some indignation that he was a Roman Catholic; and for the rest of the journey never spoke to me.

From our ventures among the tourist class we came back with stories, and sometimes with captives. Correia's captive was an Indian boy called Kripal Singh from British Guiana, who so endeared himself to the company that he was invited to tea.

'So handsome,' Mrs Mackay said over and over. 'So fair.'

'This boy,' Correia said, 'comes from one of the best families in B.G. You never hear of them? Biggest people in the ground provision business. Singh Brothers, man. Singh, Singh, and Singh.'

Kripal Singh looked correctly modest, his manner suggesting that what Correia said was true but that he didn't want to boast. He was tall and slender; his features were fine, his mouth as delicate as a girl's. He smoked with nervous elegance.

'Tell me about your family, Kripal,' Correia said.

Kripal, bowing slightly, offered cigarettes. He was a little drunk. So was Correia.

'They don't *grow* the ground provisions, you know,' Correia said, taking one of Kripal's cigarettes. 'They does only buy and sell. Tell them, Kripal.'

'So fair,' Mrs Mackay said.

For the rest of the voyage Kripal remained attached to the first class, only sleeping with the tourists and eating with them. He could find no suitable drinking companions among them; and he shared a cabin with the British Guianese butcher, whom he detested.

'The man s-say he went to England for holiday,' Kripal said, recalled to the subject by the sight of the butcher running around the deck. 'And he s-spend all s-seven weeks drawing dole.'

Kripal himself had gone to England to study. This studying in England is one of the strange activities of West Indian youth, of well-to-do Indians in particular. It can last until early middle age. Kripal had studied deeply in England and the Continent until his father, alarmed at the expense, had summoned him home to the business and marriage. By travelling tourist Kripal was having his last subsidized fling; his studies were almost over.

One morning, not long after we had left the Azores, I found Correia in a sparkling mood.

'How, how, man? You is a son of a bitch, you know. You never tell me you was a educated man. Let we go and have a drink, nuh.'

Correia had been lucky in me. He became sea-sick: I had

Marzine pills. He had headaches: I had Disprin tablets. He developed a corn: I had Dr Scholl's cornplasters. When he wanted to drink and couldn't find Kripal Singh, he came to me. Drinking with him had its dangers. He drank rapidly and became drunk in a matter of minutes. And he seldom had money on him: he preferred to settle later.

'You know,' he said at the bar. 'I had a damn good wash-out this morning. First try.' This explained his mood. 'You are a damn good writer, boy. Yes, man. I watch you at the post office in the Azores. Writing off those cards so damn fast I couldn't even read what you was writing.'

Philip joined us. He had been reading the *Kama Kalpa* in his cabin. I thought he had been reading the wrong book, but he said, 'This Indian philosophy is a great thing.'

'It *is* a great thing,' Correia said, drunk already. 'What is the first thing you going to do when you get back home, Philip?'

'I think I have to see about insuring the car, first of all.'

'I'm going to have a damn good purge-out with some Epsom Salts, boy.'

Both Correia and Philip had married daughters in England, Correia's daughter had been married not long before; Philip had just attended his daughter's wedding.

'You know what it makes a father feel to lose his daughter, Naipaul?' Correia asked. 'You know how he does feel when she cry out at the train, "Don't go, Pa"? You don't know, Naipaul. *"Don't go, Pa. Don't leave me."* His one and only daughter.' He beat his feet on the rung of his stool and burst into tears. 'He don't know, Philip.'

'No, old man. He don't know.'

'Where your daughter living, Philip? Mine living in a kiss-me-arse place called Dudley.'

Philip didn't answer. He left the bar and came back some moments later with an album stamped on the white leather cover: The Wedding of Our Daughter. Philip was anxious about his daughter and now, looking through the album, recognizing the working-class faces, clothes and backgrounds, I understood why. What had been desirable in the West Indies appeared differently in England.

Everyone seemed to be thinking about his children that day. The Mackays had left their son in England. Mr Mackay had made his last voyage; he would never see his son again.

'He's picking up all sorts of English habits,' Mrs Mackay said with pride. 'Everything for him is a "flipping" this and a "flipping" that. I just can't keep up with his English slang and English accent.'

Mr Mackay smiled, remembering.

It is possible for an escaped English convict to be welcomed by the white community in Trinidad and set up in business. And the West Indian, knowing only the values of money and race, is lost as soon as he steps out of his own society into one with more complex criteria.

The captain, an aristocrat in visage and bearing, invited no passenger to his table. He dined with his senior officers. I didn't know whether this was Spanish naval etiquette or whether it was the etiquette of the immigrant ship. I think it was the latter. From the wireless officer and the purser, the only officers who permitted us to approach them, we learned that just before loading up with the West Indian immigrants we had seen at Southampton, the ship had taken several hundred Moroccan pilgrims to Mecca. Some of these pilgrims had died on the way and had to be thrown overboard; afterwards the ship had to be deloused.

As England receded, people prepared more actively for the West Indies. They formed colour groups, race groups, territory groups, money groups. The West Indies being what they are, no group was fixed; one man could belong to all. A small group of Indians, dropping the competitive talk of London and Paris and Dublin and brilliant children studying in England, Canada and America, discussed the political situation in Trinidad. They spoke of Negro racism, and on the subject of miscegenation repeatedly wound themselves up to hysteria. The British Guianese Indians, among them a man who spent much of the voyage playing Monopoly and reading the first volume of Radhakrishnan's *Indian Philosophy*, were less impassioned. Believing that racial coexistence, if not cooperation, is of urgent importance to the West Indies, I was disturbed by these Indian views and wanted to explore them further. But I had to drop out of the group because of the unpleasantness with Mr Hassan.

Mr Hassan had lent me a copy of *Time* magazine. I had lent it to Philip (in exchange for his *Kama Kalpa*), and when on the following day Mr Hassan asked for his magazine, it couldn't be found. Thereafter, four, five, six times a day, Mr Hassan asked for his magazine. He waited for me on deck. He waited for me before and after the film show. He waited for me outside the dining room. He waited for me in the bar. I bought him drink after drink. But he never relented. I promised to buy him a copy in Trinidad. But he wanted his particular copy of *Time*. I told him it was lost. That didn't matter. He wanted his *Time*. After three days of this persecution I burrowed deep down into the tourist class and, miraculously, found someone who had a copy of the magazine. It was then, needless to say, that Mr Hassan's own copy turned up. Mr Hassan's main subject of conversation had been his wealth and his persecution, at the hands of government departments, customs officials, shipping companies, his wife's family, his children's teachers. From the depths of my heart I wished his persecutors greater strength and a long life.

And one day there was very nearly a racial incident in the bar. It seemed that a group of tourist-class passengers, made restless by the long journey and the approach of their various native lands, and provoked by the comparative emptiness of the first-class bar, had decided to rush it. A group burst in that evening, singing. They came running in and bobbed up and down before the bar. They called loudly for drinks. The barman refused to serve them. The group, still bouncing abruptly stilled, their high spirits gone, stood silently in front of the bar for a few seconds. One man withdrew. The others followed him. They walked in a body down the deck, then back again. They stood in the doorway and muttered. At length one man left the group and, buttoning his jacket, walked up to the bar and said, 'Gimme a pack of cigarettes, please.' The barman handed over the cigarettes. The man looked at the cigarettes, surprised. For a second he hesitated. Then, with careless swinging steps, he strode out. The group, moral victory theirs, went running off to the tourist bar, singing loudly.

And poor Miss Tull became more and more worried about her return journey. No one could console her. Philip suggested that she should abandon her sunshine cruise at Trinidad and fly back to England.

'I'm not going to lie to you,' Mr Mackay said. 'When I saw that pack of orang-outangs getting off the ship at Southampton, I didn't feel good. It was a damn frightening thing to see. You can't blame some people for not wanting to call themselves West Indians.'

'Angus always tells people he's Brazilian,' Mrs Mackay said. 'He could pass for one too.' Angus was her son, who spoke English slang with an English accent.

* * *

We were near St Kitts. A drink, a sunset as flamboyant as one could have wished, the Caribbees pastel-grey outlines around us, the waters where the navies of Europe acquired their skills in the seventeenth and eighteenth centuries: it wasn't enough to take our minds off the horror that was nearly upon us. That evening we would take on our first load of emigrants. St Kitts, the mother colony of the British West Indies, 'the first and best earth' (according to an inhabitant of 1667) 'that ever was inhabited by Englishmen amongst the heathen cannibals in America', today an overpopulated island of sixty-eight square miles, producing a little sea-island cotton, having trouble to sell its sugar, and no longer growing the tobacco, the first

crop of the settlers, which Thomas Warner took back to England
in 1625 to prove the success of his enterprise. The romance of its
history – Warner and his Amerindian mistress, their son 'Indian'
Warner – is buried. There are reminders only of the brutality of that
history: the slaves shanghaied there, their descendants abandoned
when prosperity went, and now *their* descendants, their belongings
packed, their good-byes said, searching the sea for the black smoke-
stack of the *Francisco Bobadilla*, prepared for another middle
passage.

It was night when we anchored, far out at sea. We saw nothing
of St Kitts except the scattered lights of its capital. We looked
for tenders; several lights deceived us. Nothing moved, except the
headlamps of motor-cars.

'Eh!' Mr Mackay said. 'They have motor cars here too?'

Tourist class, first class, we were one now, lining the rail,
watching the lights of the toy capital where people took themselves
seriously enough to drive cars from one point to another.

Mr Mackay, joining us later in the bar, reported that one of the
lunatics had been taken off. A launch had taken him away with
his keeper; the keeper had returned alone. Presently the keeper
himself turned up in the bar. In spite of the gravity of his charge,
he had come prepared for the tropical climate, and we had
observed his degeneration from grey-flannelled, soft-soled official
into red-shirted, sandalled cruise passenger.

A commotion, and some shouts, told us that the emigrants had
arrived.

Part of the port deck had been roped off; the companion-way
had been lowered. Bright lights made the deck dazzle, bright lights
played on the black water. There they were, rocking in the water, in
three large rowing-boats. Men sat on the gunwales and with long
oars steadied the boats. Policemen had already come aboard. Tables
had been placed just in front of the companion-way, and there the
purser and his officials sat, consulting long typewritten sheets.
Below, the boats rocked. We could see only white shirts, black faces,

hats of many colours, parcels, suitcases, baskets. The men with the oars shouted occasionally, their voices dying quickly in the darkness. But from the passengers we heard no sound. Sometimes, for a second or two, a face was upturned, examining the white ship. We saw women and children, dressed as for church. They all looked a little limp; they had been dressed for some time. The lights played on them, as if for their inspection. Beyond there was darkness. We picked out suits, new broad-brimmed felt hats, ties whose knots had slipped, shining faces.

'They could at least have brought them out in launches,' Miss Tull said. 'At least in launches!'

The tourist class looked down, chattering, laughing whenever a rowing-boat struck the side of the ship or when an emigrant tried to get on the companion-way and was turned back.

Presently they started coming up. The companion-way quickly became packed, a line of people from ship to boat. They looked tired; their clothes were sweated, their faces blank and shining. With policemen on either side, they produced tickets and brand-new passports. Separated from them by ropes, we stood and watched. The blue-dungareed crew leaned over the rails, exclaiming at the beauty of black women and pointing; we had never seen them so animated.

The deck became crowded. Passengers recognized an emigrant here and there.

'What, you come back already?'

'I just went up on a lil holiday, man.'

'I think I would go up and try my luck. You see Ferdie or Wallace or any of them up there?'

But most of them were subdued. One or two tried to duck under the ropes before presenting their papers. The tourist class, with sudden authority, bullied them back. The deck was choked with plastic bags in plaid patterns, brown paper parcels, cardboard boxes tied with string. The crowd grew. We lost sight of the purser and his table. The crowd pressed against the rope. One man with a blue suit, a slipped tie and a hat was jammed against me. He pushed his frightened, red-eyed face close to mine. He said hoarsely, anxiously, 'Mister, this is the ship that going to England?' Sweat was running down his face; his shirt stuck to his chest. 'It all right? It does go straight?'

I broke away from the group behind the rope and walked round to the starboard deck, where it was still and dark and silent, and looked at the lights of the island.

'Well!' someone said loudly.

I turned to see a tourist. We had not spoken during the voyage.

'The holiday is over,' he said. 'The wild cows are coming on board.'

He spoke in earnest. And what was he, this tourist? A petty official perhaps, an elementary school teacher. *The wild cows are coming on board*. No attitude in the West Indies is new. Two hundred years before, when he would have been a slave, the tourist would have said the same. 'The creole slaves,' says a writer of 1805, 'looked upon the newly imported Africans with scorn, and sustained in their turn that of the mulattoes, whose complexions were browner; while all were kept at a distance from the intercourse of the whites.' On this ship only the Portuguese and the Indians were alien elements. Mr Mackay and his black fellers, the tourist and the wild cows; these relationships had been fixed centuries before.

The emigrants were running all over the ship. They peered in at the window of the bar, stood in the door-way. The ship was suddenly crowded. The first-class bar was the only place of refuge, and to it now came many of the tourists who had come with us from Southampton. No one objected. There were now only two classes: travellers and emigrants.

The barman vented his rage on two small emigrant children who had drifted into the bar, still in their fussy emigrant clothes. He lifted the counter flap, shooed the young emigrants to the door, and, blind to their charm, lifted them firmly and with an expression of distaste out on to the deck.

Sometimes for as much as three months at a time a slave ship would move from anchorage to anchorage on the West African coast, picking up its cargo. The *Francisco Bobadilla* would be only five days. It would go from St Kitts to Grenada to Trinidad to Barbados: one journey answering another: the climax and futility of the West Indian adventure. For nothing was created in the British West Indies, no civilization as in Spanish America, no great revolution as in Haiti or the American colonies. There were only plantations, prosperity, decline, neglect: the size of the islands called for nothing else.

What are the points in the history of an island like Jamaica? 'This isle,' we are told in 1597, in *A True Relation of the Voyage Undertaken by Sir Anthony Shirley*, 'is a marvellous fertil Isle, & is as a garden or store house for divers parts of the maine. We have not found in the Indies a more pleasant and holsome place.' From that, to Trollope in 1859: 'If we could, we would fain forget Jamaica altogether. But there it is; a spot on the earth not to be lost sight of or forgotten altogether, let us wish it ever so much.' From Trollope in 1859 to the Ras Tafarian of 1959, who rejects Jamaica entirely and wishes to return to Africa, to a heaven called Ethiopia: 'Jamaica was a nice island, but the land has been polluted by centuries of crime.'

When Columbus put his ideas to King John II of Portugal in 1483, King John, telling Columbus nothing, sent a ship out into the Atlantic. Within weeks of the discovery of the New World in 1492, Columbus's companion Pinzón, deserting, took the *Pinta* off on his own to look for gold in an unknown sea. And there, in the treachery of the Portuguese king, in Pinzón's courage, treachery and greed, are all the elements of the European adventure in this part of the New World.

There is a myth, derived from the Southern states of America, of the gracious culture of the slave society. In the West Indian islands slavery and the latifundia created only grossness, men who ate 'like cormorants' and drank 'like porpoises'; a society without standards, without noble aspirations, nourished by greed and cruelty: a society of whose illiteracy metropolitan administrators continued to complain right until the middle of the last century; illiteracy which encouraged Governor Vaughan of Jamaica to suggest the placing of a collection of books in the English language 'in the most conspicuous places where such of the gentry as are studious may always resort, since there is nothing more ridiculous than ignorance in a person of quality'; grossness to which traveller after traveller testifies and which made a seventeenth-century observer say of Barbados: 'This Iland is the Dunghill whareone England doth cast forth its rubidg: Rodgs and hors and such like peopel are those which are gennerally Broght heare. A rodge in England will hardly make a cheater heare; a Baud brought over puts one a demuor comportment, a whore if hansume makes a wife for sume rich planter.'*

How can the history of this West Indian futility be written? What tone shall the historian adopt? Shall he be as academic as Sir Alan Burns, protesting from time to time at some brutality, and setting West Indian brutality in the context of European brutality? Shall he, like Salvador de Madariaga, weigh one set of brutalities against another, and conclude that one has not been described in all its foulness and that this is unfair to Spain? Shall he, like the West Indian historians, who can only now begin to face their history, be icily detached and tell the story of the slave trade as if it were just another aspect of mercantilism? The history of the islands can never be satisfactorily told. Brutality is not the only difficulty. History is built around achievement and creation; and nothing was created in the West Indies.

* * *

* These quotations, and many others in this book, are taken from Sir Alan Burns's *History of the British West Indies.*

In the morning I was calmer. The emigrants had got out of their going-away clothes and were sitting in the sun in simpler, less constricting garments, so that the deck looked like a West Indian slum street on a Sunday. One or two of the women had even put on slacks; the cloth was new, not yet washed, and one could detect the suitcase folds.

I fell into conversation with a man who was wearing khaki trousers, blue shirt and unlaced white canvas shoes. He was very big, with thick hands and slow thick speech. He was a baker. In a good week he could make thirty dollars. This I thought to be a very good wage in the West Indies, and I wondered why he had given up his job to go to England.

'Look, eh,' he said. 'I ask God, you hear. I went down on my two knees and ask God. And I always do what God tell me. Don't mind the Jamaicans gone and stink up England. I bound to get through. Morning and evening I does go down on my two knees and consult God.' His eyes became smaller, fixed on the horizon, and he was slowly raising his enormous hands in what could have been a suppliant or a strangulatory gesture.

I tried to change the subject to baking.

He didn't listen. In biblical language he spoke of his religious experiences and his colloquies with God. Then, breaking off, he asked, 'You know Sloughbucks?'

'Slough, Bucks?'

'Is there I going. You think they have bakeries there? How much you think they would start me off at? Twelve pounds? Fifteen?'

'I don't know. You could bake good bread?'

'With the help of the Lord.'

He worried me. But many of the emigrants I spoke to had consulted God and He had advised them to throw up their jobs – no one I spoke to was unemployed – and go to Sloughbucks. In Sloughbucks wages were high. And once they made it clear that they were not Jamaicans, they would be treated with regard. Only

Jamaicans were beaten up in race riots, and deservedly, for they were uneducated and ungrateful and provoked the English people.*

The young Baptist missionary, with his collar on, worked hard that morning, explaining in what direction England play, where London was, and unscrambling the apocalyptic name of Sloughbucks. He drew innumerable diagrams of the London Underground, and advised one man against taking a taxi from Southampton to Sloughbucks.

From the St Kitts *Labour Spokesman* ('Sound Speech That Cannot Be Condemned' – Titus ii, 8), 14 September 1960:

> Considerable difficulties throughout the reaping of the 1960 sugar cane crop came to an end last Monday morning when the Basseterre Sugar Factory gave the final signal that the mills at the factory have ceased grinding operations . . .
>
> Declining interest on the part of some workers became evident at the early stage of crops as (a) there is the possibility of migrating to the U.K. and (b) the obvious difficulty to recruit young agricultural workers in the Sugar industry . . . Without being seriously affected by the number which left for England steady production results were maintained down to April when

* In her articles for the London *Evening Standard*, 'I Sail with the Immigrants', Anne Sharpley gives a Jamaican view:

' "These little dunce breadfruit niggers" (he meant the small islanders). "I *voted* for Federation, but since I come on this ship I seen what barefoot niggers them be. When us said no to Federation I so hurted I couldn't eat for a day.

' "But now them's so insulted me – all from these little islands, St Kitts, Montserrat, Antigua – them's so small that if you started running on them and develop speed you'd land up in the sea.

' "They're going to a dream in London, they don't know what they're going to, but when they ask them in London where them comes from, these yam and breadfruit little niggers, them's got to say Jamaica, 'cos nobody heard of dem islands." ' ('The Night the Knives Came Out', 26 October 1961).

at short notice managers were informed of the intention of workers to leave for the United Kingdom.

Larger was the outflow in May and some estates were evidently in trouble to reap the total crop.

The second year of the existence of the production Committee, establish [*sic*] by the Union and the Association, was somewhat disastrous as some managers disregarded the importance of the work of the Committee, and its full function therefore became fruitless. This however worked out to be detrimental to most of the estates as both managers and workers could not easily bridge some of the gaps in industrial relationships. It is on most of these estates that a substantial amount of cane remain [*sic*] unreaped last Monday . . .

Two hundred and twenty-three workers were recruited from Barbados . . .

OUR QUESTION BOX

Is it true: That the complexed Estate manager who was concerned only with his monthly salary is now trying to accuse the Union for the 600 tons of unreaped cane?

Encouraged by the example of the missionary, I went among the emigrants after lunch – they were fed at long tables, in relays: '*Son buena gente*, they are good folk,' a member of the crew said – to find out what had made them leave St Kitts, what they hoped to find in England. I had no official position, no clerical collar, and I attracted the attention of the emigrants' leader, a tall, high-bottomed brown-skinned young man.

'Don't tell him nothing,' he said, running up, some of his flock at his heels. 'Don't tell him nothing. What he want?'

He was an educated man. He travelled first. He spoke very quickly.

'What you want? Why you discouraging the poor people?'

He didn't give me a chance to speak.

'The poor people just come on board the ship and you discouraging them?'

'I wasn't doing nothing, and he came up and start asking me all sort of question. Why I was going to England and things like that.' This was from the God-inspired baker.

'Don't worry with him,' said the leader. 'He is a propagandist.'

This appeared to be a well-known word of abuse among the emigrants.

'What happen, man?'

'We pick up a propagandist.'

'A propagandist?'

'You come from Kenya, nuh?' the leader asked. 'I bet you you come from Kenya.'

'He call me a nigger,' a man said. (I had jotted down his details on the *Labour Spokesman* an emigrant had given me: $3.90 a day during the crop season, $2.82 during the slack season. His destination was Sloughbucks. He had not consulted God.)

'What is this? What is this?'

'A propagandist from Kenya called Boysie a nigger.'

'He call me a nigger,' Boysie said, his voice now touched with genuine hurt.

'Well, this ain't Kenya, you hear,' the leader said. 'I mad to get the boys to give you a ducking. The British Government send you out here as a propagandist, eh? Let him prove that he don't come from Kenya?'

I was rescued by the missionary.

'I know the type of provocator,' the leader said, addressing his flock. 'He don't care about the poor people. He don't care that a hurricane blow way the whole of Anguilla.'

I decided that the attitude of Mr Mackay and Philip and Correia and most of the tourist class was healthier. They had ignored the emigrants altogether, and were in the bar. I joined them.

'That Baptist boy keeping busy like hell,' Correia said. 'He must be really like the work.'

'He say he would like to go up England with them,' Philip said.

'Better he than me,' Mr Mackay said. 'Tomorrow afternoon please God I getting off this ship, and that is that.'

It was from the emigrants' leader that I first heard of the hurricane, Donna, which had struck Anguilla and caused many deaths. The *Labour Spokesman* carried further details: the cables received and sent, and an account of the rescue operations. The cables interested me; for their style, first of all: an early longwindedness, urgency expressing itself only towards the end, in the omission of a few prepositions; and because they showed the delight West Indian politicians take in their new titles. St Kitts is sixty-eight square miles, Montserrat thirty-two.

> From Chief Minister, Montserrat. To Chief Minister, St Kitts. Sent on 9th September 1960. Please accept and convey to the distressed people of Anguilla the sympathy of the Government and people of Montserrat damage sustained hurricane Donna. Chief Minister.

> From Chief Minister, St Kitts. To Chief Minister, Montserrat. Sent on 10th September 1960. Thanks very much your sympathy expressed in telegram of 9th. Chief Minister.

And so it went on, an exchange of salutations. Mr Manley of Jamaica was more positive:

> From Manley, Premier of Jamaica. To Southwell, Chief Minister, St Kitts. Sent on 8th September 1960. My profound sympathy for the disaster you have suffered. Please let us know what help you need. Manley.

The Chief Minister of St Kitts was determined to show Mr Manley more honour than Mr Manley had shown him:

> From Chief Minister, St Kitts. To Hon. Manley, Premier,

Jamaica. Sent on 8th September 1960. Thanks kind sympathy. Food, clothing, cash useful. Southwell.

Another cable repaired omissions.

From Chief Minister, St Kitts-Nevis-Anguilla. To Hon. Manley, Premier, Jamaica. Sent on 9th September 1960. Further my cable. Grateful include tarpaulins if possible. Chief Minister.

The story was rounded off by an article on the relief work. The writer was Mr John Brown who, according to an announcement in the same paper, was lecturing, even while the boatloads of emigrants were rocking in the shadow of the *Francisco Bobadilla*, on 'Dialect, Drama and West Indian Culture' and was inaugurating a Literary Club.

What was less inspiring [*Mr Brown wrote*] was that there was little semblance of an overall plan of organization. There were organizers of various sorts of work – too many of them if anything, and too few carrying out the work ... It seems self-evident that a central hurricane relief planning unit is needed for the colony ... and it is essential that the exact nature of its relationship with the voluntary agencies – Red Cross, Jaycees, etc. – should be very clearly defined to prevent confusion of responsibility and action.

I had some idea who the 'etc.' were. But the Jaycees were new to me. It was hard, on this immigrant ship, to associate the West Indies with well-dressed young businessmen, well-dressed and helpful young wives, and well-publicized acts of public service.

The emigrants' leader had his tea in the first-class dining room. He had excellent manners and skipped no part of the tea ritual. His followers peered approvingly through the windows at him. He concentrated on his tea. Sitting apart from us, and without the occasion to talk, he looked a little constrained. But I felt he would go far and that one day he too would be sending off cables. As soon as he had finished his tea and had daintily pressed a paper napkin to his lips, he rejoined his followers and started jabbering again, walking round and round the deck. We had occasional glimpses of his high bottom bobbing up and down outside windows. Then the class barriers on the deck came down and his walks were cut short. He stayed with his followers in their reserve.

Someone didn't approve of the barriers, however. He was the pipe-smoking Negro who had kept to himself throughout the voyage and read *The Ten Commandments*. It was his habit to walk around the deck for hours. Now he broke the barriers outside the dining room, outside the bar. The barman put the barrier up; the pipe-smoker broke it again. A squabble started. The pipe-smoker continued to walk, shouting over his shoulder. He was met at the dining-room barrier by the chief steward. He raised his voice; the chief steward replied. Angrily the pipe-smoker wrenched the barrier up, snapping the thin cord, and crashed it down. He walked past the steward; he was screaming now, incoherent with anger. Groups of emigrants, their faces growing as blank as when they had come up from the rowing-boats, began to gather. Officers were summoned. The pipe-smoker walked measuredly round the deck, breaking barriers, his calm stride unrelated to his hysterical words, which carried across the ship. When he came round to the dining-room barrier again, he had a crowd of frightened emigrants behind him. The emigrants' leader ran up eagerly, as he had run up to me; his followers opened a way for him; but he only halted and his jabbering ceased. The pipe-smoker walked alone. With an access of added fury he broke the barrier. On one side of the barrier the deck was black with emigrants. On the other side officers and stewards stood in a cool white circle. The pipe-smoker, in black, approached them at an unfaltering pace.

'He's gone mad,' Mr Mackay said.

The emigrants were beginning to buzz.

'Don't handle him roughly,' the purser shouted. 'Captain's orders. Don't handle him roughly.'

The pipe-smoker walked steadily on.

'I'm gonna get you!' the chief steward said. He didn't speak menacingly. He was only speaking an American expression.

'Terrible, terrible,' Mr Mackay said at dinner. 'To see that fine beast trapped.' His heart was bad; he had been disturbed by the incident and could only nibble at a lettuce leaf. His words were a matter of habit; they were separate from the distress in his voice. 'I talked to him once or twice, you know. He wasn't a bad feller. Such a beautiful Negro. Terrible, terrible.' His mouth was twisted with pain. 'He must have had a damn hard time in England. Now they're taking him back to his mother.'

'They gave him an injection and put him in the sick bay,' Philip said. 'I must say I wasn't expecting that at all. Insulting these Spanish officers in front of everybody.'

'Saving on the bad food, if you ask me,' Correia said. 'I wish they could give me a injection. I not been sleeping on this ship at all. Is the food. All this hispanol this and hispanol that.'

After dinner I went down to the sick bay. The doors were open. All the beds were empty except for one, in the corner, on which the pipe-smoker lay, still in his black serge trousers and blue shirt, a bit of plaster on his forehead. No doors were needed to keep him there.

Very late that evening or very early next morning we were to load up with more emigrants at Grenada, the spice island. It was our last night on board and we had a little party in the bar. The barman had not prepared for us and we quickly exhausted his brandy and Spanish champagne. We roused purser and stewards but could get no more drink. While we were talking to a steward an emigrant from St Kitts said he could help us, if we wanted brandy.

'Let the poor feller keep it,' Mr Mackay said, his soft mood persisting. 'Is probably the first and last bottle of brandy he ever going to buy. When the cold start busting his skin in England he going to be damn glad of that brandy.'

But the emigrant insisted. He was short, middle-aged and fat, with spectacles and a scratched skin.

Kripal Singh and I went down to the emigrant's cabin, going lower and lower, picking our way past babies down polished, hot corridors, catching glimpses of choked little cabins, heads below sheets, one above the other, opened suitcases, hearing sounds of thick muted activity all round us, seeing men and women hurrying to and from lavatories. The emigrant did not let us into his cabin. He half opened his door — four bunks, each dotted with a head emerging out of sheets, and many suitcases — squeezed in, shut the door, and presently came out with a bottle whose label was all gone except for one corner with the word 'brandy'.

Kripal Singh, whom I regarded as an expert in these matters, looked satisfied. He gave the emigrant five dollars and the emigrant, retiring, shut the door of his cabin.

We ran up with the bottle to the deck, where the fresh air revived us.

Philip said, 'This is rum. Even Spanish brandy isn't that colour. This is a thing they call sugarcane brandy.'

We all three went down again to the hot, airless lower decks. We knocked. The emigrant opened. He was in vest and pants, without his spectacles. He gave us our money back and took his bottle, without a word.

'You see what I mean, Miss Tull,' Mr Mackay said. 'You see how these beasts treat their own people? And he ain't even get to England. When a few white fellers jump on him and mash his arse he will start bawling about colour prejudice.'

We were leaving Grenada in its early morning stillness when I got up next morning. The sun was not out. The sea was bright grey, the sky light, the hills a cool green, the water at their feet shadowed and still. It was like a Sunday morning. After breakfast the sun was high and hot and the emigrants were thick in the bow of the ship.

Skirts and dresses flapped in the breeze; they chattered and pointed; they might have been on a day cruise.

We now acknowledged Mr Mackay as our West Indian expert. Philip asked him, 'How about these Grenadians? They does get on with people from St Kitts?'

'You have me there. People from St Kitts don't like people from Antigua. But I don't know about Grenadians. I only hope they don't start fighting before we reach Trinidad.'

Suddenly at lunchtime the water changed from deep blue to olive, and the new current of colour was edged with white froth. We were in the flood waters of the Orinoco River. I had no idea they reached so far north; and I wondered whether it was true, as Columbus reported, that one could find fresh water on one side of the white line and salt on the other.

We were approaching South America: a low grey range of hills in the distance. It was impossible to tell where South America ended and where Trinidad began. The hills could even have been another island. There was nothing, apart from the colour of the water, to tell us that we were near a continent. The hills grew higher, a dip became a separation, and we saw the channel. Columbus gave it its name: the Dragon's Mouth, the treacherous northern entrance to the Gulf of Paria. Venezuela was on our right, a grey haze. Trinidad was on our left: a number of tall rocky islets untidily thatched with green, and beyond them the mountains of the Northern Range blurred in a rainstorm.

It was from the South, through what he called the Serpent's Mouth, that Columbus came into the Gulf of Paria in 1498. The strong currents set up by the flood waters of the Orinoco River as they forced their way into the Gulf of Paria delayed him and nearly wrecked his ship. The currents roared continuously, he wrote; and once, in the middle of the night, when he was on deck, he saw 'the sea rolling from west to east like a mountain as high as the ship, and approaching slowly; and on the top of this rolling sea came a mighty roaring wave . . . To this day I can feel the fear I then felt.' When at last he came into the Gulf he found that the water was fresh. It was this that encouraged him to announce his most startling discovery. He had discovered, he wrote Ferdinand and Isabella, the approaches of the terrestrial paradise. No river could be as deep or as wide as the Gulf of Paria; and, from his reading of geographers and theologians, he had come to the conclusion that the earth here was shaped like a woman's breast, with the terrestrial paradise at the top of the nipple. The fresh water in the Gulf of Paria flowed down from this paradise which, because of its situation, could not be approached in a ship and certainly not without the permission of God.

Keeping close to Trinidad, hearing the thunder roll around us out of a blue sky, and watching the lightning play on the hills, we swung in a slow wide arc to the left, so that standing amidships on the port deck we could see our wake quickly subsiding to a dimpled glassiness.

The emigrants gesticulated.

'I hope Immigration keep an eye on these fellers,' Mr Mackay said. 'Trinidad is a sort of second paradise to them, you know. Give them the chance and half of them jump ship right here.'

We took on the pilot. We took on the immigration officials.

'Let them look,' Mr Mackay said, referring to the emigrants. 'We have launches here. No damn rowing-boats.'

Flag fluttering stiffly, the launch marked POLICE in heavy, reassuring white letters raced beside us, its occupants immaculately uniformed.

'It ain't a bad little island, you know,' Mr Mackay said.

'I hear they taking college boys in the police these days,' Philip said.

Port of Spain is a disappointing city from the sea. One sees only trees against the hills of the Northern Range. The tower of Queen's Royal College pierces the greenery; so does the blue bulk of the Salvatori building. At the bauxite loading station at Tembladora the air was yellow with bauxite dust.

We docked. The emigrants massed on deck and choked their way down the gangplank to get a glimpse of Trinidad (and a few, according to Mr Mackay, to stay).

'Let the small islanders go first,' he said.

'The prop, man,' someone whispered in my ear. 'The old propagandist.'

It was Boysie.

In my disembarkation suit and with my typewriter (never to be used) I felt I looked the part.

Correia was in a temper. The ship's agent had not arranged for his aeroplane ticket to British Guiana. His angry voice boomed out over the ship, down the gangplank; and I continued to hear it even when he disappeared into a customs shed, Kripal Singh at his heels, looking respectable and unhappy in his suit, smoking nervously, his studying days over. And that was the last I saw of them. Philip disappeared. The Mackays disappeared. Miss Tull disappeared; seventeen days with the emigrants awaited her.

The sky was pastelled in spectacular shades of scarlet and gold; the palm trees and the saman trees were black against it. The bar was empty and alien as it had been that afternoon in Southampton. The barman wanted someone to buy him a short-sleeved Aertex shirt. He was negotiating with the lunatic-keeper who, already red-faced, was in his tourist clothes: red shirt, straw hat, khaki trousers, sandals, with a camera slung over his shoulder.

We drove out of the dock area. The way was choked with emigrants, many of them Indians who had flown from British Guiana. Emigrants everywhere, and everywhere the people who had come to see them off. Cars everywhere. We drove very slowly. At the gates we were stopped, our passes checked.

A policeman said, 'Will you out your cigarette please?'

I outed it.

2. TRINIDAD

Because several of their generations had lived in a transitional land, pitching their tents between the houses of their fathers and the real Egypt, they were now unanchored souls, wavering in spirit and without a secure doctrine. They had forgotten much; they had half assimilated some new thoughts; and because they lacked real orientation, they did not trust their own feelings. They did not trust even the bitterness that they felt towards their bondage.

Thomas Mann: *The Tables of the Law*

In place of distaste for the Latin language came a passion to command it. In the same way, our national dress came into favour and the toga was everywhere to be seen. And so the Britons were gradually led on to the amenities that make vice agreeable – arcades, baths and sumptuous banquets. They spoke of such novelties as 'civilization', when really they were only a feature of enslavement.

Tacitus: *Agricola*

As soon as the *Francisco Bobadilla* had touched the quay, ship's side against rubber bumpers, I began to feel all my old fear of Trinidad. I did not want to stay. I had left the security of the ship and had no assurance that I would ever leave the island again. I had forgotten nothing: the wooden houses, jalousied half-way down, with fretwork along gables and eaves, fashionable before the concrete era; the concrete houses with L-shaped verandas and projecting front bedrooms, fashionable in the thirties; the two-storeyed Syrian houses in patterned concrete blocks, the top floor repeating the lower, fashionable in the forties. There were more neon lights. Ambition – a moving hand, drink being poured into a glass – was not matched with skill, and the effect was Trinidadian: vigorous, with a slightly flawed modernity. There were more cars. From the number plates I saw that there were now nearly fifty thousand vehicles on the road; when I had left there were less than twenty thousand. And the city throbbed with steel bands. A good opening line for a novelist or a travel-writer; but the steel band used to be regarded as a high manifestation of West Indian Culture, and it was a sound I detested.

When one arrives for the first time at a city, and especially if one arrives at night, the people in the streets have, just for that moment, a special quality: they are adepts in a ritual the traveller doesn't know; they are moving from one mystery to another. But driving now through Port of Spain, seeing the groups lounging at corners, around flambeau-lit stalls and coconut carts, I missed this thrill, and was distressed, not so much by the familiarity, as by the feeling of continuation. The years I had spent abroad fell away and I could not be sure which was the reality in my life: the first eighteen years in Trinidad or the later years in England. I had never wanted to stay in Trinidad. When I was in the fourth form I wrote a vow on the endpaper of my Kennedy's *Revised Latin Primer* to leave within five years. I left after six; and for many years afterwards in England, falling asleep in bedsitters with the electric fire on, I had been awakened by the nightmare that I was back in tropical Trinidad.

I had never examined this fear of Trinidad. I had never wished to. In my novels I had only expressed this fear; and it is only now, at the moment of writing, that I am able to attempt to examine it. I knew Trinidad to be unimportant, uncreative, cynical. The only professions were those of law and medicine, because there was no need for any other; and the most successful people were commission agents, bank managers and members of the distributive trades. Power was recognized, but dignity was allowed to no one. Every person of eminence was held to be crooked and contemptible. We lived in a society which denied itself heroes.

It was a place where the stories were never stories of success but of failure: brilliant men, scholarship winners, who had died young, gone mad, or taken to drink; cricketers of promise whose careers had been ruined by disagreements with the authorities.

It was also a place where a recurring word of abuse was 'conceited', an expression of the resentment felt of anyone who possessed unusual skills. Such skills were not required by a society which produced nothing, never had to prove its worth, and was never called upon to be efficient. And such people had to be cut down to size or, to use the Trinidad expression, be made to 'boil down'. Generosity – the admiration of equal for equal – was therefore unknown; it was a quality I knew only from books and found only in England.

For talent, a futility, the Trinidadian substituted intrigue; and in the exercise of this, in small things as well as large, he became a master. Admiration he did have: for boys who did well at school, such academic success, separate from everyday life, giving self-respect to the community as a whole without threatening it in any way; for scholarship winners until they became conceited; for racehorses. And for cricketers.

Cricket has always been more than a game in Trinidad. In a society which demanded no skills and offered no rewards to merit, cricket was the only activity which permitted a man to grow to his full stature and to be measured against international standards. Alone on a field, beyond obscuring intrigue, the cricketer's true worth could be seen by all. His race, education, wealth did not matter. We had no scientists, engineers, explorers, soldiers or poets. The cricketer was our only hero-figure. And that is why cricket is played in the West Indies with such panache; that is why, for a long time to come, the West Indians will not be able to play as a team. The individual performance was what mattered. That was what we went to applaud; and unless the cricketer had heroic qualities we did not want to see him, however valuable he might be. And that was why, of those stories of failure, that of the ruined cricketer was the most terrible. In Trinidad lore he was a recurring figure; he appears in the Trinidad play, *Moon on a Rainbow Shawl*, by Errol John.

Though we knew that something was wrong with our society, we made no attempt to assess it. Trinidad was too unimportant and we could never be convinced of the value of reading the history of a place which was, as everyone said, only a dot on the map of the world. Our interest was all in the world outside, the remoter the better; Australia was more important than Venezuela, which we could see on a clear day. Our own past was buried and no one cared to dig it up. This gave us a strange time-sense. The England of 1914 was the England of yesterday; the Trinidad of 1914 belonged to the dark ages.

There was an occasional racial protest, but that aroused no deep feelings, for it represented only a small part of the truth. Everyone was an individual, fighting for his place in the community. Yet there was no community. We were of various races, religions, sets and cliques; and we had somehow found ourselves on the same small island. Nothing bound us together except this common residence. There was no nationalist feeling; there could be none. There was no profound anti-imperialist feeling; indeed, it was only our Britishness, our belonging to the British Empire, which gave us any identity. So protests could only be individual, isolated, unheeded.

It was only towards the end of the war that stories of limited success began to be known, stories of men who had served with distinction in the R.A.F., of men who had become lecturers in English and American universities, of singers who had won recognition abroad. These people had all escaped. 'Conceited' at home, they had won distinction abroad; and as theirs was not the despised local eminence Trinidad accepted them with a ready generosity and exaggerated their worth.

The threat of failure, the need to escape: this was the prompting of the society I knew.

From the *Trinidad Guardian*:

LITERATURE IS OUR HERITAGE

Editor, 'Guardian'

In the 'Trinidad Guardian' of October 22, the heading covering the falls of gold prices read [*sic*] 'Golds Lose Glitter', and this reminded me of the well-known quotation: 'All that glitters is not gold.'

As a matter of literary interest, the passage is misquoted, and should read: 'All that glisters is not gold.' It comes from 'The Merchant of Venice'. True enough, both 'glitters' and 'glisters' convey the same idea, but if I may say so, 'glitters' is not Shakespearean. 'Glisters' is the word that has come down to us and it behoves us to pass it on without change or alteration.

This is not to be taken as reproof towards those who have mistaken one word for the other.

Rather it is a plea for the preservation of those words and phrases that constitute, in part, our literary legacy.

Norman A. Carter, *St Augustine*

No one was deeply interested in the emigrants on the *Francisco Bobadilla*. There was more concern about the number of immigrants in Trinidad. The population had jumped from 560,000 in 1946 to 825,000 in 1960. Immigrants had come from England, America, Canada and Australia as well as the other West Indian islands. Two new white suburbs had been established, but Trinidad directed all its annoyance against West Indian immigrants, and Grenadians in particular. Grenada, immemorially, has been as funny a word in Trinidad as Wigan is in England; and the occasional expulsion of Grenadians and other small islanders is a subject for calypso.

Shortly before my arrival there had been another police campaign, reportedly of exceptional rigour, against illegal immigrants. The attitudes to immigrants are the same the world over – the stories about West Indians in England ('twenty-four to a room') are exactly matched by the stories about Grenadians and others in Trinidad – and there was great public enthusiasm as Grenadians scattered in terror all over the island and went into hiding. (Many were harboured by employers who valued the cheapness of their labour. In the remote Ortoire district I was to come upon a nest of Vincentians gathering oysters from mangrove roots for a local entrepreneur.) The calypsonian called Lord Blakie sang:

> Move, lemme get me share.
> They beating Grenadians down in the Square.
> Lemme pelt a lash, lemme get a share.
> They beating Grenadians down in the Square.
> Since they hear we have Federation
> All of them packing up in this island.

Grenadians were altogether in the news. The latest Trinidad personality was a Grenadian of twenty-four who had married a Trinidad woman of eighty-four. Their photographs were often in the paper; cinema managers were trying to get them to make personal appearances; and a rumour, started perhaps by a government supporter, had it that the acting leader of the opposition had asked the Grenadian to stand as one of the party's candidates at the next general election. In an interview with the *Sunday Guardian* – with photographs of the bride feeding her chickens, the groom acting as linesman in a football match – the Grenadian said he had four children in Grenada (thus giving the lie to one persistent rumour). He had left their mother because she, and her family, had wanted to 'rush' him into marriage.

They were discussing this in a Port of Spain taxi one morning.

'She have too much vice in she old tail, if you ask me,' the fat woman beside me said. 'God! What she must be does look like in the morning? I ain't fifty, and it does frighten me like hell to see my face when I get up.'

'When that man I have started getting fresh,' the woman in front said, 'I does be mad to give him a clout. Is only backside for him, you hear. And I breathing deep and pretending I sleeping sound sound.'

'You right, child. A neighbour was telling me that this Grenadian only want to go away to study. He go away, doing this studying, and she stay home, feeding those chickens. You see she in the *Guardian*, feeding chickens?'

From the *Trinidad Guardian*:

FASHION SHOW

The management of the Starlite Drive-In and Pollyanna, a new children's dress shop, put on a delightful children's fashion parade at the cinema on Sunday afternoon before the first show. Apart from the very lovely frocks, and they were adorable, the little models, boys and girls, one little youngster not quite 2, were positively amazing, perfectly self-possessed, and poised. The array of garments ranged from bathing suits 'Balon', a Brigitte Bardot type, but certainly B.B. could not have done fuller justice to her suit than did Christine Cozier and Renata Lopez; not to mention Master Barry Went in his Marlon Brando bikini . . . Among the most appreciative audience were Mrs Isaac Akow and her grands, Mr and Mrs A. Dickson, Mr and Mrs Dennis Crooks and their kids, Mr and Mrs Frank de Freitas and their family.

Trinidad considers itself, and is acknowledged by the other West Indian territories to be, modern. It has night clubs, restaurants, air-conditioned bars, supermarkets, soda fountains, drive-in cinemas and a drive-in bank. But modernity in Trinidad means a little more. It means a constant alertness, a willingness to change, a readiness to accept anything which films, magazines and comic strips appear to indicate as American. Beauty queens and fashion parades are modern. Modernity might also lie in a name like Lois – pronounced Loys in Trinidad – which came to the island in the 1940s through Lois Lane, the heroine of the American *Superman* comic strip. Simple radio is not modern. Commercial radio is: when I was a boy not to know the latest commercial jingle was to be primitive.

To be modern is to ignore local products and to use those advertised in American magazines. The excellent coffee which is grown in Trinidad is used only by the very poor and a few middle-class English expatriates. Everyone else drinks Nescafé or Maxwell House or Chase and Sanborn, which is more expensive but is advertised in the magazines and therefore acceptable. The elegant and comfortable morris chairs, made from local wood by local craftsmen, are not modern and have disappeared except from the houses of the poor. Imported tubular steel furniture, plastic-straw chairs from Hong Kong and spindly cast-iron chairs have taken their place.

In an article in the *Caribbean Quarterly*, a journal of the University College of the West Indies, Dr Alfred P. Thorne studies the economic consequences of this 'apparent psychological trait'. 'Large numbers of middle- and upper-class islanders,' he writes, 'avoid regular consumption of many local roots or ground provisions, and prefer imported items of corresponding food value (and usually higher cost).' He suggests that political leaders and the new élite should set an example, which would be more effective than 'fervent imprecations and exhortations'.

Is there any good reason why, in the prestige system, sweet potatoes and the like should not be among the foods of the middle and upper income classes of the communities? Do not elegant English barons and earls, and, indeed, even most gracious royal princesses share common 'Irish' potatoes with English dock labourers? Not even the 'Cockneys' renaming these humble roots as 'spuds' have diverted the aristocratic consumer.

It is an old West Indian problem. Trollope complained about it in Jamaica in 1859:

> But it is to be remarked all through the island that the people are fond of English dishes, and that they despise, or affect to despise, their own productions. They will give you ox-tail soup when turtle would be much cheaper. Roast beef and beefsteaks are found at almost every meal. An immense deal of beer is consumed. When yams, avocado pears, the mountain cabbage, plantains, and twenty other delicious vegetables may be had for the gathering, people will insist on eating bad English potatoes; and the desire for English pickles is quite a passion.

Charles Kingsley, who ten years later spent a winter in Trinidad, tells the story in *At Last* of a German who, because Trinidad produced sugar, vanilla and cocoa, decided to make chocolate in Trinidad. He did, and his price was a quarter that of the imported. 'But the fair creoles would not buy it. It could not be good; it could not be the real article, unless it had crossed the Atlantic twice to and from that centre of fashion, Paris.' One of the complaints of tourists in Jamaica is that they cannot get Jamaican food. And once in a small intellectuals' club in Port of Spain I asked for guava jelly: they had only greengage jam.

Modernity in Trinidad, then, turns out to be the extreme susceptibility of people who are unsure of themselves and, having no taste or style of their own, are eager for instruction. In England and America there are magazines for such groups; in Trinidad instruction is now provided by advertising agencies, which have been welcomed by the people not only for this reason but also because the advertising agency is itself a modern thing.

There was a time when Trinidad had no agencies and the nearest we got to copy-writing was Limacol's 'The Freshness of a Breeze in a Bottle' and Mr Fernandes's 'If you don't drink rum that is your business; if you do drink rum that is our business.' For the rest we made do with each store's list of bargains and the usual toothpaste sagas about bad breath. This has now changed. It has been said that a country can be judged by its advertisements, and a glance at Trinidad advertising is revealing. A man with a black eye-patch is used to advertise, not Hathaway shirts, but an alcoholic drink. Bermudez biscuits are described as a 'Family of Fine Crackers', with the 'Mopsy' biscuit for 'the young in heart', which is as puzzling as the slogan for Trinidad Grapefruit Juice: 'The Smile of Good Health – in a Tin'. 'Crix' (of the Bermudez family) is 'a meal in itself'. One examines the copy for the point; and it seems that this is to persuade Trinidadians that Bermudez biscuits are really 'crackers', American things which Americans in films and the comic strips eat. Old Oak Rum was introduced with a Showdown Test. (It might have been a ten-second showdown test, but I may be confusing it with other tests.) In this Showdown Test a number of laughing, well-dressed Trinidadians, carefully chosen for race, stood at a bar. None was clamorously black. A genuinely black man was used for the garage-hand in the 'I'm going well, I'm going Shell' advertisement; black faces are normally used only in advertisements for things like bicycles and stout.

This is the work of expatriate advertising agents, and Trinidad is grateful and humble. At a time when the whole concept of modern advertising is under fire elsewhere, Trinidad offers a haven: it is officially recognized that Trinidadians are without the skill to run advertising agencies. And, indeed, without outside assistance commercial radio might not have been so easily established. At a quarter past seven in the morning, in those early days, Doug Hatton was there with his *Shopping Highlights*, a programme of music and 'information'. Sometimes, he telephoned people to ask whether they knew the name of the 'number' he was playing; if they did they got a prize, provided by some firm willing to contribute to the public merriment. At eight Hatton went off the air, to make way for a little local news, a little more information and the death announcements. But at half past eight Hatton's associate Hal Morrow came on, with *Morrow's Merry-Go-Round*, a programme of information and music. This lasted until nine, and for the rest of the day there would be no more of Hatton and Morrow until they came on in the evening with a quiz, perhaps, a talent show, records and more information. They retired, Hatton and Morrow, somewhat prematurely; but Trinidad has never ceased to honour them: simple people of whose work the wider world shall never know, who turned their backs on metropolitan success and renown and devoted their energies to the service of a colonial people.

So Trinidad, though deserted by much of the talent it produces, has always been fortunate in attracting people of adventurous spirit.

'I'm a second-rater,' a successful American businessman said to an Englishman, who told it to me. 'But this is a third-rate place and I'm doing well. Why should I leave?'

With this emphasis on America, English things are regarded as old-fashioned and provincial. One of the more pleasing aspects of Trinidad modernity is that it is possible to eat well and from a number of national cuisines. I found myself one day in an English restaurant. Trollope's remarks about the potato still apply; and the restaurant, which was an 'and chips' place, attracted depressed expatriates and some of the English-minded Trinidad élite. The waiters were dressed up. My joylessness was matched by the waiter's until I asked what there was for a sweet. He looked embarrassed; and when at last he said, 'Bread and butter pudding,' his voice half-broke in a laugh, disclaiming all responsibility for such an absurdity.

So Trinidad gives the impression of a booming, vigorous, even frenzied little island. Helped by a series of fires, the main streets of central Port of Spain have been rebuilt, and the Salvatori building stands for all that is modern. Elsewhere the flat-façaded stonewalled houses remain: dwelling-houses turned into stores to meet the needs of an expanding city. Traffic crawls in the choked streets; parking is a problem. In the stores the quality of unbranded goods is not high, the prices extravagant; the mark-up is fifty or a hundred per cent, and on some goods, like Japanese knick-knacks, as much as three hundred per cent: Trinidadians will not buy what they think is cheap. In December 1959, after the civil servants had received another of their pay rises, Port of Spain was sold out of refrigerators. In betting shops you can bet on that day's English races. And there are numerous race meetings in Trinidad itself; when I was a boy there were only three a year. Horse-racing, one of the island's few entertainments, has always been popular and now, with more money circulating, gambling has become universal. It is respectable; it is almost an industry; and I was told that as a result not a few civil servants are in the hands of moneylenders.

We went to the races, leaving Port of Spain by the dual-carriageway Wrightson Road that runs between the town and the reclaimed area of Docksite, the former American army base. We passed the Technical College, still being built – a few years later than British Guiana's, but a promise of the future; we passed the modernistic headquarters of the Seamen and Waterfront Workers Trade Union, the new Fire Brigade headquarters. Then we drove along the Beetham Highway, the new road built over reclaimed swampland to relieve the overburdened Eastern Main Road. To our right lay the city rubbish dump, misty with smoke of rubbish burning in the open. On our left was Shanty Town, directly outside the city, extending right across and up the hills: oddly beautiful, each shack with its angular black shadow on the reddish hill, so that one would have liked to sketch the scene into a rough wet canvas. Corbeaux patrolled the highway. These black vultures are never far away in Trinidad; they perch on the graceful branches of coconut trees on the beaches; and when on the highway, as we saw, one of the city's innumerable pariah dogs is run over, the corbeaux pounce and pick the starved body clean, flapping heavily away from time to time to avoid the traffic. Scarlet ibises flew with an awkward grace over the mangrove to our right. And at regular intervals on the highway English-style traffic signs urged motorists to keep to the left except when overtaking.

We had music while we drove, from the two radio stations. With their songs, commercials, constant weather reports (as though this was at any moment liable to spectacular change) and news 'every hour on the hour', they suggested that we were in an exciting, luxurious metropolis which was supported by a vast, rich hinterland. Soon this hinterland appeared: occasional horse-carts, small houses, people working in small vegetable gardens. We with our car-radio on the highway were in one world; they were in another.

An approaching car blinked its lights.

'Police,' my friend said. 'Speed trap.'

Every car that met us gave the warning. And soon, sure enough, we passed a disconsolate, ostentatiously plain-clothed policeman sitting on the verge looking at something in his hand.

Country people, mainly Indians brilliantly dressed, were walking towards the races. We turned off the main road and found the way blocked as far as we could see with cars, new, of many colours, shining in the sun. This was nothing like the Trinidad I knew.

When Charles Kingsley went to the Port of Spain races in 1870 he came upon a dying horse surrounded by a group of coloured men whom he advised 'in vain' to cover the horse with a blanket, 'for the poor thing had fallen from sunstroke'. Kingsley did not go to the races to bet – it was the first time he had been to a raceground for thirty years – and he does not speak of gambling. He speaks of a run-down French merry-go-round ('a huge piece of fool's tackle'), people sitting on the grass ('live flower-beds'), and the 'most hideous' smell of new rum. He had gone to the races, he says, 'to wander *en mufti* among the crowd'. He was greatly taken by their racial variety, and the engraving which accompanies the chapter shows a group of Trinidadians – Negroes, Indians and

Chinese – at the races. The Negro man and the Negro boy are wearing straw hats, loose collarless shirts and three-quarter-length trousers, a tropical abridgement of eighteenth-century European garb which has been revived in night clubs as a folk costume. A Negro woman is wearing a turban and many well-starched skirts such as Anthony Trollope, getting off the West Indian steamer at the island of St Thomas late in 1858, saw on the flower-seller on the quayside; these skirts 'gave to her upright figure', he said, 'that look of easily compressible bulk which, let *Punch* do what it will, has grown so sightly to our eyes'. The Indian men are in turbans, Indian jackets, and dhotis, and carry the quarterstaff; the Indian woman wears the long skirt of the United Provinces and the *orhni*. The Chinese are in Chinese peasant clothes; the man has a pigtail and carries an open umbrella.

No dying horses surrounded by helpless jabbering men will be found on a Trinidad race-ground today. No pigtails; no calypso folk costumes; and turbans are rare. Dress is uniform, national tastes emerging only in colours. The three groups in the Kingsley engraving stand in three isolated cultures. Today these cultures, coming together, have been modified. One, the Chinese, has almost disappeared; and the standards of all approximate to the standards of those who are absent in the engraving: the Europeans.

* * *

Outside the Royal Victoria Institute in Port of Spain an anchor, still in good condition, stands embedded in concrete, and a sign says this might be the anchor Columbus lost during his rough passage into the Gulf of Paria. So much, one might say, for the history of Trinidad for nearly three hundred years after its discovery. The Spaniards were more interested in the profitable territories of South America, and the island was never seriously settled. The abundance today of Amerindian names speaks of this absence of early colonization: Tacarigua, Tunapuna, Guayaguayare, Mayaro,

Arima, Naparima. In Trinidad you do not find the Scarborough and Plymouth of Tobago, the Hampstead and Highgate of Jamaica, the Windsor Forest and Hampton Court of the British Guiana coastland.

There was a little excitement in 1595. The Spanish governor, Berrio, was using the island as a base for his search for El Dorado. Raleigh came; used the pitch from the Pitch Lake to caulk his ships, pronouncing it better than the pitch from Norway; tasted the small oysters that grew in flinty clusters on the mangrove roots, liked them; and since 'to leave a garrison at my back, interested in the same enterprise, I should have savoured very much of the asse', he sacked the small Spanish settlement and took Berrio off with him as a guide up the Orinoco River.

It was 1783, when the islands had a population of 700 whites, Negroes and coloureds and 2,000 Amerindians, that immigration began on any scale. The immigrants came from the French West Indian islands, royalists fleeing the revolution and the slave rebellion in Haiti. The island became Spanish only in name, and even after the British conquest in 1797 retained its French character, of which Trollope so strongly disapproved in 1859.

> As Trinidad is an English colony, one's first idea is that the people speak English; and one's second idea, when that other one as to the English has fallen to the ground, is that they should speak Spanish, seeing that the name of the place is Spanish. But the fact is that they all speak French ... As this was a conquered colony, the people of the island are not allowed to have so potent a voice in their own management. But one does see clearly enough, that as they are French in language and habits, and Roman Catholic in religion, they would make an even worse hash of it than the Jamaicans do in Jamaica.

In spite of the black legend of Spain in the New World, the Spanish slave code was the least inhumane. Doubtless for this reason it was seldom followed. For some time after the British conquest the island continued to be administered under Spanish law, and the first British governor, Picton, scrupulously followed the Spanish code. (He even used a little torture, which the code permitted; and this ruined his reputation in England.) It was easier under the Spanish code for a slave to buy his freedom, and in 1821 there were 14,000 free coloured in Trinidad. Estates were small: in 1796 there were 36,000 acres cultivated, divided between 450 estates. The latifundia never had a chance to be established. And in 1834 slavery was abolished. So that in Trinidad society never hardened around the institution of slavery as it had done in the other West Indian islands; there was no memory of bitterly suppressed revolts.

After the abolition of slavery Spanish law was replaced by English law. This established the basic rights of the individual; and because the island, as a conquered crown colony, was ruled directly from London, where the government was under steady pressure from anti-slavery societies, the planter group could be controlled. It is hard in Trinidad today to find reminders of slavery; in British Guiana, Surinam, Martinique, Jamaica, the past cannot be avoided. In 1870 Kingsley thought that the Trinidad Negro lived better than the working-man in England. Froude, in 1887, 'seeing always the boundless happiness of the black race', could only warn that 'the powers which envy human beings too perfect felicity may find ways one day of disturbing the West Indian Negro.'

Throughout the century immigration continued. As early as 1806 attempts had been made to get Chinese labourers, the government no doubt anticipating emancipation and being unwilling to increase the Negro population. French labourers were imported from Le Havre, Portuguese from Madeira. After the abolition of slavery the Negroes refused to work on the estates, and the resulting labour shortage was solved by the importation of indentured labour from Madeira, China and India. The Indians proved to be the most suitable; and, with a few breaks, Indian immigration continued until

1917. In all, 134,000 Indians came to Trinidad; most of them were from the provinces of Bihar, Agra and Oudh.*

So Trinidad was and remains a materialist immigrant society, continually growing and changing, never settling into any pattern, always retaining the atmosphere of the camp; unique in the West Indies in the absence of a history of enduring brutality, in the absence of a history; yet not an expanding society but a colonial society, ruled autocratically if benevolently, with the further limitations of its small size and remoteness. All this has combined to give it its special character, its ebullience and irresponsibility. And more: a tolerance which is more than tolerance: an indifference to virtue as well as to vice. The Land of the Calypso is not a copy-writer's phrase. It is one side of the truth, and it was this gaiety, so inexplicable to the tourist who sees the shacks of Shanty town and the corbeaux patrolling the modern highway, and inexplicable to me who had remembered it as the land of failures, which now, on my return, assaulted me.

From the *Trinidad Guardian*:

> Residents of Fisher Avenue, St Ann's, must have wondered who on earth their new neighbours in No. 1a were on Saturday night, as the strains of Choy Aming's tape recorded music shattered the suburban peace. Little did they know that four gay bachelors — men-about-town — Jimmy Spiers, Nick Proudfoot, David Renwick and Peter Galesloot had moved in and were having a house warming. Batting Scotch and assorted chasers were Malcolm Martin, Eddie de Freitas, Pat Diaz, Maureen Poon Tip, Joan Rawle, Gillian Geoffroy, Joan Spiers and others. You should have seen the floor the next morning.

---

* These facts about immigration are taken from *The West Indies in the Making*, by four hands. London, 1960.

Port of Spain is the noisiest city in the world. Yet it is forbidden to talk. 'Let the talkies do the talking,' the signs used to say in the old London Theatre of my childhood. And now the radios and the rediffusion sets do the talking, the singing, the jingling; the steel bands do the booming and the banging; and the bands, live or tape-recorded, and the gramophones and record-players. In restaurants the hands are there to free people of the need to talk. Stunned, temples throbbing, you champ and chew, concentrating on the working of your jaw muscles. In a private home as soon as anyone starts to talk the radio is turned on. It must be loud, loud. If there are more than three, dancing will begin. Sweat-sweat-dance-dance-sweat. Loud, loud, louder. If the radio isn't powerful enough, a passing steel band will be invited in. Jump-jump-sweat-sweat-jump. In every house a radio or rediffusion set is on. In the street people conduct conversations at a range of twenty yards or more; and even when they are close to you their voices have a vibrating tuning-fork edge. You will realize this only after you have left Trinidad: the voices in British Guiana will sound unnaturally low, and for the first day or so whenever anyone talks to you you will lean forward conspiratorially, for what is being whispered is, you feel, very secret. In the meantime dance, dance, shout above the shuffle. If you are silent the noise will rise to a roar about you. You cannot shout loud enough. Your words seem to be issuing from behind you. You have been here only an hour, but you feel as exhausted as though you had spent a day in some Italian scooter-hell. Your head is bursting. It is only eleven; the party is just warming up. You are being rude, but you must go.

You drive up the new Lady Young Road, and the diminishing noise makes it seem cooler. You get to the top and look out at the city glittering below you, amber and exploding blue on black, the ships in the harbour in the background, the orange flames issuing from the oil derricks far out in the Gulf of Paria. For a moment it is silent. Then, above the crickets, whose stridulation you hadn't noticed, you begin to hear the city: the dogs, the steel bands.

You wait until the radio stations have closed down for the night – but rediffusion sets, for which there is a flat rental, are never turned off: they remain open, to await the funnelling of the morning noise – and then you wind down into the city again, drowning in the din. All through the night the dogs will go on, in a thousand inextricably snarled barking relays, rising and falling, from street to street and back again, from one end of the city to another. And you will wonder how you stood it for eighteen years, and whether it was always like this.

When I was a boy the people of Port of Spain used to dress up and walk around the Savannah on a Sunday afternoon. Those who had cars drove around in them slowly. It was a ritual parade which established the positions of the participants. It was also a pleasant walk. To the south lay the fine buildings of the wealthy and the Queen's Park Hotel, to us the last word in luxury and modernity. To the north were the botanical gardens and the grounds of Government House. And to the west lay Maraval Road.

Maraval Road is one of the architectural wonders of the world. It is a long road with few houses: it used to be the street of the very wealthy. At the north it begins with a Scottish baronial castle. Then comes Whitehall, an odd Moorish-Corsican building; before it was turned into government offices – the name Whitehall, however, came first – it was hung with tapestries depicting shepherds and shepherdesses, and had papier-mâché logs in dummy fireplaces. Beyond Whitehall there is a palace with much wrought-iron decoration; it has a strong oriental flavour but is said to be copied from a French château. Then there is a monumental ochre-and-rust Spanish Colonial mansion. And the street ends with the blue-and-red P.W.D. Italianate of Queen's Royal College, whose clock has Big Ben chimes.

This was the taste of the old Trinidad: individual, anarchic, not arising out of the place – in spite of the fireplaces every office in Whitehall needs two or three fans – but created out of memories. There were no local standards. In the refinements of behaviour, as in architecture, everything was left to the caprices of the individual. In the immigrant society, memories growing dim, there was no guiding taste. As you rose you evolved your own standards, and they were usually those of modernity.

There was no guiding taste because there was no taste. In Trinidad education was not one of the things money could buy; it was something money freed you from. Education was strictly for the poor. The white boy left school at an early age, 'counting on his fingers', as the Trinidadian likes to say; but this was a measure of his privilege. He went to work in a bank, in Cable and Wireless or in a large business firm; and for many Trinidadians to be a bank clerk or a salesman was therefore the peak of ambition. Those of the white community who eccentrically desired an education nearly always left the island. The white community was never an upper class in the sense that it possessed a superior speech or taste or attainments; it was envied only for its money and its access to pleasure. Kingsley, in spite of all his affection for his white hosts in Trinidad, observed: 'French civilization, signifies practically, certainly in the New World, little save ballet-girls, billiard-tables and thin boots: English civilization, little save horse-racing and cricket.' Seventy years later James Pope-Hennessy repeated and extended the observation. 'Educated people of African origin would speak to him of subjects about which he was accustomed to talk in his own country: about books, music or religion. English persons on the other hand spoke mainly of tennis-scores, the country-club, whisky or precedence or oil.' Education was strictly for the poor; and the poor were invariably black.

With the opening up of the colonial society the white community finds itself at a disadvantage, and the attitude to education has changed. It is now seen as not discreditable, possibly even useful, and the white community has decided to expose itself to it. A new boarding-school, which appears to be whitish in intention, has been opened. While I was there the principal, brought down from England to direct this Custer's last stand, was issuing unrealistic statements about building character. Unrealistic because too late: the taste of the society has hardened.

The cultures represented by the buildings in Maraval Road and the figures in the Kingsley engraving have not coalesced to form this taste. They have all been abandoned under the pressure of every persuasive method: second-rate newspapers, radio services and films.

It might have been expected that journalism would provide an outlet for the talent that could not find expression elsewhere. But local talent, like the local eminence, was automatically condemned. Experts were continually imported, the English Hattons and Morrows; and journalism in Trinidad remained under-valued and underpaid, never ranking as high as motor-car-selling. The news-papers relied to a great extent on space-filling syndicated American and English columns, comic strips, the film gossip of Louella Parsons and beauty hints about the preservation of peaches-and-cream complexions.

Again and again one comes back to the main, degrading fact of the colonial society; it never required efficiency, it never required quality, and these things, because unrequired, became undesirable.

The radio came later, and it was worse. America sent Hatton and Morrow. Britain sent Rediffusion. A generation has now been brought up to believe that radio, modern radio, means a song followed by a jingle, soap-operas five and fifteen minutes long, continually broken for commercials, so that in a five-minute morning serial like *The Shadow . . . of . . . Delilah!*, to which I found all Trinidad thrilling, two minutes, by my reckoning, were given over to advertising. This type of commercial radio, with its huckstering geniality, has imposed its values so successfully that there was widespread enthusiasm when Trinidad, not content with one such radio service, acquired two.

Newspapers and radio were, however, only the ancilliaries of the cinema, whose influence is incalculable. The Trinidad audience actively participates in the action on the screen. 'Where do you come from?' Lauren Bacall is asked in *To Have and Have Not*. 'Port of Spain, Trinidad,' she replies, and the audience shouts delightedly, 'You lie! You lie!' So the audience continually shouts advice and comments; it grunts at every blow in a fight; it roars with delight when the once-spurned hero returns wealthy and impeccably dressed (this is important) to revenge himself on his past tormentor; it grows derisive when the hero finally rejects and perhaps slaps the Hollywood 'bad' woman (of the *Leave Her to Heaven* type). It responds, in short, to every stock situation of the American cinema.

Nearly all the films shown, apart from those in the first-run cinemas, are American and old. Favourites are shown again and again: *Casablanca*, with Humphrey Bogart; *Till the Clouds Roll By*; the Errol Flynn, John Wayne, James Cagney, Edward G. Robinson and Richard Widmark films; vintage Westerns like *Dodge City* and *Jesse James*; and every film Bogart made. Films are reputed for their fights. *The Spoilers* is advertised as having the longest fight ever (Randolph Scott and John Wayne, I believe). *The Brothers* was one of the few British films to win favour; it had a good fight and was helped not a little by the scene in which Maxwell Reed prepares to beat Patricia Roc with a length of rope ('You must be beaten'): the humiliation of women being important to the Trinidad audience. And there are serials – *Dare-devils of the Red Circle*, *Batman*, *Spy-catcher* – which are shown in children's programmes in the countries of their origin but in Trinidad are one of the staples of adult entertainment. They are never shown serially but all at once; they are advertised for their length, the number of reels being often stated: and the late-comer asks, 'How much reels gone?' When I was there *The Shadow*, a serial of the forties, was revived; the new generation was being urged to 'thrill to it like your old man did'.

In its stars the Trinidad audience looks for a special quality of style. John Garfield had this style; so did Bogart. When Bogart, without turning, coolly rebuked a pawing Lauren Bacall, 'You're breathin' down mah neck,' Trinidad adopted him as its own. 'That is man!' the audience cried. Admiring shrieks of 'Aye-aye-*aye*!' greeted Garfield's statement in *Dust Be My Destiny*: 'What am I gonna do? What I always do. Run.' 'From now on I am like John Garfield in *Dust Be My Destiny*,' a prisoner once said in court, and made the front page of the evening paper. Dan Duryea became a favourite after his role in *Scarlet Street*. Richard Widmark, eating an apple and shooting people down in *The Street With No Name*, had style; his chilling dry laugh was another endearing asset. For the Trinidadian an actor has style when he is seen to fulfil certain aspirations of the audience: the virility of Bogart, the man-on-the-run romanticism of Garfield, the pimpishness and menace of Duryea, the ice-cold sadism of Widmark.

After thirty years of active participation in this sort of cinema, the Trinidadian, whether he sits in the pit or the house or the balcony, can respond only to the Hollywood formula. Nothing beyond the formula is understood, even when it comes from America; and nothing from outside America is worth considering. British films, until they took on an American gloss, played to empty houses. It was my French master who urged me to go to see *Brief Encounter*; and there were two of us in the cinema, he in the balcony, I in the pit. As Trinidad was British, cinemas were compelled to show a certain footage of British film; and they compiled with the regulations by showing four British films in one day, *Brief Encounter* and *I Know where I'm Going* in the afternoon, say, and *The Overlanders* and *Henry V* in the evening.

This attitude to British films is understandable. I had enjoyed *Our Man in Havana* in London. Seeing it again in Trinidad, I was less enchanted. I saw how English and narcissistic it was, how provincial, and how meaningless to the audience were the English jokes about Englishness. The audience was silent through all the comedy and came to life only during the drama. There were even approving shouts during the game of draughts played with miniature bottles of liquor, each piece being drunk when taken: this, for the Trinidadian, was style.

A Board of Censors, which knows about the French, bans French films. Italian, Russian, Swedish and Japanese films are unknown. Indian films of Hollywood badness can be seen; but Satyajit Ray's Bengali trilogy cannot find an exhibitor. Nigerians, I believe, are addicted to Indian films as well as to those from Hollywood. The West Indian, revealingly, is less catholic; and in Trinidad the large and enthusiastic audiences for Indian films are, barring an occasional eccentric, entirely Indian.

If curiosity is a characteristic of the cosmopolitan, the cosmopolitanism on which Trinidad prides itself is fraudulent. In the immigrant colonial society, with no standards of its own, subjected for years to the second-rate in newspapers, radio and cinema, minds are rigidly closed; and Trinidadians of all races and classes are remaking themselves in the image of the Hollywood B-man. This is the full meaning of modernity in Trinidad.

From the *Trinidad Guardian*:

CHILDREN ENCHANT AUDIENCE WITH DANCE
By Jean Minshall

This is not a review of 'Dance Time 1960' which was presented at Queen's Hall on Thursday night for the first time. It is the only way in which I can show my appreciation and that of the capacity audience that was there – for an enchanted evening of purely delightful entertainment.

Which was the outstanding number? Each and every one – they were all perfect.

Could anything be lovelier than the 'Ballet of the Enchanted Dolls' with well over 100 of the junior pupils taking part – the fairy dolls, the fluffy little yellow ducklings, the fat little black and white pandas, the golden brown teddy bears, the smart tin soldiers, the little French dolls and raggedy Anns.

Could you imagine anything more delightful than the pair of petite and adorable Japanese dolls, the twirling tops, or

Topsy, Mopsy and Dinah with their banjos, all of them dancing with such obvious delight – their costumes each and every one so carefully designed and executed?

Came the 'Wedding of the Painted Doll' and no Hollywood's 'Broadway Melody' ever staged it better!

The dainty bridesmaids pirouetting in their rainbow hued ruffled tutues. Red Riding Hood and Buster Brown, and the Halsema twins as the bride and groom – how can I describe them – without repeating myself again and again?

In the country it was quieter except when a loudspeaker van, volume raised to a fiendish pitch, ran slowly about the roads advertising an Indian film. I often went to the country, and not only for the silence. It seemed to me that I was seeing the landscape for the first time. I had hated the sun and the unchanging seasons. I had believed that the foliage had no variety and could never understand how the word 'tropical' held romance for so many. Now I was taken by the common coconut tree, the cliché of the Caribbean. I discovered, what every child in Trinidad knows, that if you stand under the tree and look up, the tapering chrome ribs of the branches are like the spokes of a perfectly circular wheel. I had forgotten the largeness of the leaves and the variety of their shapes: the digitated breadfruit leaf, the heart-shaped wild tannia, the curving razor-shaped banana frond which sunlight rendered almost transparent. To ride past a coconut plantation was to see a rapidly changing criss-cross of slender curved trunks, greyish-white in a green gloom.

I had never liked the sugarcane fields. Flat, treeless and hot, they stood for everything I had hated about the tropics and the West Indies. 'Cane is Bitter' is the title of a story by Samuel Selvon and might well be the epigraph of a history of the Caribbean. It is a brutal plant, tall and grass-like, with rough, razor-edged blades. I knew it was the basis of the economy, but I preferred trees and shade. Now, in the uneven land of Central and South Trinidad, I saw that even sugar cane could be beautiful. On the plains just before crop-time, you drive through it, walls of grass on either side; but in rolling country you can look down on a hillside covered with tall sugar-cane in arrow: steel-blue plumes dancing above a grey-green carpet, grey-green because each long blade curves back on itself, revealing its paler underside.

The cocoa woods were another thing. They were like the woods of fairy tales, dark and shadowed and cool. The cocoa-pods, hanging by thick short stems, were like wax fruit in brilliant green and yellow and red and crimson and purple. Once, on a late after-noon drive to Tamana, I found the fields flooded. Out of the flat yellow water, which gurgled in the darkness, the black trunks of the stunted trees rose.

After every journey I returned to Port of Spain past Shanty Town, the mangrove swamp, the orange mist of the burning rubbish dump, the goats, the expectant corbeaux, all against a sunset that reddened the glassy water of the Gulf.

Everyone has to learn to see the West Indies tropics for himself. The landscape has never been recorded, and to go to the Trinidad Art Society Exhibition is to see how little local painters help. The expatriates contribute a few watercolours, the Trinidadians a lot of local colour. 'Tropical Fruit' is the title of one painting, a title which would have had some meaning in the Temperate Zone. Another, startlingly, is 'Native Hut'. There are the usual picturesque native characters and native customs, the vision that of the tourist, at whom most of these native paintings seem to be aimed. The beach scenes are done with colours straight out of the tube, with no effort to capture the depth of sky, the brilliancy of light, the insubstan-tiality of colour in the tropics. The more gifted painters have ceased to record the landscape: the patterns of the leaves are too beguiling. In art, as in almost everything else, Trinidad has in one step moved from primitivism to modernism.

Many years ago, in Jamaica, Mrs Edna Manley had to judge some local drawings and paintings. Not one, she reported, portrayed a Jamaican face. 'Even worse, there was one little study or sketch of a Jamaican market scene, and believe it or not, the market women under their scarlet bandanas had yellow hair, pink faces, and even blue eyes.' It would appear at first that this has changed, for in Trinidad even the advertisements are now in blackface. But the impulse that prompted the Jamaican artist to give yellow hair and pink faces to people he knew to be irremediably black still exists and is, if anything, stronger.

It was the blackface advertisements that disturbed me. I suppose I was too used to seeing white people winning new confidence after using Colgate's and keeping that schoolgirl complexion with Palmolive. The trouble was, paradoxically, that the advertisements were not in blackface but only in blackish face. The people undergoing the Showdown Test for Old Oak rum were not really black; their features were not noticeably un-European and lighting made them scarcely distinguishable from white. The only truly black person was the garage-hand in the Shell advertisement. Who, then, were these people of the middle class, for whom these advertisements were meant, who would be offended by the black image of themselves?

They sat around in night clubs and applauded at the end of a 'number', just like Americans in films, particularly those old musicals where the heroine burst into song in the restaurant and looked surprised and embarrassed when the clapping started. They had drive-in cinemas. They had barbecues — a custom of the Caribs, and a word from the Caribs, returning with changes to the Caribbean. Their houses, decorations, amusements and food were copied from American magazines. This was the Hollywood B-world. With one difference.

A new magazine appeared in Trinidad while I was there. It was called *West Indian Home and Family* and was described as 'the West Indian magazine for women ... *your* magazine, created and printed right here in Trinidad'. Already in the first issue 'family problems are answered by a qualified psychologist'. Trinidad has two psychiatrists, I believe; and from internal evidence, both problems and psychologist in this magazine comes from America in the form of a syndicated column. 'Dreams are interpreted by Stephen Norris, who has been writing on the fascinating subject for over 20 years.' This column is a little harder to place. 'I dreamed,' Mrs. J. H. writes, 'that my husband and I were in Egypt, fighting off attacking Arabs . . .' The romantic serial, *Latin Love Song*, has for heroine Marcy Connors, an American night-club singer, a brunette, 'slim, with dark tresses piled high on her head . . . a picture of true, patrician beauty'. All this in a magazine for women, 'created and printed right here in Trinidad'.

Certain concessions have been made. There is a black woman on the cover; but lighting has given her a copperish colour. In the advertisement for Valor Stoves — *My Mummy Has a Lovely Valor* — there are two black children with, however, 'good' (not negroid) hair. The advertisement for Texgas — *How do you manage to look so cool . . . cooking? Why tell him? Little secrets like these only give busy housewives a captivating air of mystery! Why spoil the illusion? But we know she uses TexGAS* — is more revealing. The copy is given point by a drawing of what is meant to be a happy West Indian family — Daddy laughing, baby waving from Daddy's shoulder, Mummy stirring, smiling — but pains have been taken, in drawing and colouring and dress, to suggest a white American family slightly tanned, perhaps by those 'long summer holidays', mentioned in the copy for Avon Moisturized Skin Care, which 'expose your skin to harsh treatment from the sun and wind'.

When James Pope-Hennessy was in Trinidad just before the war he thought the sight of Negro girls singing '*Loch Lomond*' 'sickening'. And for a long time in Trinidad there has been a campaign against poems about daffodils — daffodils in particular: Wordsworth's poem appears to be the only poem most Trinidadians have read — because daffodils are not flowers Trinidad schoolchildren know. I cannot myself see why anyone should deny himself the pleasures of any literature or song. Absurdity would enter only if

the girls singing '*Loch Lomond*' pretended to be Scottish. Trinidadians know this; those who wish to wear the kilt do so only in
Scotland. To the Trinidadian mind, however, no absurdity attaches
to the pretence of being American in Trinidad; and while much
energy has been spent in the campaign against Wordsworth, no one
has spoken out against the fantasy which Trinidadians live out every
day of their lives.

They can never completely identify themselves with what they
read in magazines or see in films. Then frustration can only deepen
for their minds are closed to everything else. Reality is always
separate from the ideal; but in Trinidad this fantasy is a form of
masochism and is infinitely more cheating than the fantasy which
makes the poor delight in films about rich or makes the English
singer use an American accent. It is the difference between the
Emily Post Institute advice on dating, published in the *Trinidad
Guardian* ('The man must call for his date at her house'), and the
calypso by Sparrow:

> Tell your sister to come down, boy.
> I have something here for she.
> Tell she is Mr Benwood Dick,
> The man from Sangre Grande.
> She know me well. I give she already.
> Mm. She must remember me. Go on, go on.
> Tell she Mr Benwood come.

The Negro in the New World was, until recently, unwilling to look
at his past. It seemed to him natural that he should be in the West
Indies, that he should speak French or English or Dutch, dress in
the European manner or in adaptation of it, and share the European's religion and food. Travel-writers who didn't know better
spoke of him as a 'native', and he accepted this: 'This is my island
in the sun,' Mr Harry Belafonte sings, 'where my people have
toiled since time begun.' Africa was forgotten. What was more

astonishing, it had been, from the early days of slavery and long before the European scramble for Africa, a reminder of shame, when one might have expected that in secret legends it would have been a mythical land of freedom and bliss. But that was the vision of Blake, not of the Negroes in the New World, apart from a few like the rebellious soldier Dagga in Trinidad in 1834, whose intention was to walk east until he got back to Africa. In 1860, twenty-six years after the abolition of slavery, Trollope wrote:

> But how strange is the race of creole Negroes – of Negroes, that is, born out of Africa! They have no country of their own, yet they have not hitherto any country of their adoption. They have no language of their own, nor have they as yet any language of their adoption; for they speak their broken English as uneducated foreigners always speak a foreign language. They have no idea of country, and no pride of race. They have no religion of their own, and can hardly as yet be said to have, as a people, a religion by adoption. The West Indian Negro knows nothing of Africa except that it is a term of reproach. If African immigrants are put to work on the same estate with him, he will not eat with them, or drink with them, or walk with them. He will hardly work beside them, and regards himself as a creature immeasurably the superior of the newcomer.

This was the greatest damage done to the Negro by slavery. It taught him self-contempt. It set him the ideals of white civilization and made him despise every other. Deprived as a slave of Christianity, education and family, he set himself after emancipation to acquire these things; and every step on the road to whiteness deepened the anomaly of his position and increased his vulnerability. 'He burns to be a scholar,' Trollope observed, with an unusual insensitivity, 'puzzles himself with fine words, addicts himself to religion for the sake of appearances, and delights in aping the little graces of civilization.' Everything in the white world had to be learned from scratch, and at every stage the Negro exposed himself to the cruelty of the civilization which had overpowered him and which he was mastering. 'These people marry now,' a white lady said to Trollope in Jamaica. 'In the tone of her voice,' he comments, 'I thought I could catch an idea that she conceived them in doing so to be trenching on the privileges of their superiors.'

Yet to the West Indian there has never been any anomaly.

> It is necessary [writes Dr Hugh Springer in a recent *Caribbean Quarterly*] to see ourselves in perspective as far as we can, and to recognize that ours is not a separate civilization, but a part of that great branch of civilization that is called Western civilization. At any rate this is where we begin our national life. Our culture is rooted in Western Culture and our values, in the main, are the values of the Christian-Hellenic tradition. What are the characteristics of that tradition? They can be summed up in three words – virtue, knowledge and faith – the Greek ideals of virtue and knowledge and the Christian faith.

This, with its unintentional irony, its ignoring of the squalid history of the region, is a good Empire Day exhortation; not surprisingly, for this willingness to forget and ignore is part of the West Indian fantasy. Surely the words of Trollope and the white lady of Jamaica can give the West Indian a better perspective on his situation.

> My Mummy has a lovely Valor. How do you manage to look so cool . . . cooking?

Twenty million Africans made the middle passage, and scarcely an African name remains in the New World. Until the other day African tribesmen on the screen excited derisive West Indian laughter; the darkie comic (whose values were the values of the Christian-Hellenic tradition) was more admired. In the pursuit of the Christian-Hellenic tradition, which some might see as a paraphrase for whiteness, the past has to be denied, the self despised. Black will be made white. It has been said that in concentration camps the inmates began after a time to believe that they were genuinely guilty. Pursuing the Christian-Hellenic tradition, the West Indian accepted his blackness as his guilt, and divided people into the white, fusty, musty, dusty, tea, coffee, cocoa, light black, dark black. He never seriously doubted the validity of the prejudices of the culture to which he aspired. In the French territories he aimed at Frenchness, in the Dutch territories at Dutchness; in the English territories he aimed at simple whiteness and modernity, Englishness being impossible.

* * *

Living in a borrowed culture, the West Indian, more than most, needs writers to tell him who he is and where he stands. Here the West Indian writers have failed. Most have so far only reflected and flattered the prejudices of their race or colour groups. Many a writer has displayed a concern, visible perhaps only to the West Indian, to show how removed his group is from blackness, how close to whiteness. The limits of this absurdity were reached in one novel when a light-skinned Negro (or, as the writer prefers to call people of this group, a 'good-class coloured') made a plea for tolerance towards black Negroes. In the context it was not the plea that mattered, but the behaviour: light-skinned Negroes, it was implied, have the same feelings as white people and the same prejudices, and behave just like white people in a certain type of novel. So the brown writer will have his brown heroes who behave whitely, if not well; they will further establish their position by being permitted to speak as abusively as possible of other groups. This yearning to be thought different and worthy is not a new thing. A hundred years ago Trollope found that 'coloured girls of insecure class' delighted in speaking contemptuously of Negroes to him. 'I have heard this done by one whom I had absolutely taken for a Negro, and who was not using loud abusive language, but gently speaking of an inferior class.' The black writer is now, of course, able to retaliate; he might speak, as one writer has done, of 'English soldiers smelling of khaki and their race'. To the initiated one whole side of West Indian writing has little to do with literature, and much to do with the race war.

The insecure wish to be heroically portrayed. Irony and satire, which might help more, are not acceptable; and no writer wishes to let down his group. For this reason the lively and inventive Trinidad dialect, which has won West Indian writing many friends and as many enemies abroad, is disliked by some West Indians. They do not object to its use locally; the most popular column in Trinidad is a dialect column in the *Evening News* by the talented and witty person known as Macaw. But they object to its use in books which are read abroad. 'They must be does talk so by you,' one woman said to me. 'They don't talk so by me.' The Trinidadian expects his novels, like his advertisements, to have a detergent purpose, and it is largely for this reason that there are complaints about the scarcity of writing about what is called the middle class.

In fact there is a good deal of West Indian writing about the middle class, but the people tend to be so indistinguishable from white and are indeed so often genuinely white that the middle class cannot recognize itself. It is not easy to write about the West Indian middle class. The most exquisite gifts of irony and perhaps malice would be required to keep the characters from slipping into an unremarkable mid-Atlantic whiteness. They would have to be treated as real people with real problems and responsibilities and affections – and this has been done – but they would also have to be treated as people whose lives have been corrupted by a fantasy which is their own cross. Whether an honest exploration of this class will ever be attempted is doubtful. The gifts required, of subtlety and brutality, can grow only out of mature literature; and there can be advance towards this only when writers cease to think about letting down their sides.

The involvement of the Negro with the white world is one of the limitations of West Indian writing, as it is the destruction of American Negro writing. The American Negro's subject is his blackness. This cannot be the basis of any serious literature, and it has happened again and again that once the American Negro has made his statement, his profitable protest, he has nothing to say. With two or three exceptions, the West Indian writer has so far avoided the American Negro type of protest writing, but his aims have been equally propagandist: to win acceptance for his group.

'Comedy,' Graham Greene says, 'needs a strong framework of social convention with which the author sympathizes but does not share.' By this definition the West Indian writer is incapable of comedy; and, as we have seen, he is not interested in it. Mr Greene's statement can be extended. A literature can grow only out of a strong framework of social convention. And the only convention the West Indian knows is his involvement with the white world. This deprives his work of universal appeal. The situation is too special. The reader is excluded; he is invited to witness; he cannot participate. It is easier to enter any strong framework of social convention, however alien. It is easier to enter the tribal world of an African writer like Camara Laye.

No writer can be blamed for reflecting his society. If the West Indian writer is to be blamed, it is because, by accepting and promoting the unimpressive race-and-colour values of his group, he has not only failed to diagnose the sickness of his society but has aggravated it.

It is only in the calypso that the Trinidadian touches reality. The calypso is a purely local form. No song composed outside Trinidad is a calypso. The calypso deals with local incidents, local attitudes, and it does so in a local language. The pure calypso, the best calypso, is incomprehensible to the outsider. Wit and verbal conceits are fundamental; without them no song, however good the music, however well sung, can be judged a calypso. A hundred foolish travel-writers (reproducing the doggerel sung 'especially' for them) and a hundred 'calypsonians' in all parts of the world have debased the form, which is now generally dismissed abroad as nothing more than a catchy tune with a primitive jingle in broken English. The knowing refusal of travel-writers nowadays to be taken in is as foolish as their previous indiscrimination, neither reaction being based on a knowledge of genuine calypso.

For this bastardization Trinidadians are as much to blame as anyone. Just as they take pleasure in their American modernity, so they take pleasure in living up to the ideals of the tourist brochure. They know that they are presented to the world as the land of calypso and steel band. They are determined that the world shall not be disappointed; and their talent for self-caricature is profound. The Americans expect native costumes and native dances; Trinidad will discover both.

Few words are used more frequently in Trinidad than 'culture'. Culture is spoken of as something quite separate from day-to-day existence, separate from advertisements, films and comic strips. It is like a special native dish, something like a *callalloo*. Culture is a dance — not the dance that people do when more than three of them get together — but the one put on in native costume on a stage. Culture is music — not the music played by well-known bands and nowadays in the modern way, tape-recorded — but the steel band. Culture is song — not the commercial jingle which, as much as the calypso, has become the folksong of Trinidad, nor the popular American songs which are heard from morning till night — not these, but the calypso. Culture is, in short, a night-club turn. And nothing pleases Trinidadians so much as to see their culture being applauded by white American tourists in night-clubs.

From the *Trinidad Guardian*:

LIMBO FOR WI FILM LIKELY
By George Alleyne
Guardian Shipping Reporter

Mr Lourenço Ricciardi, Italian film director, and Mrs Ricciardi, photographer, flew into Trinidad on Tuesday to look for talent and possible locations for a movie that the Baltea Film Company of Rome plans making in the West Indies. Within hours they were taken by friendly Mr Oliver Burke, secretary of the Tourist Board, to the new Miramar Club, South Quay, Port of Spain, where they saw the Limbo being performed by Lord Chinapoo, one-time Limbo 'king', and his troupe.

'Wonderful,' cried Ricciardi. 'I will consider incorporating the limbo in the film. Nothing is decided though,' he said yesterday.

The Ricciardis are on the last leg of an exploratory tour of the Caribbean.

They have been so far on their trip to Cuba, Jamaica, St Thomas, Puerto Rico, Martinique, St Lucia, Grenada and Barbados.

This talk of culture is comparatively new. It was a concept of some politicians in the forties, and caught on largely because it answered the vague, little-understood dissatisfaction some people were beginning to feel with their lives of fantasy. The promotion of a local culture was the only form of nationalism that could arise in a population divided into mutually exclusive cliques based on race, colour, shade, religion, money. Under pressure any Trinidadian group could break up into its component parts; there was no more pathetic demonstration of this than during the London race riots of 1958. White, coloured, Portuguese, Indian, Chinese thought that no rioters would attack them; there were Negroes who thought that only Jamaican Negroes would be attacked; some students and professional men thought that only lower-class Negroes would be attacked; and among respectable West Indians generally, white, brown and black, there was a feeling that the 'black fellers' had what was coming to them, and that the English people had been 'provoked'. At a time when West Indians should have drawn together, many were anxious to contract out; Mrs Mackay's son Angus, it will be remembered, used to tell people that he was Brazilian.

Nationalism was impossible in Trinidad. In the colonial society every man had to be for himself; every man had to grasp whatever dignity and power he was allowed; he owed no loyalty to the island and scarcely any of his group. To understand this is to understand the squalor of the politics that came to Trinidad in 1946 when, after no popular agitation, universal adult suffrage was declared. The privilege took the population by surprise. Old attitudes persisted: the government was something removed, the local eminence was despised. The new politics were reserved for the enterprising, who had seen the prodigious commercial possibilities. There were no parties, only individuals. Corruption, not unexpected, aroused only amusement and even mild approval: Trinidad has always admired the 'sharp character' who, like the sixteenth-century picaroon of Spanish literature, survives and triumphs by his wits in a place where it is felt that all eminence is arrived at by crookedness.

When in 1870 Kingsley visited San Fernando, a 'gay and growing little town', he was distressed only by the Negro houses, which were 'mostly patched together out of the most heterogeneous and wretched scraps of wood'.

> On inquiry I found that the materials were, in most cases, stolen; that when a Negro wanted to build a house, instead of buying the materials, he pilfered a board here, a stick there, a nail somewhere else . . . regardless of the serious injury which he caused to working buildings; and when he had gathered a sufficient pile, hidden safely away behind his neighbour's house, the new hut rose as if by magic . . . But I was told too, frankly enough, by the very gentleman who complained, that this habit was simply an heirloom from the bad days of slavery, when the pilfering of the slaves from other estates was connived at by their own masters, on the ground that if A's Negroes robbed B, B's Negroes robbed C, and so all round the alphabet; one more evil instance of the demoralizing effect of a state of things which, wrong in itself, was sure to be the parent of a hundred other wrongs.

The picaroon delight in trickery persists. These are constant 'leakages' of examination papers; in 1960 the Cambridge School Certificate biology paper was known throughout the island days before the examination. Slavery, the mixed population, the absence of national pride and the closed colonial system have to a remarkable degree re-created the attitudes of the Spanish picaroon world. This was an ugly world, a jungle, where the picaroon hero starved unless he stole, was beaten almost to death when found out, and had therefore to get in his blows first whenever possible; where the weak were humiliated; where the powerful never appeared and were beyond reach; where no one was allowed any dignity and everyone had to impose himself; an uncreative society, where war was the only profession.

So in Trinidad you must always walk careful of your dignity, and you must impose yourself whether you are in a store or a bank, whether you are crossing the road or driving a car. The treatment of the sick poor in drug-stores is notorious. In a bank it is always better to be served by an expatriate; he may know that your account is negligible, but he will be civil. On the highway no one will dip his lights for you; you must blind in return, and learn the Trinidad highway game of driving into the blinding lights, to make your opponent swerve.

Throughout the picaroon society violence and brutality are accepted. Twenty years ago an extremely popular calypso urged the reintroduction of corporal punishment:

> The old-time Cat-o'nine!
> Lash them hard! And they bound to change their mind.
> Send them Carrera [*prison island*] with licks like fire,
> And they bound to surrender.

In 1960 the Grenadian illegal immigrant who was hounded by the police was a subject for calypso; and the brutality of the police was applauded:

If you see how they holding the scamps and them,
Friends, you bound to bawl.
Some of them can read and spell,
But they can't pronounce at all.
The police telling them, 'Say pig, you stupid man,'
And as they say hag, is licks in the police van.

Sentimentality and brutality go together. The man who, during an emotional mother-and-son scene in a B-film, turns to you and says hoarsely, 'A mother is a helluva thing, you know, boy. You only have one,' is the same man who, watching Belsen camp scenes, will roar with derisive laughter.

To bring political organization to the picaroon society, with its taste for corruption and violence and its lack of respect for the person, has its dangers. Such a society cannot immediately become responsible; but it can be re-educated only through responsibility. Change must come from the top. Capital punishment and corporal punishment, incitements to brutality, must be abolished. The civil service must be rejuvenated. In the colonial days the civil servant, his way blocked by the expatriate who was sometimes his inferior and occasionally corrupt as well, expended all his creative energies on petty picaroon intrigue and worked off his aggression on the public. His duties were those of a clerk; he was never required to be efficient; he never had to make a decision. Pitch-forked now into the ministerial system, turned from clerical or at best executive grade officer into administrative, the average civil servant is out of his depth. Contempt for the public lingers on, as well as the tradition of responsibility-dodging. The public, obliged to beg favours, continues to hold authority in dread and contempt. What is true of the civil service is true of most of the business houses.

The need to be efficient will change some of these attitudes. An efficient civil service is in some ways a considerate civil service. The assistant in a drugstore, if required to be efficient, will see that her position is not simply one of authority over the poor who are sick;

the policeman will see that he is more than a licensed bully; and perhaps, gradually, there will be a lessening of the need now felt by everyone all down the line to display his authority by aggression.

From the *Trinidad Guardian*:

SAM COOKE TO GIVE FREE SHOW

Sam Cooke, one of America's leading vocalists and his Summertime show, will put on a free performance for any one of Trinidad's Orphan homes at the conclusion of the Trinidad leg of his tour upcoming November 9 and November 10.

This was made known in a letter from the Sam Cooke Inc., New York, to Mr Valmond (Fatman) Jones, Secretary of the Sam Cooke Fan Club in Trinidad who are sponsors of the show.

The free show comes off on November 11, the day after Mr Cooke's last local performance at San Fernando.

From the *Trinidad Guardian*:

SAM COOKE'S 'AGENT' FLIES TO MARTINIQUE

Valmond 'Fatman' Jones, secretary of the Sam Cooke Fan Club, flew unexpectedly to Martinique yesterday morning, 36 hours before his singing idol was booked to perform before a sell-out crowd at the Globe Cinema, Port-of-Spain.

Mr Jones, popular carnival masquerader, is the 'impresario' behind Sam Cooke's advertised visit to Trinidad.

The American singer, according to arrangements made by Mr Jones, is expected to give two performances at the Globe Cinema, Port-of-Spain, tonight and two at the Empire cinema, San Fernando, tomorrow. He was due to arrive at Piarco Airport, according to correspondence, with a six-piece band on Monday. Up to last night, the singer and his musicians had not turned up.

It is understood that both shows at the Globe, 4.30 and 8.30

p.m., were completely sold out. Tickets for the San Fernando show were selling like 'hot bread', it was also reported.

Before he left, Mr Jones had disclosed that Cooke would give a charity show for orphans after concluding his four engagements.

A publicity agent in Port-of-Spain, who spent more than $1,000 to advertise the Sam Cooke shows in Trinidad, was surprised to hear of Mr Jones' departure. He immediately stopped all further promotion of the shows.

A cocktail party to welcome Mr Cooke fixed for last night at the Bretton Hall Hotel, Port-of-Spain, did not come off. Several invited guests turned up, but were disappointed when they learned that Mr Cooke had not yet arrived.

Perhaps the most disappointed among the people who came to Bretton Hall expecting to see Mr Cooke was an American Naval Officer from the U.S. Base at Chaguaramas, who said he had deposited a 'few hundred dollars' with Mr Jones on the agreement that the singer would give a brief performance at the Base.

Three youths were talking about this affair one afternoon around a coconut-cart near the Savannah.

The Indian said, 'I don't see how anybody could vex with the man. *That* is brains.'

'Is what my aunt say,' one of the Negro boys said. 'She ain't feel she get rob. She feel she pay two dollars for the *intelligence*.'

She feel she pay two dollars for the intelligence. And at once analysis is made ridiculous. For here is a natural sophistication and tolerance which has been produced by the picaroon society. How could one wish it otherwise? To condemn the picaroon society out of hand is to ignore its important quality. And this is not its ability to beguile and enchant. For if such a society breeds cynicism, it also breeds tolerance, not the tolerance between castes and creeds and so on –

which does not exist in Trinidad anyway – but something more profound: tolerance for every human activity and affection for every demonstration of wit and style.

There is no set way in Trinidad of doing anything. Every house can be a folly. There is no set way of dressing or cooking or entertaining. Everyone can live with whoever he can get wherever he can afford. Ostracism is meaningless; the sanctions of any clique can be ignored. It is in this way, and not in the way of the travel brochure, that the Trinidadian is a cosmopolitan. He is adaptable; he is cynical; having no rigid social conventions of his own, he is amused by the conventions of others. He is a natural anarchist, who has never been able to take the eminent at their own valuation. He is a natural eccentric, if by eccentricity is meant the expression of one's own personality, unhampered by fear of ridicule or the discipline of a class. If the Trinidadian has no standards of morality he is without the greater corruption of sanctimoniousness, and can never make pleas for intolerance in the name of piety. He can never achieve the society-approved nastiness of the London landlord, say, who turns a dwelling-house into a boarding-house, charges exorbitant rents and is concerned lest his tenants live in sin. Everything that makes the Trinidadian an unreliable, exploitable citizen makes him a quick, civilized person whose values are always human ones, whose standards are only those of wit and style.

As the Trinidadian becomes a more reliable and efficient citizen, he will cease to be what he is. Already the gap between rich and poor – between the civil servant, the professional man, and the labourer – is widening. Class divisions are hardening and, in a land where no one can look back too far without finding a labourer or a crook, and sometimes a labourer who became a crook, members of the embryonic middle class are talking of their antecedents. Standards are being established by this class, and the fluidity of the society has diminished. With commercial radio and advertising agencies has also come all the apparatus of the modern society for joylessness, for the killing of the community spirit and the shutting up of people in their separate prisons of similar ambitions and tastes and selfishness: the class struggle, the political struggle, the race struggle.

When people speak of the race problem in Trinidad they do not mean the Negro–white problem. They mean the Negro–Indian rivalry. This will be denied by the whites, who will insist that the basic problem remains the contempt of their group for the non-white. Now that complaints about white prejudice are rarely heard, it is not uncommon to find whites scourging themselves for the prejudices of their group before black audiences. This they do by reporting outrageous statements made by members of their group and dissociating themselves from their sentiments.

The fact is that in Trinidad power is so evenly distributed – whites in business, Indians in business and the professions, Negroes in the professions and the civil service – that racial abuse is without meaning. What the Calypsonian Sparrow predicted quite recently has already come to pass:

> Well, the way how things shaping up,
> All this nigger business going to stop.
> And soon in the West Indies
> It will be 'Please, Mr Nigger, please.'

In spite of the abuse in which the white indulges, particularly for the benefit of the outsider, there is no general feeling against the local whites. Against 'expats', however, there is a growing animosity; their presence in positions of power is a threat and a humiliation, a reminder of the days when top posts were reserved for expatriates, and a reminder of prejudice encountered in England. But this animosity is not widespread; it does not go beyond certain insecure sections of the middle class.

The virtual by-passing of white prejudice was inevitable. The cultural involvement of the Negro was with the white world in general and not so much with the local whites, who had shown little interest in education and who rarely entered the professions. The break-up of the colonial system made plain their inaptitudes at the same time that it released the pent-up ambitions of the better equipped non-white. The chaotic social divisions also help. Each of the island's many cliques believes that it is the true élite. The expatriates believe they are the élite; so do the local whites, the businessmen, the professional men, the higher civil servants, the politicians, the sportsmen. This arrangement, whereby most people don't even know when they are being excluded, leaves everyone reasonably happy. And most important of all, the animosity that might have been directed against the whites has been channelled off against the Indians.

Throughout the Caribbean today the Negro's desire to assert himself is a constant quantity. This brings him in collision with white, coloured, Chinese, Syrians and Jews in Jamaica, white and coloured in Martinique, Indians in Trinidad. The animosity between Negroes and Indians is, at first sight, puzzling. At all levels they share the same language, the same ambitions – *My Mummy has a lovely Valor* – and, increasingly, the same pleasures. Their interests don't clash. The Negro is a town-dweller; the Indian is an agriculturist. The Negro with a good handwriting and a head for intrigue goes into the civil service; the Indian similarly equipped goes into business. Both go into the professions.

Of late, with Indians entering the civil service and small-island Negroes muscling in on the taxi business, there has been a certain direct rivalry; but this is outweighed by a long-standing division of labour which is taken so much for granted that Trinidadians are hardly aware of it. Coconut-sellers, for instance, are Indian; it would be unnatural and perhaps unwise to receive a coconut from a black hand. No one, not even an Indian, will employ a mason or a carpenter who is not a Negro. The lower down the scale one goes, the nicer the divisions of labour become. Negroes sell ice and its immediate byproducts: shaved ice, 'presses', snowballs. Indians sell iced lollies. Before the war Indians swept the streets of Port of

Spain; Negroes emptied the cesspits. Each felt a hearty contempt for the other; and when, during the war, Negroes from the smaller islands began sweeping the streets, it was felt by some Indians that this was another example of Indians losing their grip, the virtues of their fathers.

In St Kitts, if the emigrant on the *Francisco Bobadilla* wasn't lying, a Negro can bake bread with moderate success. But St Kitts is St Kitts. In Trinidad a Negro who opens a bakery runs a considerable risk, and he is begging for trouble if he opens a laundry. Whatever goes on in the back rooms, Trinidadians like to feel that their clothes are washed and their bread handled by white or Chinese hands. Equally, for all the complaints about white and whitish staff in the banks, there is a strong feeling among Negroes that black people, even when they can be trusted, don't know how to handle money. In money matters generally there is almost a superstition among both Indians and Negroes about the unreliability of their own race; there is scarcely a Trinidadian who has not at one time felt or said, 'I don't have any luck with my race.' It is an aspect of the multi-racial society to which sociologists pay little attention.

All this speaks of accord. But Trinidad in fact teeters on the brink of racial war. Politics must be blamed; but there must have been an original antipathy for the politicians to work on. Matters are not helped by the fierce rivalry between Indians and Negroes as to who despises the other more. This particular rivalry is conducted by the liberal-minded, who will not be denied the pleasure of appealing to their group to show more tolerance towards the other group, and who are deeply annoyed when it is claimed by liberals of the other party that it is the other group which has to do the tolerating. There is also considerable rivalry as to who started the despising.

It is sufficient to state that the antipathy exists. The Negro has a deep contempt, as has been said, for all that is not white; his values are the values of white imperialism at its most bigoted. The Indian despises the Negro for not being an Indian; he has, in addition, taken over all the white prejudices against the Negro and with the convert's zeal regards as Negro everyone who has any tincture of Negro blood. 'The two races,' Froude observed in 1887, 'are more absolutely apart than the white and the black. The Asiatic insists the more on his superiority in the fear perhaps that if he did not the white might forget it.' Like monkeys pleading for evolution, each claiming to be whiter than the other, Indians and Negroes appeal to the unacknowledged white audience to see how much they despise one another. They despise one another by references to the whites; and the irony is that their antagonism should have reached its peak today, when white prejudices have ceased to matter.

Few non-Indians know much about the Indians, except that they live in the country, work on the land, are rich, fond of litigation and violence. There were undoubtedly small criminal and army elements among the Indian immigrants – one or two low Indian army ranks survive as surnames – and parts of the Indian country-side, with their recurring unsolved murders, used to have a *mafia*-like atmosphere. Everyone in Trinidad knows that to run over an Indian in an Indian village and to stop is to ask for trouble; whether it has ever occurred that the driver who stopped was beaten up I don't know.* Nothing is known about Hinduism or Islam. The Muslim festival of Hosein, with its drum-beating and in the old days stick-fighting, is the only Indian festival which is known; Negroes sometimes beat the drums. Indian weddings are also known. There is little interest in the ritual; it is known only that at these weddings food is given to all comers. Even the simple distinction between Hindu and Muslim names is not known; and the Negro makes less

---

* 'A clever and sympathetic Indian journalist took me to Agra to see the Taj Mahal. A hundred and twenty miles by car, through the parched, dust-clouded countryside. At every village, the driver slowed down to ten miles an hour and kept his thumb on the horn. "If a car ran over a man in one of these places," my friend said, "the people would burn the car and kill the occupants." ' John Wain: 'A visit to India': *Encounter*, May 1961. The old province of Agra was one of the areas from which Trinidad Indians came.

effort than the average English person to pronounce Indian names correctly. This is partly because of the attitude that nothing which is not white is worth bothering about; partly because Indians are difficult to know; and partly because so many Indians have been modernizing themselves at such a rate that Indian customs have come to be regarded as things out of which people grow. So although Indians make up more than one-third of the population, their customs and ceremonies remain quaint and even exotic.

Everything which made the Indian alien in the society gave him strength. His alienness insulated him from the black–white struggle. He was taboo-ridden as no other person on the island; he had complicated rules about food and about what was unclean. His religion gave him values which were not the white values of the rest of the community, and preserved him from self-contempt; he never lost pride in his origins. More important than religion was his family organization, an enclosing self-sufficient world absorbed with its quarrels and jealousies, as difficult for the outsider to penetrate as for one of its members to escape. It protected and imprisoned, a static world, awaiting decay.

Islam is a static religion. Hinduism is not organized; it has no fixed articles, no hierarchy; it is constantly renewing itself and depends on the regular emergence of teachers and holy men. In Trinidad it could only wither; but its restrictions were tenacious. Marriage between unequal castes has only just ceased to cause trouble; marriage between Hindu and Muslim can still split a family; marriage outside the race is unthinkable. Only the urban Indian, the Indian of the middle class, and the Christian convert were able to move easily out of the Indian framework. The Indian Christian was more liberal and adaptable in every way; but, following far behind the Negro on the weary road to whiteness, he was more insecure.

Living by themselves in villages, the Indians were able to have a complete community life. It was a world eaten up with jealousies and family feuds and village feuds; but it was a world of its own, a community within the colonial society, without responsibility, with authority doubly and trebly removed. Loyalties were narrow: to the family, the village. This has been responsible for the village-headman type of politician the Indian favours, and explains why Indian leadership has been so deplorable, so unfitted to handle the mechanics of party and policy.

A peasant-minded, money-minded community, spiritually static because cut off from its roots, its religion reduced to rites without philosophy, set in a materialist colonial society: a combination of historical accidents and national temperament has turned the Trinidad Indian into the complete colonial, even more philistine than the white.

Much of the West Indian Negro's drive arises out of his desire to define his position in the world. The Indian, with no such problem, was content with his narrow loyalties. Whether he knew his language or practised his religion, the knowledge that a country called India existed was to him a pole. He felt no particular attachment to this country. It is said that Indian Independence in 1947 encouraged Indian racialism in Trinidad; but the explanation is too simple. The Trinidad Indian who was concerned about the Independence struggle and contributed large sums to various funds, washed his hands of India in 1947. The struggle was over, the shame was removed, and he could settle without self-approach into the easy, undemanding society of Trinidad. Indians who went to India returned disgusted by the poverty and convinced of their own superiority. The relationship between Indians from India and Indians from Trinidad quickly developed into the relationship of muted dislike between metropolitans and colonials, between Spaniards and Latin Americans, English and Australians.

1947 is not the date. 1946 is the date, when the first elections were held under universal adult suffrage in Trinidad. Then the bush lawyers and the village headmen came into their own, not only in the Indian areas but throughout the island. Then the loudspeaker van reminded people that they were of Aryan blood. Then, as was reported, the politician, soon to be rewarded by great wealth, bared his pale chest and shouted, 'I is a nigger too!'

Though now one racialism seems to be reacting on the other, each has different roots. Indian politicians have created Indian racialism out of a harmless egoism. Negro racialism is more complex. It is an overdue assertion of dignity; it has elements of bitterness; it has something of the urban mob requiring to be satisfied with bread and circuses. It has profound intellectual promptings as well, in the realization that the Negro problem lies not simply in the attitude of others to the Negro, but in the Negro's attitude to himself. It is as yet confused, for the Negro, while rejecting the guilt imposed on him by the white man, is not able to shake off the prejudices he has inherited from the white man, a duality which is responsible for what the Jamaican novelist John Hearne, on a visit to British Guiana in 1957, described as 'the pathetic nostalgia that corrupts so many Negroes. The retreat into apologies for their condition, their endless "historical" explanations and their lack of any direction. The sentimental camaraderie of skin which provides the cheap thrill of being "African".'

In the Negro–Indian conflict each side believes it can win. Neither sees that this rivalry threatens to destroy the Land of the Calypso.

It is characteristic of the Trinidad sense of humour, with its ability to turn grave international crises into private jokes, that the unsavoury and dangerous night-club stretch of Wrightson Road in Port of Spain should be called the Gaza Strip – *Gunplay in Gaza Strip* was a headline I saw – and that by this local association the name should be repeated in country cafés by proprietors anxious to give a touch of drama to their unpretentious establishments. It was not surprising, therefore, with the Congo occupying the headlines for weeks, that the sonorous names of the Congolese leaders, Kasavubu, Lumumba, Mobutu, should have caught the Trinidad imagination. Anyone in authority, particularly foremen

and policemen, became Mobutu: 'Look out, boys. Mobutu coming.'
The names of Kasavubu and Lumumba could be applied to anyone;
and I came across one person whose temporary nickname was
Dag (Hammarskjöld). This sophisticated play-acting is part of that
Trinidad taste for fantasy, already noted, which finds its full
bacchanalian expression on the two days of Carnival.*

Then comedy turned to tragedy. Lumumba was captured, his
humiliations were photographed, and he was killed. Some weeks
after the news of Lumumba's death I came upon a procession in one
of the main streets of Port of Spain. It was an orderly procession
made up wholly of Negroes. They were singing hymns, which
contrasted with the violence of their banners and placards. These
were anti-white, anti-clerical and pro-African in an ill-defined,
inclusive way. I had never before seen anything like it in Trinidad.
It was a demonstration of that 'sentimental camaraderie of skin
which provides the cheap thrill of being "African"' of which John
Hearne had written. It represented all that was barren in Negro
racialism. The Gaza Strip and the policeman who was Mobutu stood
for the Old Trinidad. This hymn-singing procession was the new.

I thought then that it was a purely local eruption, created by the
pressures of local politics. But soon, on the journey I was now
getting ready to make, I came to see that such eruptions were
widespread, and represented feelings coming to the surface in
Negro communities throughout the Caribbean: confused feelings,
without direction; the Negro's rejection of the guilt he has borne
for so long; the last, delayed Spartacan revolt, more radical than
Toussaint L'Ouverture's; the closing of accounts this side of the
middle passage.

* George Lamming, the Barbadian writer, encountered at Lord's cricket
ground in 1957 on the day Sobers scored a hundred against the M.C.C., told of
the West Indian who exclaimed delightedly: 'A century on his first appearance
in the Kremlin of cricket, man. *In the Kremlin.*' So the drama of the cold war is
adapted to homelier events.

3. British Guiana

If there were but a snug secretaryship vacant there – and these things in Demerara are very snug – how I would invoke the goddess of patronage; how I would nibble round the officials of the Colonial Office; how I would stir up my friends' friends to write little notes to their friends! For Demerara is the Elysium of the tropics – the West Indian happy valley of Rasselas – the one true and actual Utopia of the Caribbean Seas – the Transatlantic Eden.

Anthony Trollope, 1860

FROM THE AIR Trinidad's Atlantic coast was outlined as on the map, the waves steadily rolling lace-patterned foam towards the shore, green edged with yellow. The waves began far out and rolled in evenly. On the bright blue water cloud shadows were like submerged rocks or like dissolving drops of ink. Soon blue water turned to brown, its progressively darker shades neatly contoured and sometimes marked off in white. Then the South American continent: a grey-green tufted carpet, worn brown in patches, with rivers like cracks in drying mud. For minute after minute we moved rapidly over the unchanging, unwelcoming land, a small corner of a vast continent, where trees grew and collapsed on muddy shores.

One can learn much about British Guiana from the air: its size, its emptiness, the isolation of its communities. Six hundred thousand people live in a country the size of Britain, and when you fly over the populated eastern coastal strip you see why there is so much unrest in a country which, from its bigness, should be a country of opportunity. The land here is fertile. The sugarcane fields, intersected by ruler-straight ditches, are like machine-made carpets. They go on and on, until the pattern is broken by a huddle of white-and-rust wooden houses, laid out as precisely as the fields: workers' houses: sugarcane land, you feel, going to waste, and the site arbitrarily chosen, for the settlement could have been put down anywhere else in that clear green expanse. 'To force the Negroes of the Virgin Islands to work,' Michael Swan writes in *The Marches of El Dorado*, 'the Danes cut down their soursop trees, and today in British Guiana sugar must use a hundred subtle methods to maintain a sufficient labour force – tropical people prefer a subsistence and little work to hard work and a higher standard of living.'

And emptiness. Fly to the interior. First you go over the sugar-cane fields beside the brown Demerara River. Abruptly the fields stop and bush begins; and in the bush there are little irregular areas of timorous destruction – indicating attitudes you will learn to associate with British Guiana – where forest has turned to marsh-land, for the soil here is poor and hardwood trees cannot easily be made to grow again. Within minutes towns, fields and clearings are passed, and you are over the forest, thick and choked and even, occasionally flawed by a river that is black or, when caught by the sun, glinting, a vein of gold or red through the dead green. And the forest continues. You cease to look, until, thirty or forty minutes later, the land breaks up into hills and valleys, beyond which lie the savannah lands, in the dry season marbled in green and brown and ochre, scratched with white trails, the beds of diminished streams lined with rich, succulent-looking palm trees. Brazil is not far away, equally empty, a vastness not to be comprehended.

It was strange then to find, as one drove from the airport to the city, that the houses were set close to one another, as on any cramped

West Indian island. Bush screened the Demerara River along which
we drove and which would have reminded us that we were on a
continent. As it was, only the elegance of the wooden houses on tall
stilts was not of the islands. The Guianese know how to build in
wood; the humblest wooden dwelling has a rightness of proportion
and style, while the newer concrete buildings have the recognizable
West Indian insipidity and clumsiness. In wood the Guianese have
built mosques with minarets and Hindu temples with balustrades
and domes; they have built a cathedral; they have even managed
Victorian Gothic. They are profoundly ashamed of these wooden
buildings, regarding them as signs of their poverty and backward-
ness, shabby substitutes for the concrete of a rich island like
Trinidad; and since everyone also agrees that wooden houses are
firetraps, it seems likely that soon only the very poor will live in
attractive houses, and that Georgetown, the most beautiful city
in the West Indies, in its elegance, unity and spaciousness, will be
destroyed.

Georgetown is a white wooden city. One would like to sketch it
on rough dark grey paper, using black ink and thick white paint, to
suggest the lightness and fragility of the two-storeyed buildings, a
fragility most apparent at night, when light comes through verandas
on the top floor, through windows, through open lattice-work, and
the effect is of those Chinese ivory palace-miniatures lit up from
within. The city was founded by the British but escaped being
built by them – British colonial architecture in the West Indies
has had few moments of glory – and was largely created by the
Dutch, whose influence remains. The streets are laid out on the grid
pattern, and in the Dutch manner canals once ran down the centre
of the main streets. Most of the canals have been filled in and
replaced by asphalt walks lined with the spreading, many-branched
saman tree, which in appearance is a nobler oak.

It was perfectly ridiculous then to feel on that first day that I was
in a frontier town of the Wild West. It was the wooden buildings, I
imagine; and the empty wide streets – I had arrived on Boxing Day.

It was also the prevalence of the name of Booker's, a name which went around the world during the crisis of 1953. Booker's are the largest firm of merchants and planters in British Guiana, and at one time virtually controlled the country; according to the People's Progressive Party, they were and perhaps still are the villains of the piece. Now, seeing the name Booker's on hardware stores, foodshops, machine-tool shops, drugstores, taxis, I felt I had come to rescue Georgetown. I walked down the main street on spurs. Old Booker, bearded, gruff-voiced and tobacco-chewing, waited with the five Booker boys to shoot me down. The natives had fled from the streets and were cowering in barbershops and saloons.

In fact the Christmas celebrations were still going on. A sour-faced white drunk leaned out of the window in the house next to my boarding-house; and in the room next to mine there was another drunk who was groaning and intermittently singing Puccini to the radio. I could hear every sound he made. The wooden partition and the ventilation gaps at the top ensured that. As a result, I found myself walking about on tiptoe, doing everything as quietly as possible, just listening to the noises next door.

Late that night I was awakened.

'I'm a bum, I'm a bum,' the man was saying. He gave a prolonged groan. 'I've just realized what a terrible bum I am.'

'You only make yourself so,' a woman said, plaintive yet consoling.

'No, no. I *am* a bum.' Then, reflectively: 'Biggest blasted bum in B.G.'

'You *make* yourself that way.' The woman sobbed a little.

Silence. A groan, a rumbling snatch of song. Then: '*Do what your mother tells you!*' the man roared.

I lay straight and still in bed, unwilling to move, to make any betraying noise.

I had been told that the Guianese Christmas celebrations last a week, and I was not surprised next morning to hear the drunk next door freshly drunk. As soon as I could I left the house. I made many telephone calls, with such success that by the middle of the morning Abdul, friend of a friend, was taking me to the Rahimtoolahs, friends of his, rich and respectable people who lived in a large house in an elegant area. The upper floor, open, jalousied and with Demerara windows, was cool and airy; but the paint was peeling and the furniture was rough. The house had large neglected spaces, and there were only calendars on the walls.

Mr Rahimtoolah, a big man with fat quivering thighs revealed by shorts, and a blotched face and a turtle-like neck, said apologetically that he was living in a wooden house only for the time being; he was soon going to pull it down and build something modern in concrete.

He introduced us to Mike, a young English National Serviceman with dull slanting eyes, big teeth, heavy lips and a line-moustache that was very faint and definitely askew. Mike had the appearance of someone much abused; he was the friend of plump-cheeked Miss Rahimtoolah.

Whisky was brought out and we were asked to admire the glasses. They carried the words 'Ballantine's Guide for Beginners': they were marked off like measuring glasses, the varying depths labelled 'teetotal', 'timid' and 'tally-ho'. On the bottom of the glass a man hung from a scaffold: this was 'the last drop'.

'You went to the Chinese last night?' Mr Rahimtoolah asked one of his Portuguese guests.

'We decided to go to the Indians after all.'

They were speaking of the clubs of Georgetown; and Mr Rahimtoolah, with much pride, explained the frenzied activities of the clubs during the festive season, while his daughter passed round fresh drinks.

In the women's corner talk began about the respective merits of Great Britain and British Guiana.

'People in B.G. are more hospitable than people in Britain,' Mr Rahimtoolah said.

'I agree,' said Mike.

Then they talked about the seasons, and how wonderful it was to have spring, summer, autumn and winter instead of just a rainy season and a dry season. I felt the conversation had been rigged for Mike's benefit: he now spoke about the seasons like an expert called in to give advice. He described snow in detail and announced that he was going to tell a 'funny story'. Miss Rahimtoolah and Mrs Rahimtoolah laughed in advance. It happened, Mike said prefatorily, 'before we moved to the new house.' He paused to allow this to sink in; his glass was filled; he drank. I was waiting impatiently for the story which already had Miss Rahimtoolah giggling, the bottle of whisky shaking in one hand, the other hand covering her mouth. At last the story came: one winter Mike's father, going out of the back door for an undisclosed purpose, had been covered by snow falling off a roof.

Mrs Rahimtoolah shrieked and said, 'I *love* England.'

Mr Rahimtoolah looked at her indulgently.

Abdul, reclining on a Berbice chair, spoiled the mood of Indo-British amity by saying that he hated England and never wanted to set foot in the country again.

He took everyone by surprise. He looked surprised himself.

'Of course I had friends,' he said, destroying the silence he had created. Then, smiling at Mike: 'But they were reserved friends.'

'That's England, though,' Mrs Rahimtoolah said, relaxing.

Mike agreed. He looked mollified, and made a little speech about the warmth of his welcome in British Guiana and the hospitality of the Guianese people.

The embarrassing moment had passed. Two national myths had been flattered: Guianese hospitality, English reserve. Mr Rahimtoolah shook his fat legs in relief.

Some overdressed young girls, evidently of families as respectable and rich as the Rahimtoolahs, came up the steps, and there were gay exclamations. Mike was taking them all to the army camp; the outing appeared to be of importance.

We ourselves left, and went on to the Ramkerrysinghs, whose Christmas week entertaining, Abdul told me, was fabulous. At any time of day or night food and drink were to be had in any quantity; and, appropriately, the Ramkerrysinghs dispensed their hospitality in what looked like a large hall, thoroughly contemporary, though, thoroughly modern. The living area was not broken up by walls; the bedrooms in one corner were marked off by partitions that followed a wavy line; in another corner was the kitchen; and in another there was a large well-stocked bar, fitted up to look like the genuine commercial thing, where guests sat on stools and the host played barman. It was the Ramkerrysinghs' claim that they had every drink in the world. This looked likely.

We were introduced briefly to the eaters outside the kitchen. Then we joined the drinkers at the bar. I couldn't take any more whisky. I asked for red wine. There was none. I was given some hock instead. 'Take some ice, nuh,' one of the drinking Ramkerrysinghs said, and he dropped two cubes in my glass. I drank quickly and then was taken on a tour of the house. In the veranda that ran down one side of the house there were many more people. From their appearance and the looks they gave us, they clearly belonged to the house; they seemed used to having peasants shown around. In a wavy-partitioned bedroom we came upon a whole group of women lying on beds. I felt I had intruded into a zenana, and the effect was heightened because the women appeared to be of many races.

I said nothing to them and they, lying in a heap like puppies, stared superciliously at me.

I returned with relief to the bar, passing various china ornaments on the way, among them an open book on which was written the Lord's Prayer.

At the bar they were talking about the soft drinks industry: it seemed that 'competitions' were killing the trade.

'Put chits in one or two corks,' said the senior Mr Ramkerrysingh, behind the bar. 'Is what *I* would do. No fuss, no bother.'

The drinkers, at his instigation, were experimenting wildly with one drink after another, wines, liqueurs, spirits. Already slightly broken by the morning's drinking, I decided to stick to hock on the rocks. The senior Ramkerrysingh pushed the ice-bowl towards me and I took two pieces of ice. As soon as I dropped them in, the drinking Ramkerrysingh who had put the ice in my first glass, said, 'I don't know where you learn to drink. You don't know you mustn't put ice in wine?'

The senior Mr Ramkerrysingh said he liked living simply himself, and that the purpose of the establishment was to entertain foreign businessmen: the hotels of Georgetown were inadequate.

'You got to impress these fellers,' he said. 'And I can tell you what I put out I more than make back. When you dealing with big people you got to treat them big. You got to think big.'

Abdul nodded and said to me, 'Mr Ramkerrysingh always thought big. He started in a small way, you know. Those of us now starting have a lot to learn from him.'

It was surprising to hear, when we sat down to eat, that the country had been going to the dogs since politics and the Jagans had come to it.

When we went to Abdul's home we found his wife distressed. Her car had hit a child. She had stopped, but the child had got up and run off. No one would tell her whose child it was or where it lived – 'You know these black people' – and so she didn't know whether the child was injured.

In the boarding-house the drunk was still drunk.

Outside Stabroek Market, its pavements bright and cluttered with fruit-sellers, their baskets, trays and boxes, I asked an elderly Negro, who was respectably dressed and pushing a bicycle, to direct me to the Government Buildings.

'I am passing by there,' he said. 'Hop on.'

I hesitated. He was very small and thin. But he insisted, and I felt I would have offended him if I refused. So I sat on the crossbar, he pushed the cycle off with a run, hopped on to the saddle, breathing heavily, and we wobbled through the traffic. In this way I arrived at Mrs Jagan's office.

I had read and heard so many malicious accounts of Mrs Jagan that I was prejudiced in her favour. Although she has suffered much from visiting writers, she received me kindly in her small air-conditioned office. She sat behind a large desk, neatly ordered, on which were photographs of her husband and children. Her bag was on the floor. I thought her far more attractive than her photographs: women who wear spectacles rarely photograph well. A plain cotton frock set off her balanced figure; large hoop ear-rings and red toenails gave her a touch of frivolity which seemed incongruous in that office, the door of which was marked: *Hon Janet Jagan, Minister of Labour, Health and Housing*. She looked tired, and her talk was frequently broken by nervous laughter.

She said she was a pessimist. No one was more surprised than she when they won the elections in 1957. The country had lost much of its drive since 1953, when the constitution was suspended, she and others were imprisoned, and the British troops came in. Many supporters, 'without stamina', had deserted at that time; and the country had lost further when the party which had come to power so completely in 1953 split in 1955 along racial lines, Indians on one side, Negroes on the other. Race had, in fact, now become a major issue in British Guiana. She spoke of this with genuine regret. It was a subject to which she often returned during our subsequent meetings, and I fancied there was more than regret at racialism: there was regret for the camaraderie and the friendships of 1953. She remembered what certain people, now enemies, ate, how they talked, what her children had said to them. Since 1953 the party had also lost the support of the intellectuals; and this was a blow, for British Guiana did not have the talent that Trinidad had.

Specifically, I had called that morning to have my trip to the interior arranged. We turned our attention to the large map on the wall behind the desk; and abruptly one was reminded of the size of the country – the Rahimtoolahs and the Ramkerrysinghs had made one forget. Mrs Jagan had travelled widely through the country; she knew it better than most of the Guianese I had met. The district of Berbice in the east was her favourite. It was the liveliest. It produced the cricketers, most of the writers, and the best politicians: her husband, of course, came from Berbice.

The side door of the office opened, and Cheddi Jagan himself came in. He was wearing a suit and carried a briefcase. He had just come in to say that he was off to the bank to sign the agreement for the loan to buy over the Georgetown Electric Company.

It was an oddly domestic scene, and I felt an intruder.

In 1953, when the British Guiana constitution was suspended and British troops went into the country, the Jagans were the pariahs of the West Indies. Trinidad was so horrified it forbade Cheddi Jagan to step off the plane at Piarco airport; it should be noted that most of the important Trinidad politicians of the time have since been discredited. The Jagans and their party were accused of fomenting strikes, undermining the public service and the public force, spreading racial hatred, and generally advancing the cause of international communism. 'Reliable sources' established that there was also a plan 'to set fire to business property and residences of prominent Europeans and Government officials . . . This information was supported by reports of unusual sales of petrol to individuals without cars who carried it away in cans or bottles.'

It is all there in the United Kingdom Government White Paper, published on 20 October 1953, twelve days after the constitution had been suspended: a document that reduces the events of exciting weeks to forty-four unemotional, numbered paragraphs, in six parts – Introduction, Activities of Ministers, The Economic Consequences, The Danger of Violence, People's Progressive Party Leaders and Communism, Action by Her Majesty's Government – each part with its sub-heads in italics, the whole accompanied by three appendices: a document that never loses its temper and never drops the 'Mr' or 'Mrs' or 'Dr' from the names of people it helped to put in jail.

The most striking thing about this document is its appearance. In British Guiana it was 'Reprinted by Command' by the Bureau of Public Information. The words are on the title-page; and this title-page, which consists of ten printed lines spaced all the way down, with its italic capitals, its four type-faces, its commas at the end of two lines and a full stop at the end of the last line, has a curiously old-fashioned appearance, recalling the typography of a hundred years ago, and seeming to relate to events as old. On the back of the title-page there is a full-length sepia photograph of the Queen; the caption is in Gothic letters. On succeeding pages there are photographs of Sir Winston Churchill (a large star at the top); Sir Alfred Savage, the Governor (he is given a smaller star); the Chief Secretary, the Hon'ble John Gotch (Churchillian star for him); the Speaker, Sir Eustace Woolford (small star); the President of the State Council (small star); the Attorney General and the Financial Secretary (squeezed into Appendix C, between the lines of paragraphs nine and ten respectively, and unstarred). The impression given by these photographs in the midst of pages speaking with White-Paper calm of reprehensible thoughts and deeds is that these persons have been unwarrantably and unfairly affronted and bullied by those whose photographs do not appear.

* * *

I had heard much of the Rupununi, the savannah country south of the forest belt, and I was going to spend a few days there, at Lethem, the administrative centre, which is on the Brazilian border some two hundred and fifty miles from Georgetown. In the old days you went to the Rupununi by river, a long and difficult journey of many weeks; later there was a cattle trail. Today you can get there in ninety minutes by the Dakotas of British Guiana Airways. But on the coast, aware only of the colonial apparatus of the country and the nearness of the Caribbean islands, you can still forget that British Guiana has a border with Brazil. For most Guianese the coast is Guiana; everything beyond is bush.

And so it is. The bush begins at Atkinson Airfield, which is just twenty miles south of Georgetown. The Americans built this field during the war and they still use it; their sleek modern aircraft, silver and orange, delicately poised on the ground, make the up-tilted Dakotas look underprivileged and overworked. The office and store-rooms of British Guiana Airways are in a cheerless shed, formerly part of the American buildings. Grass grows through the steel-mesh of the runway, which has buckled here and there; and there is bush all around.

It was raining and the passengers stood among their boxes and baskets on a raised gallery. They were not a crowd one associated with British Guiana. Many of them were white; there were four Amerindians; and the pilot, a tall, plump man wearing a red shirt, was a European. The coast – sugarcane, irrigation ditches, workers' houses, political rivalries, communism – was already far away. Under cheap black umbrellas, roughly painted B.G. AIRWAYS in huge letters, not to promote pride, one felt, but to prevent theft, we went out to the plane. There were no seats inside. A narrow metal ledge ran down either side of the plane; on this thin rubber cushions had been placed, linked one to the other and equipped with safety belts. The front of the plane was stuffed with cargo. I noticed cartons of beer, a bed, a sewing-machine and many bags of flour: everything in the interior, from safety pins to Land-Rovers, has to be flown in by these valiant Dakotas, at nine cents a pound.

An elderly American sat next to me. He was very tall and had a stoop, but his enormous chest still suggested great power. If I had known that he was eighty-five, and that he was Ben Hart, one of the Rupununi pioneers and one of its famous characters, I would have paid him greater attention.* As it was, I was more interested in the four Amerindians who sat facing me. This was my first sight of these people, known fearfully to Trinidadians as 'wild Indians' and contemptuously referred to as 'Bucks' by coastland Guianese. The man was barefooted; he wore khaki trousers and a loose white shirt and held a handkerchief to his face. The two women stared at the floor. The small girl in a pink frock and broad-brimmed straw hat stared at the other passengers, but as soon as you caught her eye she pulled in her lower lip and looked down. They became animated only when, as we began to fly low over the savannah, the plane became suffocatingly hot, the ride grew bumpy, and some people were sick. Then the women smiled slyly at the other passengers and covered their mouths with their hands as though to hide giggles.

Our first stop was in a field at a place called Good Hope, and it was like stepping out into another country, into the scene of a Western. The flat red land, dotted with tussocks of coarse grass, stretched away to pale blue-grey mountains. The sun was fierce and we sheltered under the wings of the plane. The plane comes to Good Hope once a fortnight, and everyone seemed to have come out to greet it. But they didn't make up a crowd; and it was hard to see where they came from, for only one house was visible, apart from the collapsed hut next to the landing field. Nearly all of them must have walked, for there was only one Land-Rover, and this belonged to César Gorinsky, a formidably handsome Russian émigré who is reputed to be one of the richest settlers in the Rupununi. The Hollywood-Western atmosphere was greatly helped by the presence of a tall, rangy, barefooted man who looked like a film Texan, dressed like a film cowboy, and talked with an American accent. He turned out to be a German from Hamburg; he was Gorinsky's assistant.

* For the Hollywood-style stories of Ben Hart and other Rupununi characters the reader is recommended to consult Michael Swan's *The Marches of El Dorado*.

Questions of nationality seemed unimportant in the setting which, though strange, was yet so familiar that the exotics were not the Amerindians whom I was seeing in quantity for the first time, but the two Negro policemen in smart black uniforms and bush hats. And this, too, was a singular reversal of the roles, this policing of Amerindians by Negroes: in the days of slavery the Amerindians were employed to hunt down runaway slaves. And now these policemen spoke to me of the Amerindians as of some primitive, unpredictable people, who needed to be watched.

One of the policemen waved a hand. 'Brazil over there, you know.' The word clearly excited him. 'One time they come over here, you know.' He laughed. 'But you know the English people and their land. We chase them back, man.' Questions of nationality didn't matter. Here the Negro policeman could speak of himself as English, and it seemed right. Everything on the other side of the border was Brazilian; everything on this side was English; and the English had no doubt which was superior.

The adjective most often used to describe the interior of British Guiana is 'vast'. 'Vast', too, are the natural resources; these are invariably 'untapped'. The impression created is that forests have simply to be cut down for a wealthy new state to grow. In fact, a good deal of the untapped interior rests on infertile white sand, and the problem of reafforestation has yet to be solved. There is bauxite, but gold and diamonds are obtained only in small quantities.

The Rupununi is typical of British Guiana. It is 'savannah', 'grassland', 'cattle country'. Yet you can drive for a day without seeing a cow. The ground, in the dry season, when I saw it, is brown-red and hard and in parts composed of pure laterite. What looks like grass turns out to be sedge. Only cashew trees and mango trees flourish, occasional startling clumps of green, in this burning wasteland. And the sandpaper trees: stunted and gnarled, they have the appearance of carefully tended fruit trees, and are at times so evenly spaced that the savannah seems an endless orchard. But this is only Nature's mimicry: the leaves of this tree have the abrasive quality of sandpaper. In between these trees there are the ant castles, conical structures of grey mud that are sometimes six feet high. Castles and bastard orchards, especially when seen on an incline, suggest that the land is fruitful and peopled. Each castle throws its black shadow like a primitive stone monument protected by a National Trust and one feels that in the next shallow valley a village will appear, an inn serving warm meals and cool drinks. But the road just goes on, past more ant castles and sandpaper trees. A grey colonnade of green-crowned palms marks the course of a stream; the blue-grey mountains bound the horizon. The illusion is past; one is really quite alone.

Sometimes the savannah is on fire: an irregular slowly-moving line of low, broken flame that divides the land into two colours: brown-green on one side, black on the other. Hawks fly above the white smoke, waiting to pounce on the snakes and other creatures that escape across the fire-line. The fires are started by ranchers who wish to burn away the grass-choking sedge; and more indiscriminately, in defiance of the law, by Amerindians, who like to see the savannah burn; at times, I was told, whole mountains are on fire. After such a fire the savannah becomes truly lunar: a landscape in which curling copper leaves hang on gnarled, artificial-looking trees rising out of the black ground.

In the valleys there is balata-bleeding and tobacco-growing, and this, together with the ranching, is enough to support a few people and to make some even rich, but scarcely sufficient to make the area valuable to the rest of the country as a whole. The Rupununi is not a land so much for the pioneer as for the romantic. The pioneer wants to see cities rise in the desert; the romantic wants to be left alone. The Rupununi settlers want to be left alone; though they depend on Georgetown, there is an unexpressed resentment at the desire of the government in Georgetown to administer the area — this administering of small, widely separated communities is a burden on a poor country – and relations between officials and settlers are not altogether easy.

Some of this resentment is undoubtedly racial. Government officials, the police in particular, are Negroes; and in the Rupununi the Negro, the black man from the coast, is still a symbol of threat and terror: the runaway slave, once the enemy of the Amerindian and now his corrupter.

In Trinidad there is no memory of slavery; in British Guiana it is hard to forget it. The very word 'Negro', because of its association with slavery, is resented by many black Guianese; the preferred word is 'African', which will cause deep offence in Trinidad. Everyone knows that Amerindians hunted down runaway slaves; it was something I heard again and again, from white and black; and on the Rupununi, and wherever one sees Amerindians, it is a chilling memory.*

Lethem, the administrative centre, named after a former governor of the colony, is a tidy, rambling settlement of a few dozen concrete houses in the ugly Caribbean style set about corrugated red laterite roads. The ranchers speak of Lethem as a city and say it is overcrowded. At first this seems an affectation, an excess of the boy-scout spirit, but after a few days of travelling through the empty savannah you begin to feel yourself that Lethem is a city, with

---

* 'The aforesaid Indians having brought the expedition to a close, sixty or seventy of them, armed with bow-and-arrow, returned to Dageraat to report to the Governor, saying that they had scoured the forests throughout, finding eleven Negroes whom they had killed, in proof of which they produced a little stick with as many nicks cut in it, and asking for some reward. The Governor gave their captains, six in number, each a piece of salamfore, two jugs of rum, some mirrors and other gee-gaws as a present, with which, being quite satisfied, they returned upcountry.' *The Story of the Slave Rebellion in Berbice – 1762*, by J. J. Hartsinck (Amsterdam, 1770). Translated by Walter E. Roth. Published in the *Journal of the British Guiana Museum and Zoo*, September 1960.

Likewise, though with less success, Moskito Indians from Central America were used to hunt down Maroon slaves in Jamaica in the 1730s.

almost too many amenities. It has an airstrip, an abattoir, a hospital and an hotel, a power plant, a cricket ground – the hard Rupununi earth makes a good pitch – and a pavilion. On the airstrip next to the abattoir, the blue-grey mountains low in the distance, the Dakotas land and take off regularly in a flurry of red dust, bringing in supplies, taking out beef; the policemen stand unobtrusively by. Occasionally a small plane flies in from across the border and a Brazilian merchant or smuggler (the frontier is unpatrolled and knows no customs checks) jumps out, as from a taxi, with a suitcase, to wait perhaps for a day or two for the plane to Georgetown.

Over the two-storeyed concrete residence of the district commissioner the Union Jack flies high enough to be visible to any Brazilian across the border. And the district commissioner, Neville Franker, a Guianese, was all that a district commissioner should be. His official manner was impeccable and reassuring; in private he was relaxed and entertaining and his conversation was edged with an agreeable cynicism. He was new to the area, and it was fitting that, playing that week in his first cricket match in the Rupununi, and going in first wicket down, he should be top-scorer with fifty-three. There could have been no more appropriate way in this part of the world for a district commissioner to call attention to his authority and no more appropriate way of showing the flag.

The centre of life in Lethem is Teddy Melville's hotel, which is at the end of the airstrip. 'Hotel' is too grand and cold a word for this establishment which looks like a large, rough dwelling-house that has been constructed with difficulty in the desert out of the plainest materials. 'Inn', with its suggestion of isolated shelter, welcome and warmth, is a better word. Here the tourist, moving about in comfort by plane and Land-Rover, can be flattered that he is a traveller. There is always room at this inn, if only a hammock on the concrete-floored, trellised veranda, and always food.

The armchairs in the veranda are of local leather, and in the small dining room the antlered hatrack is hung with ropes and holsters. A friendly pig wanders in and out, hoovering the floor;

and occasionally a baby anteater makes a shy appearance, edging shakily along the wall on column-like legs that look like those of a stuffed toy but conceal sharp curving claws which in the adult animal make it a match for the jaguar. There seem to be Melville boys everywhere, handsome, well-built, with light, elastic movements: the illusion of the 'Western' is strong. In the bar, where you drink excellent Brazilian beer at a dollar and thirty cents a litre, Portuguese (or Brazilian) is heard as often as English. This, like the Portuguese label (*Industria Brasileira*) on the unfamiliarly large beer bottle, is no illusion: Lethem is a frontier town.

The New Year Dance is a big thing in Lethem. It takes place in the hotel, and hand-written bills stuck to the door of the bar said that there was to be a Brazilian band, which was coming all the way from Boa Vista, two rivers, five hard hours and eighty miles away. Lorry-loads of Brazilians were coming as well, for each of these frontier towns, Lethem and Boa Vista, enviously regards the other as a place of vice and adventure; it had already been whispered to me that Boa Vista had brothels.

The Brazilians arrived in the middle of the afternoon and at once overran the hotel. The women besieged the bathroom, twittering and squawking; and when, hours later, it seemed, they had all repaired the ravages of the drive from Boa Vista, the bathroom was littered with tangles of hair and tufts of cotton wool. In the corridor there was an empty green-and-white carton, *Leite de Rosas* – perfume, I imagine – and *Industria Brasileira*, needless to say.

I had heard that in the old days these frontier dances were rough affairs and sometimes ended in brawls. Things were quieter now and I felt that Lethem regretted its former reputation, though the dance was still not considered by some to be suitable for respectable women. The earliest dancers were Amerindian, with the respectable looking on with aloof indulgence, as though they didn't know why they had bothered with the long drive, the stay in the bathroom and the *Leite de Rosas*.

In the veranda, removed from the hubbub of the dance floor,

I came upon a respectable Brazilian man and two respectable Brazilian women — Portuguese with a dash of Amerindian, like so many Brazilians in this part — sitting idly in Teddy Melville's leather chairs. We attempted to talk. Attempted: they spoke Portuguese and knew little English, and I had only some Spanish. The man was an engineer. His wife, who had a grave, fine beauty, was a civil servant; his sister, unfortunately still unmarried, came from Belém and was spending some time with them. We exchanged addresses. They pressed me to visit Brazil, a great country. When I did so I was to come and see them. We wandered back to the dance floor, and separated.

The Amerindian women danced dourly, looking down at the floor, concentrating on their steps, and seeming to ignore their partners. They brought their bare feet flat down on to the ground, in a slight stamping action. I did not find them attractive.

I had tried hard to feel interest in the Amerindians as a whole, but had failed. I couldn't read their faces; I couldn't understand their language, and could never gauge at what level communication was possible. Among more complex peoples there are certain individuals who have the power to transmit to you their sense of defeat and purposelessness: emotional parasites who flourish by draining you of the vitality you preserve with difficulty. The Amerindians had this effect on me.

My most depressing memory of the Rupununi is of the Amerindian village to which Franker took me one day. 'NOTICE', said a roughly written board outside. 'WE DO NOT WANT ANY STRANGERS TO BE TRESPASSING ON THE VILLAGE, EXCEPTING THE PRIESTS, THE DOCTORS, AND THE DISTRICT COMMISSIONER, ORDERED BY THE VILLAGE CHIEF. FELIX.' The notice was not government-inspired; its purpose was to protect the villagers from the importuning of certain politicians they weren't going to vote for anyway. It was a small village of thatched huts and some rough wooden houses. The teacher, an Amerindian, lived in the largest wooden house, which was some distance from the village. And in another wooden house there was the school, empty now, but with maps and posters and time-tables on the walls, just like many other elementary schools. But this one led its pupils to nothing but confusion and self-contempt.

Father Quigly, the Roman Catholic missionary, was passing through the village; he had spent the night in the school, and his hammock was still hung across the room. As he spoke to us, men and boys gathered around, some in the schoolroom, some in bright sunlight outside, the young interested and expectant, the old not looking, as though they felt they had to express their courtesy to the district commissioner and were doing so merely by being present.

'Faustino,' Father Quigly asked, 'you want to go to Georgetown?'

'Yes, Father,' said a boy in grey flannel trousers.

Yet what would Faustino, and others like him who were dissatisfied with their village and with their condition as Amerindians, do in Georgetown? There they would be objects of contempt; some might become traffic policemen; but that was all. Father Quigly thought they should be given more say in the country, some sort of semi-responsible protected employment by the government.

Felix, the village chief, in whose name the bold sign barring strangers had been written, didn't appear interested. While we spoke he sat slumped and round-shouldered on a bench, staring at the floor, his short legs, loosely trousered, dangling. Later in his trance-like way he took us to his hut. It was dark and dirty and dusty and disordered, like most Amerindians' huts. The sight of exposed food in the midst of dust and mud has the same effect on me as the screech of chalk on a board; I could scarcely stay to admire the Wai-Wai grater – sharp bits of stone stuck into a board – which I had been told was a rare and desirable souvenir. I felt then that reverence for food – rules for its handling, interdictions – was one of the essentials of civilization.

The music went on all through the night. I awoke intermittently to it: it was comforting, like the sound of rain; but there were also curious grunting noises such as one hears in Japanese films. And in the morning there was silence. The Brazilians, band and dancers, civil servant and engineer, had got into their lorries and had gone back to Boa Vista. There were empty beer bottles around the dance floor, in the veranda, in the road; and little groups of Amerindians were contentedly regarding the chaos to which they had contributed.

In the dining room there was a new guest. He was a trader, Syrian by origin, who had come in by a small plane that morning, on the way to Georgetown. He tried over coffee to persuade me to become a trader and live in Brazil. I mentioned difficulties: with transport from Georgetown to Lethem at nine cents a pound, I said, trading couldn't be very easy.

'Whatsa trouble?' he said. 'You pay one dollar in Georgetown. So? So you pay another dollar for the transport. So you charge three dollars. Whatsa trouble?'

In Boa Vista that week there was a fair of some sort – cattle or agriculture – and the Lethem officials had been invited. Hewson, the young English agricultural officer who wore correct khaki but went about barefooted by preference, was going with two of his assistants, and he agreed to take me along. We didn't need passports to get into Brazil but we had to ford the Takutu River. It was less than a hundred yards across at the fording point, and sticks marked the route over the treacherous little sandbanks in which the Land-Rover would be trapped if it halted at all. When the Land-Rover began to sink and the water level rose, I tried to remember that the river was forded twice a week by the big lorry from Boa Vista.

At last we made the bank. We were in Brazil. The ground carried no marks of difference, nothing to confirm that we were in Brazil. The savannah was as flat and bright and bare, the sky was as high, and the ground was as hard as on the other bank. The road stretched between bristling tussocks of coarse brown-green grass: two parallel white tracks separated by a strip of low, chassis-brushed vegetation. And as we penetrated deeper into Brazil I felt as a fact, what the maps had already told me, that the savannah was really Brazilian and the British Guianese portion of it trifling.

We passed small settlements of thatched houses and sometimes we were stopped by people, Amerindian with a dash of Portuguese, who sang out requests for *pasagem a Boa Vista*. 'No passage, no passage,' Hewson said; and they withdrew without showing rancour or disappointment, to wait for goodness knows how long for some vehicle that would take them to Boa Vista, whose lights, here in the savannah, must have seemed very bright indeed. One of those who stopped us was a very old, white-headed Negro. One is so used in the New World to hearing Negroes speak English that it is startling to hear them speak anything else; it is to see afresh the condition of the Negro, who in the New World has been made in so many images. In this savannah the old man was demonstrably an alien, an exotic who yet knew nothing else, neither of landscape nor language.

Suddenly, and incredibly, there was a large unpainted concrete building. It was marked POSTO MEDICO in clumsy blue letters, and on the walls there were election posters with photographs of well-dressed politicians with unreliable faces. This was a hospital. But it had no equipment, no doctors, no patients: Brazil, a great country, administering every section of its great area, on paper.

Wherever you look in the savannah you see a mountain range, low and faint and far away. Without these ranges the flatness would be insupportable, particularly when even the sandpaper trees disappear, and the twisted branches of one dead white tree at the side of the road, remarked long before you come to it, cinematically frame and give scale to the emptiness. And then you see, not a mountain range, but a single hill, neat, abrupt, isolated; you cannot take your eyes off it; it grows, it spreads; it is not neat at all. It isn't a hill which is known to people; its little slides of rock, the appearance and fading of its scant vegetation, do not matter; it has only this landmark existence.

The savannah landscape continually changes. In damp depressions there is bush which is like forest. But the pleasances are the creeks. The land around them is green, and palm trees are reflected in the clear water. We stopped at one to wet our faces and soak our feet; and while we were doing so a Land-Rover came around the greenery, shot across the shallow ford and raced away in a cloud of dust. This was César Gorinsky of the Rupununi, bound like us for Boa Vista. We followed but couldn't catch up. Gorinsky knew the road, and the whorls of dust from his Land-Rover seemed to express his flamboyant skill.

The land grew greener. We passed a *fazenda*: a whitewashed house with blue facings set between banana trees and an orange orchard. Children watched us from the yard, and a signboard gave the name of the place: Good Hope. And all at once we were on the bank of the Rio Branco, a tributary of the Amazon. Small islands barred a direct view across, and the awesome breadth of the river could be gauged only by the straggling line of unremarkable white and brown houses high on the other bank, tenderly lit by the setting sun: Boa Vista, city of adventure, with a whole street of brothels. Between our bank and the nearest island white sandbanks rose out of the muddy water, and for a moment one indulged the child-like fantasy that it was possible to hop from one sandbank to the other and so on to the island, which was low and flat.

And now we saw the reason for Gorinsky's speed. He had been hoping to catch the ferry, which took only two vehicles at a time; and he was second in the queue behind a brightly coloured Willys jeep (*Industria Brasileira*, even down to its tyres). The ferry had just left and would not be back for at least an hour. The driver of the Willys jeep, a Brazilian army officer, said with glum resignation that the service might even be suspended until the morning. We sat on the bank, eating oranges, the houses of Boa Vista growing mellower and mellower as the sun sank.

A small boat with an outboard motor came alongside, offering to take passengers across, and Hewson decided to send me over with

one of his assistants. As we left, messages were shouted to the
boatman to remind the ferry to come back. We zigzagged across
the river, between the islands and the sandbanks, and it was twenty
minutes before we reached the other bank. A multitude of women
and children were bathing close to the shore. It was now dusk.
Trees and moored boats were silhouetted against the bright sky and
river. We climbed up the steep bank and came into a dirt street
which was as full of holes and bumps as a construction site.

Boa Vista is a preposterous city: separate huddles of shabby
houses along wide streets that have been marked out according to
the design of a master town-planner. Only, the streets have not yet
been built, except in short, abrupt and arbitrary stretches. The
planners have planned for the year 2000, and what in that year
will be magnificent avenues in the meantime connect nothing to
nothing through red Brazilian dirt. One curious result is that though
in terms of population Boa Vista is a small city, its distances are
metropolitan, without the alleviation of a metropolitan bus service.
Lamp standards line the well-planned desolation, part of the
promise of the future, and a number of grand buildings, among
them an abattoir and a hospital, both uncommissioned, have been
put up, awaiting the future and an increase of population, which at
present consists mainly of civil servants administering one another
and smugglers who keep the civil servants supplied; the Brazilian
Government, for reasons of economy and convenience, tolerating
smuggling in this territory.

A taxi, an open Willys jeep – only jeeps can operate on these
streets – took me to the hotel, one of the impressive buildings put
up for AD 2000. In that year, no doubt, it will occupy a commanding
position in a splendid town centre, where smart and incorruptible
policemen will control traffic through tree-lined avenues and
fountains will play in well-kept gardens; but at the moment this
town centre was an immense featureless dustbowl, across which
gaily-coloured open jeeps packed with cheerful Brazilians regularly scuttled, whirling up clouds of red dust that blotted out the

lamp standards and electric poles with which the town bristles and the houses, small in the distance, at the other end of the bowl. The hotel, new and pink, already felt like a ruin, like a relic of a retreating civilization. It smelt of disuse. Two barefooted children, dirty and shy, wearing clothes into which, following the Boa Vistan pattern, they had yet to grow, showed me to my room: a bed, a chair, a bulbless reading lamp, an ugly unshining wardrobe, a hot-water tap that didn't run and had possibly never run, a window that overlooked a patch of wasteland where much garbage had been dumped. After this it seemed an impertinence when, on my way out, the man behind the desk asked for my passport. Abandoning Spanish, which I had used previously with him, I said in English and with some annoyance that I had none. He shrugged his shoulders, withdrew the request and went on picking his teeth.

Darkness hid the dust and the absence of buildings. In all directions and as far as the eye could see Boa Vista blazed with electric lights that seemed to mark the boulevards, squares and crescents of a metropolis offering rich sensual pleasures. I wished to avoid the dustbowl, however, and was making for a short street of disintegrating wooden shacks to the right of the hotel, when Hewson's assistant, deflecting me slightly, said with embarrassment, 'The women in that street are *bad*.'

'Bad?' I said.

He became extremely confused. 'Well, they are bad,' he said, and I thought disingenuously. Then, as though explaining matters to a child, he added, 'You see, *bad* men go to that street to meet these *bad* women.'

I didn't press the point. We walked across the dustbowl to an asphalted street. The flat surface, so rare in the city, had been put to extensive use; it was covered with enormous election slogans in white paint. After we had had a beer in a dingy bar that smelled of dog-dirt — all the bars, I later discovered, smelled of dog-dirt — Hewson's assistant left me, and I decided to call on the Brazilian engineer and his civil servant wife whom I had met in Lethem.

They lived in a small white house in a street crammed with small white houses. Like all the houses in that street, and like most of the buildings in Boa Vista, it was marked with the letters P.N., which stood for National Patrimony, the Brazilian way of saying Government Property.

I surprised them enjoying the cool of the evening in their dusty yard below a mango tree, from one branch of which a pendent light bulb of powerful wattage burned fiercely. Never was a city so prodigal of light, so strung with electric wire. I called from the unpaved pavement and they, shading their eyes against the electric glare, uttered cries of disbelief rather than delight. The sister-in-law from Belém sat at a sewing-machine, working bits of material she had bought in Lethem. The engineer was wearing the clothes I had seen on him the night of the dance: white trousers and a striped green shirt. His wife, the civil servant, wore fluffy bedroom slippers. I thought these unsuitable for the dust, which was inches thick, a chaos of footprints, every one of which was thrown into black-and-white relief by the powerful light.

At their subdued cries of welcome a number of people came out of the small house of the National Patrimony: an entire and separate family, it seemed, but the civil servant, whose gravity I now interpreted as melancholy, introduced them as members of her husband's family. The husband himself was sent to get beer; and she, going into the front room – which instantly incandesced, dazzling rays leaping across the inchoate street and through the side window into the yard – returned presently with a bottle of white liquid, a special Brazilian drink, she said, that she had prepared herself. It turned out to be soursop, which grows in every backyard in the Caribbean islands and requires no care. We drank the soursop squash; when the engineer returned with the beer we drank it quickly, to prevent it going warm; and we talked as best we could.

None of them were natives of Boa Vista, which they told me was a joke among Brazilians, who looked upon it as somewhere behind the back of beyond. They feared I was getting a poor impression of

Brazil; had I seen pictures of Brasilia? Then the engineer asked whether I had read Shakespeare. In the original? He regarded me with envy and wonder. He was fond of books himself. Yes, his wife said, he *was* a great reader. 'Camoëns, Dante, Aristotle,' the engineer said, 'Shelley, Keats, Tolstoy.' And for a full minute we exchanged names of writers, the engineer greeting every name he recognized with an 'Ah!' Yes, he said at the end, reading was a great thing; it improved man.

Mangoes fell among us as we spoke; the resulting laughter bridged the gaps in the conversation and gave it animation. Before I left, the civil servant said she would be very glad to show me around the next day. I said this would be very nice, but what about her job? She smiled and shrugged; she would call for me at the hotel at nine.

On the way back through the dead, lunar-bright city, I walked down the street of brothels. Miniature black streams, glinting in the light, had cut deep channels through the hard dirt. In one or two decaying wooden shacks there was music, not loud, and a few people were dancing, not riotously. The women were fat, not young, and nondescript. They didn't look clean and had made so little attempt to look 'bad' that I couldn't be sure they were prostitutes; the appearance and allure of prostitutes vary so much from culture to culture. I went straight on to the hotel. When I turned the light on in my room cockroaches ran off in all directions. The mosquitoes didn't move. I closed the window against the odours of the garbage in the empty lot and rubbed myself all over with insect repellent, adding another smell to the warm mustiness of the room. The label on the bottle promised me protection for at least four hours.

The dining room was large and high and lighted by many windows; it would have looked like a gymnasium if the enormous L-shaped table hadn't made it look like a partially dismantled college hall. I found one man there next morning. He welcomed me with the warmth of one made frantic by solitude. In Spanish he told me he came from Rio, was a trader (I suppose he meant smuggler) and had been three days in Boa Vista waiting for a plane. He had been to the single cinema, he had made the round of the bars; there was nothing else to do and he was going mad. I asked whether he had gone to the brothels. Yes, he said joylessly, he had; and was going to say more when there was a brisk metallic fluttering behind us. We turned and saw a bird, or so it seemed, beating its wings against a glass window. The man from Rio got up, walked to the window and put his hand over the creature, stilling its agitation. 'Cockroach,' he said, putting it in his trouser pocket. His bright eyes dimmed as soon as he got back to the table, and he spoke as one appealing for sympathy. Yes, he had been to the brothels; last night, in fact; but the women were *viejas, feas y negras*, old, ugly and black.

Being shown around by the civil servant meant missing the fair, which might have given me another view of Boa Vista; Hewson said later that it was impressive. The civil servant came for me shortly after nine, after she had finished her work for the day. Like most of the civil servants in Boa Vista, she said, she had little to do. So we started tramping through the hot dust. The smell of dog-dirt was inescapable, as was the sight of starved mongrels locked in copulation, their faces blank and foolish. Few of the thin children I saw were without some skin disease; one or two were deformed. We went to the primitive printery which produced the ragged government gazette; most of the people there appeared to be doing nothing. We went to a small insanitary market in which everything apart from some Amerindian straw fans had been imported; a maternity hospital, run by nuns, which was admirably ordered and clean; and lastly to the Government Palace, the nerve-centre of the administration.

The palace was a large, undistinguished concrete building, full of civil servants, typewriters, files and silence. In a carpeted room I was shown the governor's desk, huge and untenanted (I imagine he was at the fair). On the wall there was an enormous coloured map of Brazil, which revealed the size of the country – what a minute portion of it we had covered yesterday! – and the remoteness of Boa Vista. Two large white albums lay on an occasional table. The civil servant urged me to open them. I expected charts and maps and photographs of industrial projects. I found beauty queens in high heels, from all the states and territories of Brazil: Miss Rio Branco, Miss Amazonas and so on. With the civil servant and a secretary smiling tolerantly at me, I turned over photograph after glossy photograph, beauty queen after beauty queen, proving my manhood, unwilling to offend Brazilian womanhood. Under a glass case in a corridor there was a model of a beautifully planned city, ideal in its simplicity and symmetry. This was the Boa Vista of the future. I couldn't recognise it and asked where on the model was the building in which we stood. No one could tell me.

We went back to the house of the National Patrimony for a drink. A pedlar called, offering contraband fabrics from British Guiana at a high price. Something was bought; the man was dismissed; and then the engineer came in. His clothes were stained with paint and his wife apologized for him, explaining that he had spent the morning repairing and painting their motor-car. We separated for lunch. Mine was unsatisfactory. No fish, because Boa Vista is a town of civil servants, ranchers and smugglers, and no one found it profitable to go fishing in the Rio Branco. No vegetables, because the Japanese immigrants weren't producing enough or because there weren't enough Japanese.

In the afternoon we went with the engineer's sister to the shack-like office of the Brazilian airline to arrange for her flight to Belém: it seemed that civil servants and their families could fly all over Brazil without paying. After the airline office our sight-seeing was over. I was glad. I had had enough of sun and dust and starved mongrels. We turned into a street of small white houses. And there, before us, was the engineer.

He was on a ladder. A cigarette hung from his lips and in his right hand he held a paint brush. He was painting the wall of a house of the Brazilian National Patrimony. He was one of three painters. What was I to do? If his wife, the civil servant, hadn't told me that he had spent the morning on their car, I could have stopped and we could have exchanged smiles.

I didn't see the engineer. I walked on. The two women fell fractionally behind; I heard low words being exchanged. In a moment I had passed the house; in another moment the women had caught up with me. We didn't speak of the engineer. Had I made a mistake? Had I been unforgivably rude? At the gate of their house we said good-bye. They didn't ask me in. I thanked them for their kindness. I wanted to make my words more than formal; but language lay between us. I was a complete stranger, and they had shown me much generosity. I walked wretchedly back through wide avenues of dust to the hotel, hoping I would never see them again.

I didn't. A strong wind started across the savannah and the city centre was lost in dust. People walked with handkerchiefs over their faces. For the rest of my stay in Boa Vista the wind never dropped and the man from Rio and myself, imprisoned in the hotel, ate oranges and watched the dust storm.

* * *

César Gorinsky drove me back to Lethem. It was an admirable piece of driving. Night fell while we were still on the Brazilian savannah and we had to ford the Takutu by the headlamps of the Land-Rover. In the hotel next day there was quite a crowd waiting for the Georgetown plane: Rupununi children going back to school on the coast, a few holiday-makers who had been staying at various ranches, and some hollow-eyed Brazilian traders with their disreputable-looking suitcases.

Just as the bush had begun at Atkinson Field, so the coast now seemed to begin in the hotel. Even its politics were with us, in copies of a newspaper called the *Sun*, whose slogan was 'A place in the sun for everyone'. The *Sun* was the organ of the United

Force ('Have Foresight – be a Forcite'), a political party that had been formed earlier that year by Mr Peter D'Aguiar, a Georgetown businessman of Portuguese extraction. The United Force was anti-Jagan, anti-Burnham, anti-left. It offered 'unity and integration for the six races' (Indian, African, Portuguese, white, mixed, Amerindian); and to these races it offered 'more work more wages more industries more land more learning more money'. Something for everyone: 'more money', one imagines, for those threatened by 'more wages'.

On the front page of the *Sun* I saw – Vol. 1, No. 8 – there was a photograph of Mr D'Aguiar smiling, pen in hand, behind a desk that carried a board with his name and the words 'Managing Director'. A steel filing cabinet and a safe are at his back. Below the photograph comes Mr D'Aguiar's New Year message, a gloomy one, belying the smile and the safe.

> It is my view that it would be hypocritical to wish a bright and prosperous New Year to Guianese generally at this period of their country's history when there is so much hardship and distress in the land through unemployment and underdevelopment and the consequent absence of the means of securing the essentials which make for brightness and prosperity.
>
> My New Year Message to my fellow Guianese is that we, one and all, bestir ourselves and endeavour to put an end to the depressing conditions which surround us in our homeland.
>
> How is this to be achieved? – is the question which will be shot at me from all angles. I reply 'our country is a potentially rich one.' An I.C.A. investigator told us recently that on looking around B.G. he was tempted to say that we were sitting on our assets. It is my view that we can have no bright and prosperous new years until our country is burst wide open and its wealth brought within easy reach of its people by the expenditure of large sums of money.

Now for the news. The front page story is '$5,500 Bonus for

Wong & Khan Employees'. One hundred workers will benefit from this sum, and on page five there is a photograph of Mr Khan, his sleeves rolled up, smiling, shaking a worker's hand and presenting a cheque. In the background someone who might be Mr Wong smiles straight at the camera. 'The workers showered praise on Mr Wong and Mr Khan and the company,' though it appears that 'Mr Khan said that the workers were drifting in their cooperation with their fellow-workers, and hoped that as from the beginning of the new year, they will look at things from a different angle and will be able to share one common understanding'.

There is also an advertisement in which, despite Mr D'Aguiar's gloom, 'the partners and staff ' of Messrs Wong and Khan 'extends [*sic*] to all our clients and friends a very happy and prosperous New Year'; and, curiously, in a photograph on page eight Mr D'Aguiar himself is seen shaking hands and offering the season's greetings.

The editorial, claiming that Dr Jagan is a communist, and that Mr Burnham 'must be handled with extreme caution' since 'the stigma of Communism is not too easily removed', gives credit to Mr D'Aguiar for putting forward 'the only constructive plan for the development of British Guiana'. There are advertisements for the United Force and the *Sun*, I-Cee soft drinks and Banks beer (both D'Aguiar enterprises). And a speech of Dr John Frederick's is reported:

> Do you want to own shares in a paying concern like Bank Breweries or have to pay taxes to keep the Government concerns which are losing money as the Railway Department and the Pasteurization Plant are doing and then be told that they are yours because they belong to Government?

Amid these preoccupations God is not forgotten. A religious column (of American origin, from its style and sentiment), whose premise is that whatever your job 'you can do something to restore to the mainstream of today's world the values you think are missing', tells the story of a young New York bank clerk who, though it meant losing $1,800 a year, gave up his job to become a teacher.

> In giving his reason, he said: 'When the little eyes in front of me light up with the realization that something new has been discovered, it is worth any sacrifice to know that I have been an instrument of this discovery.'

Another story, from the days of sail, tells of the young seaman who panicked when he went up the mast during a storm. 'Don't look down, boy!' the mate shouted. 'Look up!' The boy did so, and came down safely.

> By 'looking up' to God and out to the cause of all mankind, your own personal problems will seem incidental, and will be more easily solved.

Among the passengers waiting in the veranda of the Lethem hotel there was a coloured girl from Georgetown. She said she didn't care for politics but supposed she was for D'Aguiar. The other leaders were communist. And: 'Look what Mr D'Aguiar has done for the country with Banks beer.'

Improbably, there was a connexion. In the Caribbean territories a brewery is invariably among the earliest industrial projects. It is a mark of progress and a promise of modernity, and the local beer is a source of much local pride: Red Stripe in Jamaica, Parbo in Surinam, Carib in Trinidad, Banks in British Guiana. Wherever in British Guiana you heard the United Force spoken of approvingly you heard about Banks beer.*

---

* In the 1961 elections Dr Jagan won 20 seats, Mr Burnham 11, the United Force four. Some months later there were Negro riots, and after that an American-supported strike. Many people were killed. Dr Jagan was finally defeated by a system of proportional representation.

In the boarding-house in Georgetown the drunk was still drunk, still groaning, still on his bed. I moved.

Georgetown, most exquisite city in the British Caribbean, is for the visitor the most exasperating. Try getting a cup of coffee in the morning. The thing is impossible. Yesterday you expressed a dislike for lukewarm 'instant' coffee, particularly when the coffee is placed on the water and not the water on the coffee; so this morning your hotel offers you half a teaspoon of last year's coffee grounds in a pint of lukewarm water, since in your folly you said that you 'used' ground coffee – 'use', revealingly, being the Guianese word for 'drink' or 'eat'. Protest is futile. The Indian waiters are sluggish from overwork and too cowed by abuse from employers and patrons to understand anything. ('I treat my people well,' one Indian complained angrily last night to the proprietress, 'but servants and me not the same class, you hear.' 'I know, I know,' she replied, sympathetic to his suffering.) When you came down this morning at a quarter past seven and inquired why you had not been awakened at half past six, as you had asked, the middle-aged waiter, with a look of terror, said it wasn't half past six as yet. One sip of the coffee, and you know you can't drink any more, in spite of the plastic doily on the yellow-checked oil-cloth.

So you start sweating through the hot white city looking for coffee. The cafés serve cold drinks only; the hotels, instant coffee. You telephone a friend, who recommends a café with an inviting name. You ask directions of several Guianese, who mislead you not out of malice or ignorance but out of pure stupidity. Eventually you arrive at Kate's Kitchen, say. You wait for fifteen minutes; you order half a dozen times; and half a dozen times some torpid waitress, Portuguese, African or Indian, her tumescent belly suggesting constipation, writes down your simple order with illiterate delibera-tion, as though her pencil were a stylus and her pad made of wax. No coffee comes, though. You are not known in Kate's Kitchen; therefore you are not served.

After half an hour you rise, sweating, for the café is hot and unventilated, and you find yourself saying passionately but precisely, 'You Guianese are the slowest people I have ever met.' You alone are affected by these words; the waitresses simply stare and you go out into the white light trembling with anger, solacing yourself with the words of abuse which have just leapt into your mind.

Inhospitable, reactionary and lethargic except when predatory: these were the words. And thereafter, whenever my frustration neared breaking point, I played with them, changing an adjective, adding another, until I was able to 'look up and out to the cause of all mankind'.

It is equally impossible to get a meal. About the only thing Georgetown restaurants and hotels offer is 'chicken in the rough', and unless you share the Guianese passion for this 'modern' dish with the American name, which is nothing more than a piece of roast chicken served up in a dirty basket (it is the baskets the Guianese like) you are going to remain hungry. No point either in telling the waiter that you are in a hurry. It will be fifteen minutes before you get a menu and an hour before you get your scrambled eggs. Don't complain: the man has been hurrying. You can't cook in your hotel room; you can't cook in the street. What do you do? These extracts from my diary, which read like extracts from the diary of an enfeebled explorer, tell their own story:

January 17. One of those dreadful Georgetown days. Shopping at Bookers. Taxi for 45 cents. No lunch. The rumshop; the Bookers snack bar; the buying of tin-opener and paper cups.

January 25. One of those Georgetown days. Woke up in dreadful temper. . . .

The malarial sluggishness of the Guianese is known throughout the Caribbean and is recognized even in British Guiana. Some employers prefer to recruit islanders, who, they say, have greater gifts of initiative and self-reliance. I was told that it is dangerous to leave a Guianese in charge of a surveying station in the bush: the surveyors will return to find the hut collapsed, instruments rusted, and the Guianese mad. The islander, on the other hand, will be found in the midst of a tidy plantation, which he will leave with reluctance.

One Guianese official I spoke to blamed malaria. But malaria isn't all. There is history as well. Slavery lasted for three hundred years and was of exceptional brutality: in this matter of slavery the Dutch record is even blacker than the French. The African, as a result, is passionate for independence, and for him independence is not so much an assertion of pride as a desire to be left alone, not to be involved. Hence the number of African prospectors in the interior of British Guiana, who never make a fortune but live happily beyond the claims of society and just within the law. Hence the existence in neighbouring Surinam of *de luie neger van Coronie*, the lazy Negroes of Coronie, who live placidly in their remote settlement, occasionally taking the odd coconut to the oil-factory for a little ready money, ask for nothing else, and are the despair of the oil-factory, planners, politicians and oil-consumers, for the unrefined oil produced by the people of Coronie is more expensive than the refined oil imported from Holland.

Then there is the land. The fertile coastal strip has to be protected against the floods of Guiana's many rivers, and, being below sea-level, has to be protected against the sea as well. Irrigation and drainage, valueless unless carried out on a large scale, are beyond the small farmer. The estates must therefore be large. And the evils of the latifundia follow: those clusters of workers' houses seen from the air, in the midst of fields that go on and on, regularly intersected by ruler-straight irrigation ditches. 'Today in British Guiana,' Michael Swan wrote in 1958, putting the case for the estates, 'sugar must use a hundred subtle methods to maintain a sufficient labour force. . . . Most of the evils in the sugar industry can be traced back to the fears of labour shortage.' The indenture system, which replaced slavery and brought over hundreds of thousands of Indians to the West Indies, operated most harshly in British Guiana (if we forget the treatment of Indians in the French islands and Chinese in Cuba). For the efficient running of the latifundia the workers must be regarded as a caste apart and must continually be reminded of their condition.

And everywhere on the coast you can see reminders of the past, of affronts deliberately offered, it seems, to the labourers of the latifundia. The 'ranges' – long rooms cut up into a number of tiny rooms, each occupied by a family – have nearly all disappeared; one or two on the outskirts of Georgetown are pointed out as curiosities. But when you travel by the decadent railway between Parika, on the Essequibo River, and Georgetown, your eyes are caught by more than the water-lilies in the grassy ditches. On one side of the tracks you see the workers' houses, small, similar, huddled; and on the other side you see the quarters of the senior staff: authority confronting subservience: a standing provocation, you would have thought, to any people of spirit.

It is easy to blame the planters, to blame Bookers. Sugarcane is an ugly crop and it has an ugly history. The foolishly authoritarian overseers mentioned by Michael Swan have a dishonourable ancestry. But in British Guiana it is the land which is ultimately to blame. The land required the latifundia; the latifundia created Bookers. And though Bookers must be given credit for their radical reforms of recent years, they must bear responsibility for what they have been and what, with the best will, they could not help being. Not harsh and unimaginative employers, which was unavoidable, even on the latifundia; but for being, for creating, a colonial society within a colonial society: a double confinement for the Guianese.

Slavery, the land, the latifundia, Bookers, indenture, the colonial system, malaria: all these have helped to make a society that is at once revolutionary and intensely reactionary, and have made the

Guianese what he is: slow, sullen, independent though deceptively yielding, proud of his particular corner of Guiana, and sensitive to any criticism he does not utter himself. When the Guianese face goes blank and the eyes are fixed on you, you know that receptivity has ceased and that you are going to be told what the speaker believes you want to hear. It is hard to know exactly what Guianese are thinking; but if you make up your mind in advance you will find much corroboration. 'Everybody lies in B.G.,' a Guianese told me. It isn't lying; it is only an expression of distrust, one of the Guianese's conditioned reflexes; and one cannot help feeling sympathy for the Colonial Office officials who went to British Guiana in 1957 and concluded that Jaganism was a spent political force.

That the Guianese people should have been politically aroused and organized is not surprising. The latifundia and the difficulty of communications bred a feeling of community which is missing in a place like Trinidad. Whether the people are politically educated is another matter. It has been discovered in America and England that political policies can be sold like any other commodity. In British Guiana the issues are never confusing and there is no need to sell anything. Political judgements are as simple as they were for the girl who was for Mr D'Aguiar because he brewed Banks beer.

One week-end Mrs Jagan went to Wakenaam, one of the flat, damp, rice-growing Essequibo islands, to open a new overhead water-tank. I went with her. For the first time Wakenaam was going to have a pure water supply and everyone had dressed for the occasion. A photographer from the Government Information Services was there. The speeches were made and applauded, but before Mrs Jagan could set the pump in motion (item eight in the typewritten programme, which was not strictly followed), a man wearing a suit and a hat rose and complained about the new rates so noisily that the ceremony was almost ruined. He continued to complain during the celebration – soft drinks downstairs, whisky upstairs – and at one point seemed to be threatening to withdraw his support for the government.

This is the level of political judgement in British Guiana. Wherever ministers go they are met with trivial complaints; whenever, in a country area, Dr Jagan stands still he is at once surrounded by people who have favours to ask. That the government is elected does not matter; the people require it to be as paternalistic as before, if a little more benevolently; and a popular government must respond. 'The people' have learned their power, and the sensation is still so new that every new voter regards himself as a pressure group. In this way the people – not the politician's abstraction, but the people who wish to beg, bribe and bully because this is the way they got things in the past – in this way the people are a threat to responsible government and a threat, finally, to their own leaders. It is part of the colonial legacy.

*   *   *

From the Georgetown *Evening Post*, 17 January 1961:

OVER THE TEACUPS

Faye Crum-Ewing received one of the biggest surprises of her life on Saturday night, during the course of her 18th birthday party, held at the Main Street residence of her two aunts, Misses Ivy and Constance Crum-Ewing.

About 10 o'clock a drawn cart pulled up at the entrance of the home and a few boys of the Royal Hampshire Regiment at Atkinson entered the hall toting a huge box. That was their birthday gift to Faye from Alan Bishop, Evan Ozon, David Perry and Dr Peter Kerkohn.

The boys insisted that she open it at once, and as she raised the lid, what do you think popped out? A live person in the form of Evan Ozon, holding up three gift boxes! What a shout there was from all the guests present! The first gift box was inscribed with the words – 'from her three high-class friends'.

And on opening this Faye saw a replica of the Alms House and some of its attendants. The second box contained a tin of harpic and a toilet brush, and the third most unusual binoculars made from two liqueur bottles held together by china ware.

Never was a surprise so well thought-out and executed, and even now we keep wondering what became of the drawn cart near the front steps of the Crum-Ewings' Main Street home.

Faye herself looked most attractive and was her usual sparkling self. She wore . . .

The Guianese scale of distance is curious. They will tell you with pride that the Essequibo, their largest river, is twenty miles across at its mouth and contains islands as large as Barbados. Yet they will speak of the settlement of Bartica, only forty easily navigable miles up the Essequibo, as bush, 'the Interior', though it was in this bush, along rivers the colour of burnt sugar, that the earliest plantations were established: the 'dream of perished Dutch plantations', in the words of the Guianese poet A. J. Seymour, 'in these Guiana rivers to the sea.' Very little remains of these plantations: heaps of bricks here and there – the flat red bricks one has seen individually delineated in so many Dutch paintings – which came from Holland as ballast in Dutch ships, and which, because of their association with carefully rendered sunlit church walls and interiors ordered or boorish, are so disturbing to find in the bush, where they recall only the brutalities of the slave plantations.

In West Indian towns history seems dead, irrelevant. Perhaps it is because the past is so unimaginable; perhaps it is the light; perhaps it is because so much is makeshift and new and the squalor so wholly contemporary. To feel the past you need the emptiness of these Guianese rivers. These rivers, this bush, these rocks are just as they were before the New World was discovered: just such a scene, the river banks bristling with dead, fallen trees, the bush not separate trees but something draped and festooned and heavy, something decaying, with living trunks like white pillars and branches like white veins in the lustreless green whose reflection in the black water is like tapestry-work.

It all seems to await discovery. But the emptiness is an illusion. The river banks are dotted with small settlements and camps, of Amerindians, miners, woodcutters. Trails and even roads run through the bush in improbable places. The road to Brazil begins at Bartica. Concrete at first (an experimental surfacing), it soon turns to clay and runs broad and red through the bush, with experimental grass verges stuck unconvincingly on the white sand on which the forest rests. The exposed trees look like prehistoric animals with enormous bodies and tiny heads; the sand is in parts as white as snow, suggesting a snowfall in high summer; and the claypits have the colours and brightness of crumpled rust-coloured tinfoil. Orange trees can grow in this soil, and the Honduras pine; as yet the hardwood trees cannot be made to grow again. Soon the broad red road dwindles to a track, and as a track it continues to the Potaro River, where it stops, eighty miles from Brazil. It is easy to feel in the Interior that British Guiana is a land of temporary forest clearings, experimental road surfacings, and roads that peter out or, like the cattle trail from the Rupununi, go back to bush.

One's ideas of numbers alter. Twenty people are a crowd; a hundred make a city. To go back to Georgetown is not only to move from past to present, but to move from the empty to the grossly overcrowded. For on the coast, where malaria has been eradicated, there is a population explosion. And there is land hunger. The number of children in Georgetown is frightening. In the afternoons the streets of the Albouystown district look like a schoolyard during break. Even now there is unemployment. Land resettlement on the coast, where much land is unused, is expensive; to open up the Interior is even more expensive. And from British Guiana, with 600,000 people in 80,000 square miles, migration is increasing. One cannot help feeling that the situation is curiously Guianese.

From the *Guiana Graphic*, 18 January 1961:

Graphic Opinion
USE THE JOBS THAT ARE THERE

We came across an interesting advertisement yesterday. It reads, 'Domestics Wanted'. It stated that good wages would be paid and free accommodation provided.

These jobs are available at Mackenzie, the mining town of the Demerara Bauxite Company Ltd.

Not only at Mackenzie are cooks and maids wanted. There are opportunities offering in many places in the City and its environs.

Cooks and maids are valuable helpers in homes. They should be accepted and appreciated.

On account of the great amount of unemployment in B.G. this is an avenue which women and girls should not despise. There is nothing inferior, in the eyes of really decent people, in this grade of employment. For if helpers are not available then the mistress of the home will have to do all the chores herself.

Could anybody say that a housewife becomes degraded because she has to do the housework? That would be an absurd line of thinking. There is nothing intrinsically degrading in any kind of work.

It would be a splendid thing if more of the unemployed women and girls of this country realized this and used such opportunities to enable them to earn a livelihood rather than elect to remain unemployed and open to attack by all sorts of evil influences.

The Jagans are the most energetic campaigning politicians in the West Indies. Every week-end they, or their ministerial colleagues, go to some part of the country. They were going this week-end to

Berbice, Dr Jagan's home county, which many people had told me was the most 'progressive' in the country, and they invited me to go with them. Dr Jagan himself was going to call for me at the hotel.

And I was late. I had gone to the restaurant across the road for a 'quick' snack. Forty-five minutes waiting, three minutes eating (scrambled eggs). When I came back Dr Jagan was half-sitting on a bar stool. He wore a sports shirt and looked relaxed. Then I remembered my laundry. I raced up to my room and came down with an untied parcel of dirty clothes, which I gave to the barman together with a tip. (It didn't work. When I came back, two days later, the clothes were still below the bar, a puzzle, I was told, to subsequent barmen.)

The Jagans live in an unpretentious one-floored wooden house standing, in the Guianese way, on tall stilts. It is open and unprotected.* There is a pet monkey downstairs, and there is nothing upstairs to distinguish the house from many other Guianese houses, apart from the packed bookcases and the magazine rack (the *New Yorker* among the magazines).

The trip to Berbice was a family affair. The two Jagan children, a boy and a girl, were going to spend the weekend with Dr Jagan's mother. They treated me with indifference; and considering what has been said and written about them, the boy in particular, I was not surprised. Presently Mrs Jagan arrived. She quickly made ready – they were to eat in the car – and spent a little time choosing a book. She chose *The Vagabond* by Colette (in Wakenaam she had been reading Doris Lessing). It was a squeeze in the car, but there were two more children to come: the children of Dr Jagan's brother, Sirpaul. We picked them up at a wooden house in another street. 'It's like a picnic,' Dr Jagan said. And, with oranges and bananas being passed around to children, it was.

I learned that one of Dr Jagan's brothers was my namesake, and we talked about names. Mrs Jagan said that when Sirpaul was in

---

* Just one week later Mrs Jagan was attacked while she was alone at home.

New York he found himself being treated with exaggerated defer-
ence by the hotel staff. The bill explained why: it was addressed to
Sir Paul and Lady Jagan.

We were not out of Georgetown yet. A Negro on a bicycle
shouted, 'The coolies don't care if Jagan bury them!'

It was the casualness, rather than the abuse, which seemed
strange: a small car packed with Jagans, and one of the territory's
major political issues finding such simple utterance. One somehow
expected something more formal.

'It's a thing you learn in England,' Dr Jagan said. 'To be polite
to your opponents.'

We went on talking about names. Mrs Jagan said that another of
Dr Jagan's brothers had changed his name from Chunilal to Derek;
all but one of the sisters had taken English names.

Exactly one hundred years ago Trollope complained about the
British Guiana coastal road – it was the only thing he disliked
in British Guiana – and the road hasn't improved since then. The
surface is of burnt earth, whose durability is only fractionally higher
than that of unburnt earth, and the road is a succession of potholes
so distributed that they cannot be avoided, however much a car
weaves about. The short smooth 'experimental' stretches provide a
brief but shattering contrast and complete one's sense of frustration.
Yet taxis and buses regularly use this road, bumping along in a slow,
determined straight line when there is traffic, and weaving about
like crazy ants as soon as the road is clear. Low-grade bauxite, in
which British Guiana abounds, would make a more lasting surface;
but burnt earth is a peasant industry and burnt earth has to be used.

We passed many Negro settlements. The name of one, Buxton,
hints at their story. Thomas Buxton was, with Wilberforce, one of
the campaigners for the abolition of slavery; and these Negro villages were established after emancipation, on abandoned plantations
co-operatively bought by former slaves who wished to work for no
master. The first of these plantations was bought in 1839. It cost
$10,000. Six thousand dollars was immediately subscribed in cash by

eighty-three Negroes, and the money triumphantly transported in wheel-barrows; the remaining four thousand was paid off in three weeks. The village movement continued in spite of opposition from planters and government. The planters were losing their labour force. The government feared the collapse of the economy and, in order to create 'a free but landless labourer', limited grants of Crown land and imposed penalties on those who squatted on unoccupied land, which was plentiful in British Guiana.*

As it was, Indian immigration solved the labour problem. And the former slaves were defeated by the land, by the problems of drainage and irrigation which only the large estates could tackle. We passed through one sad grey village, just like the villages Trollope had seen: grey, weatherbeaten wooden houses standing on stilts on islands of trampled grey mud in a grey swamp. Dr Jagan told me there was no sea-wall in this area, and the inhabitants didn't want one: they were not agriculturists now, but fishermen.

New Amsterdam, British Guiana's second town, stands on the Berbice River. Dr Jagan had been told that the ferry left at five minutes past two. We got to the river in good time, and there we learned that the ferry left at 1.25 and 3.45. 'The inefficiency of people in this country,' Dr Jagan said. However, a launch of the Blairmont Estate was due to make the crossing soon; and to get the necessary permits we drove to the estate office, a low white building, the ditches around the well-kept lawn cool with the broad flushed discs of the Victoria Regia lily, which the explorer Schomburgk discovered on this very Berbice River. Mrs Jagan told me with a girlish giggle that they tried to keep their relations with the estates as correct as they could; and I felt, though she didn't say so, that this asking of a favour, and the promptness with which it was granted, was an embarrassment.

---

* These facts, and the quotation, are taken from an article, 'The Village Movement', by Allan Young. Mr Young has dealt with the matter more fully in his book, *The Approaches to Local Self Government in British Guiana.*

As soon as we got to the other bank a man came up to Dr Jagan and gave him two dollars for the party, and we were met by an elderly Negro, a party-worker. New Amsterdam was a stronghold of the opposition, and we learned that Mr Burnham himself, the leader of the opposition, was in town (he had probably caught the 1.25 ferry) and was to make a speech that evening. Mrs Jagan said that sometimes on these campaigning tours government and opposition had to share the same government rest house. There was no danger of that here, however. We were staying at Government House.

Government House in New Amsterdam is the old Davson estate house, white and grand and elegant, two-storeyed, standing on tall pillars, the broad veranda wire-netted, the floors shining, the rooms high and large, and everywhere the rich smell of old wood, the unmistakable smell of the tropical estate house. Something remained of the Davsons. In the drawing room, on walls otherwise unfurnished, there were two framed photographs of Dovedale; and in the room I was given there was a coloured print, bluish and faint and misty, of Eton. In the veranda, shadowed by wide eaves and protected from insects by wirenetting which nevertheless permitted one to see the garden and the tennis court, the party-worker and I talked. He sat on the wicker chair as one who entered the house now by right; but his hat was on his knees, and his talk was mostly of the Davsons. He spoke of them with more than affection, with relish; while Dr Jagan slept in one of the rooms upstairs, and the hot afternoon stillness was emphasized by the muffled booming of a loudspeaker announcing Mr Burnham's speech that evening.

The loudspeaker went on and on. The party-worker turned to politics, reluctantly I fancied, for the party's prospects in New Amsterdam were not bright. It was the old issue of race: New Amsterdam was predominantly Negro and the Negroes were afraid of Indian dominance. He himself didn't see what dominance had to do with it. In B.G. it was open to anyone to 'progress' – in the West Indies to be progressive is to be determined and able to acquire –

and there were Negroes who were as 'progressive' as the Indians. He just wished there were more progressive Negroes; and there could be, for though the Indian owned more, the Negro earned more.

I had heard this before in Georgetown, and from supporters of the other side. In their uncertainty, their fear of being twice over-taken, not as individuals but as a community, first by the Portuguese (between whom and the Negroes there were riots in 1856 and 1889) and now by the Indians, in their feeling that time was against them, many Guianese Negroes were in this mood of self-analysis. At Christmas there had been a campaign urging the Negroes to save, to buy only what was absolutely necessary. The campaign had failed, and the stores had complained of racialism.

In Georgetown a Negro woman of energy, charm and sensibility had spoken to me for an hour, with urgency and something like despair, about the shortcomings of the Guianese Negro. She wished the Negro to behave with dignity. It nauseated her to see Negro women jumping up in street bands at Carnival time: no Indian or Portuguese or white or Chinese woman did that. (But they do in Trinidad, where it is a sign of modernity and emancipation.) The Negro wasted his money on drink, which was for him a symbol of wealth and whiteness. (This is, of course, an over-simplification, though it should be said that Dr Jagan recognizes alcoholism as one of the country's problems.) She wished the Negro could have the thrift and determination of the Indian; many respected coloured families had wasted their substance and were completely in the hands of Indian money-lenders. Above all, the Negro lacked the family feeling of the Indian; this was the root of his vulnerability. Three hundred years of slavery had taught him only that he was an individual and that life was short.

And now, in the veranda of the Davson house, the party-worker was speaking of the same problem, less analytically, but with less urgency and despair. There were progressive people everywhere, he was saying; no one race had the monopoly of progress. So the talk turned to the great families of Guiana, and came back to the Davsons. Mrs Jagan joined us – the children had been sent on to their grandmother's – and we had tea.

Dr Jagan had to make two speeches later that afternoon, not in New Amsterdam but in outlying villages. The car had come over by the 3.45 ferry; and, leaving Mrs Jagan to Colette, we went to the party office, a run-down wooden building, to pick up party-workers and loudspeaker equipment. On the way out of town we picked up the local speakers, among them Mr Ajodhasingh, the member for the region, who, I was told, was in disgrace with his constituents because he had not visited them for some time.

There was a lorry-load of blue-uniformed policemen at the village where the second meeting was to be held; and another lorry-load at the village where we stopped. The policemen had taken up positions on either side of a red shop-and-rumshop of wood and corrugated iron. Some boys were sitting on the rails of the shop gallery and such crowd as there was was so scattered, in yards across the road, on the steps of houses nearby, that at first it seemed there were more policemen than audience. Dr Jagan was at once surrounded in the yard of the shop by a delegation of rice-farmers; himself a tall man, he was hidden by these farmers, who had put on their visiting clothes: pressed khaki trousers, stiff shining shoes, ironed shirts that were white or bright blue, well-brushed, new-looking brown felt hats.

The party-workers hung up the loudspeaker and tested it. Mr Ajodhasingh was introduced, and while he made a fighting, over-energetic speech about the achievements of the government, copies of the party newspaper, *Thunder*,* were hawked around. The rice-farmers released Dr Jagan only when he had to speak. As soon as he began, the party-workers and Mr Ajodhasingh drove off, to

---

* From William Morris: Hark the rolling of the thunder:
                        Lo the sun and lo thereunder
                        Riseth wrath and hope and wonder.

'warm up' the second meeting. Dr Jagan's passion contrasted with the pastoral scene and the placidity of his audience, separated from him by the road. Along this road there passed a scampering cow and seconds later a running herdsman; a pundit in turban, dhoti and white jacket, briskly pedalling a bicycle; a tractor, two lorries. Dr Jagan spoke about the buying over of the Demerara Electric Company; the land resettlement scheme; the electoral boundaries report. Night fell while he spoke. He spoke for an hour – the children in the shop gallery continually whispering, giggling and being hushed – and his speech was well received.

Abruptly he turned and walked into the shop, alone and still and withdrawn, and drank a Banks beer. Fortunately for him there was no photographer. Earlier that week Mrs Jagan had been photographed drinking an I-Cee beverage, a D'Aguiar product, like Banks beer, and the newspapers had made much of it.

In the next village the warming up had not been successful. The loudspeaker was out of order, and the party-worker was speaking, unheard, standing on a box below the eaves of a large new concrete foodshop, which was brilliantly lit and had its doors wide open. The small crowd, mainly Negro, was scattered in talkative little groups about the bright yard and dark road. Whenever a vehicle approached, its headlamps blinding, a group on the road broke up, moving to the grass verges, and never quite reformed. Movement was as constant as the chatter. The speaker, a Negro, was casually though repeatedly heckled with accusations of discrimination by the government against Negroes. One man, clearly a village character, from the humorous ovation given him whenever he spoke, asked again and again from the darkness of the roadside: 'What has the government done for the region?' And: 'How many people from this region have been granted lands?' His vocabulary was impressive – 'lands' had a startling legalistic ring – and doubtless hinted at the basis of his popularity. The party-workers attempted ineffectually to deal both with questioners and the faulty loudspeaker. The loudspeaker was eventually abandoned; and Dr Jagan, unaided, delivered his earlier speech with a similar passion. He received more attention than the speakers before him, but the crowd remained disorderly. There were more accusations of discrimination against Negroes, and from the roadside groups even some mild cursing.

We drove back in silence to New Amsterdam. In Government House, in the big, dimly-lit dining room, its freshly painted walls bare except for an old Dutch map of New Amsterdam (*Hoge Bosch* around a tiny settlement) our food was waiting, covered by cloths at one end of the long, polished table. Mrs Jagan came down, looking as though she expected news of disaster: I saw now what she meant when she said she was a pessimist. Her hair was freshly brushed; I suspected that she had been reading Colette in bed.

'How did it go?'

'All right.' Dr Jagan was brief, fatigued; he seemed to be able to move continually from passion to repose.

Mr Burnham's meeting had already begun. We could hear his amplifiers booming indistinctly across the otherwise silent town.

After dinner Dr Jagan went out visiting, and at Mrs Jagan's suggestion I went to Mr Burnham's meeting. It was in one of the main streets and the Jagans' chauffeur drove me there. Mr Burnham, in a plain short-sleeved sports shirt, was speaking from a high platform. He spotted the chauffeur and made a comment too full of local allusion for me to understand. But the chauffeur was mortified; though he was a seasoned political campaigner himself, he remained curiously sensitive to any intemperate or aggressive language. At the disorderly meeting earlier that evening he had clapped his hands to his ears when a woman spoke an obscenity.

Mr Burnham is the finest public speaker I have heard. He speaks slowly, precisely, incisively; he makes few gestures; his head is thrust forward in convinced, confiding, simple but never condescending exposition; he is utterly calm, and his fine voice is so nicely modulated that the listener never tires or ceases to listen.

The manner conceals an amazing quickness, all the more effective for never revealing itself in an acceleration of pace or a change of pitch.

'Burnham!' a youth shouts as he cycles past. 'Mister to you,' is the reply, the voice so even that it is some seconds before one realizes that the words are not part of the speech. 'You lie! You lie!' someone calls from a passing car. This is not dealt with at once. Burnham completes the sentence in hand. 'And,' he continues, the car now diminished in the distance, 'as that jackass will never understand . . .' The timing has been perfect; the crowd roars. Someone in the audience starts to object. Burnham ceases to speak. Slowly he swivels his head to gaze at the offender, and the bright light plays on a face that expresses fatigued yet somehow tolerant contempt. The silence lasts. Then Burnham, his expression now one of annoyance, turns to the microphone again. 'As I was saying,' he begins. His reputation in British Guiana undoubtedly accounts for part of his success. His speeches are known to be entertaining and the crowds come to be entertained, as this New Amsterdam crowd undoubtedly was; a large, good-humoured, mixed crowd.

Unfortunately Mr Burnham had little to say. He indicated a general disapproval of what was going on, without documenting his case effectively. He spoke of the need for education, and promised to establish an economic planning unit when he came to power. He spoke of Mrs Jagan, his former associate, as 'that little lady from Chicago, an alien to our shores'; and he played indirectly though not the less unpleasantly on the racial issue. 'I warn the Indians . . . Jagan has said he wants to gain control of the commanding heights of the economy. The commanding heights. Let me translate for you: *your* businesses, *your* land, *your* shops.' To the Negroes in the audience the message was clear.

In 1953, after the British Guiana Constitution had been suspended, I heard both Mr Burnham and Dr Jagan speak at Oxford. Though power and responsibility have brought about certain changes, Dr Jagan remains what he then was. The same cannot be said of Mr Burnham. In 1953 he spoke, however uncertainly, like a man with a case. In 1961 I felt he had none. What had happened in the interval? What caused the Jagan–Burnham split of 1955?

In British Guiana it is almost impossible to find out the truth about any major thing. Investigation and cross-checking lead only to fearful confusion. Dr Jagan blames Mr Burnham's opportunism; Mr Burnham, he says, was badly advised by West Indian politicians. And it is true that after his election victory of 1957 Dr Jagan sought a reconciliation with Mr Burnham. On the other hand, in his Georgetown chambers, where he more or less repeated the arguments of his New Amsterdam speech, Mr Burnham – in private a man of such charm that one almost regretted that he was a politician – said that his 'political demise' had been planned by the Jagans even before the 1953 elections. Reconciliation was therefore out of the question; besides, Dr Jagan was 'a Stalinist' and Mrs Jagan not an intellectual. This, however, does not explain Mr Burnham's failure, granted his great gifts, to provide constructive or stimulating opposition. My own conclusion, for which I can offer no evidence, is that between these men, who have shared an important Guiana experience, there remains a mutual sympathy and respect stronger than either suspects, each perhaps regretting the other for what he was.

However, the rift exists, and it has divided the country racially, creating a situation which reflects, as in a mirror, the Trinidad situation: in Trinidad the Negroes are the majority group, in British Guiana the Indians. With almost one half of the population contracting out of the self-government experiment, the country is dangerously weakened. Racial antagonisms, endlessly acting and reacting upon one another, and encouraged by the cynical buffoons who form so large a part of the politically ambitious in every population, are building up pressures which might easily overwhelm the leaders of both sides and overwhelm the country; though British

Guiana, because of its physical size and the isolation of its communities, can better withstand disturbance than Trinidad.

On Sunday morning we drove east along the Corentyne coast to
Port Mourant, Dr Jagan's birthplace. Port Mourant is a sugar-cane
estate of flat, hideous vastness, miles long and miles deep. The
people are proud of the vastness, and believe too that Port Mourant
produces the finest Guianese. They are only slightly less proud
of their cricketers than they are of Dr Jagan. The house of Joe
Solomon, who miraculously threw down the last Australian wicket
in the tied test match at Melbourne, was pointed out to me more
than once by people who had known Solomon ever since he was a boy.

The population of Port Mourant is mainly Indian, and Dr Jagan
was going to open a Hindu temple that morning in one of the
workers' settlements: white wooden houses set about a rectangular
pattern of narrow asphalted streets. We found a large crowd of men,
women and children, dressed mainly in white, waiting on the road
and in the scuffed grounds of the new, white-washed temple. The
temple was of concrete. I thought it heavy and inelegant, as so many
Guianese concrete buildings are; but it was interesting because,
though Hindu, it was clearly Muslim-inspired. Muslim architecture,
as formalized and distinctive as Muslim doctrine, can be more easily
remembered than Hindu, and more easily reproduced. Apart from a
few simple Hindu temples, the mosque is the only non-Western type
of building that most Indians in Trinidad and British Guiana know.

Dr Jagan was welcomed without formality by his brother Udit,
a tall, well-built man who still works on the estate. Udit wore a blue
shirt, and his khaki trousers were folded above his ankles; he was
barefooted. Mrs Jagan introduced me to her mother-in-law, a short,
sturdy woman in white. She wore the Indian long skirt, bodice and
orhni. Her son had inherited the features which, on her, were a trifle
heavy. Her manner was simple, patient and self-effacing. As soon as
she had greeted her son she withdrew. Dr Jagan and his wife were
garlanded. Then on the threshold of the temple Dr Jagan made a

very short speech about the importance of self-help and his pleasure at opening a building which was an example of that. He cut the ribbon – West happily blending with East – and helped to take the image inside. We took off our shoes and followed. The concrete floor was covered with linoleum in three widths of different patterns and colours. Men sat on the left, women on the right. Mrs Jagan sat next to her mother-in-law. A gentle young brahmin with shoulder-long hair brushed back flat, and a frogged white silk jacket, acted as master of ceremonies. A middle-aged singer of local renown, accompanying himself on the harmonium, sang a Hindi ballad he had composed for the occasion. Its subject was Dr Jagan; the words 'nineteen fifty-three' occurred often, and in English. At the end some people, including myself, started to clap.

'No! No!' cried a blue-suited, bespectacled man on my right. 'This is a temple.'

The clapping instantly died down and many of us tried to pretend that we hadn't been clapping.

The brahmin urged us to cooperate.

Dr Jagan spoke again. It made a change, he said, to hear songs of praise. The temple was a fine building, and a good example to the people of Guiana, who needed to practise self-help. In spite of all that had been said to the contrary, his party guaranteed religious freedom; his presence was proof of that.

'Say a few words in Hindustani,' the blue-suited fanatic whispered in English. 'They would appreciate it.'

Dr Jagan sat down.

There was another song. Then, to my surprise, the secretary read a report on the temple's activities; this was necessarily very brief, but it was too much for the women, who began to chatter among themselves.

'Silence!' the fanatic called, jumping up.

The brahmin urged the people to cooperate and called gently for order.

The fanatic rose to his stockinged feet to move the vote of

thanks. He began with a Hindi couplet and chastised us at length for desecrating the temple in the very hour of its opening by clapping. Then he spoke about the Sanatan Dharma, the faith. Staring hard at Dr Jagan, he said: 'The Hindus of this country will fight for their religion. Let no one forget that.'

Dr Jagan stared straight ahead.

Immediately after the ceremony Dr Jagan was besieged by people talking about land. The rest of us put on our shoes and went to an old wooden shed that adjoined the temple, and there we were fed on halwa, chipped coconut, bananas and soft drinks. We went out to the car and waited in the hot sun for Dr Jagan. The crowd around him was growing, and his attempts to step backwards to the road were frustrated. The chauffeur was sent to get him away. The chauffeur, a small man, worked his way into the crowd and disappeared. Someone else was sent. 'Is always the biggest crooks who hold him back like that,' Dr Jagan's mother said. She had prepared lunch for him at home; she was impatient to take him off; and it was hot in the car. Eventually, after many minutes, Dr Jagan freed himself and came out to the road, some people still at his heels.

Dr Jagan's mother and the family of his brother Udit live in one of the workers' houses across the main road from the compound of the estate senior staff, which is fenced around with wire mesh and guarded at the gate by a watchman. The workers' houses, standing on stilts, and sheltered by many fruit trees, give the impression of being choked together. Each house, however, stands on a fair amount of land: the feeling of oppression is created by the maze of narrow, dusty, improperly drained tracks between the houses, the fences on either side of the tracks, and above all the trees, rustling in the wind which carries the smell of cesspits. Yet it was easy to see why the Jagan children are always eager to come down to Port Mourant to stay with their grandmother. For a city child there would be enchantment in the flat, well-swept dirt yard, cool with water-channels and low fruit trees.

The house was a simple one, roughly built; and inside bright with fresh paint that had been applied to old, unpainted wood. In the small drawing room there was a set of morris chairs on the uneven floor; a photograph album and an untidy stack of old American pulp magazines rested on a small centre-table; the walls carried no decoration apart from some Roman Catholic calendars. There was no sink or running water; so we used pitchers to wash our hands out of the window of the dining-area. Constantly encouraged by Dr Jagan's mother, we ate. The food was good, indeed extravagant. It completed my exhaustion. I couldn't face the afternoon sports meeting, to which the Jagans were going, and asked whether I could rest. Udit showed me to a tiny bedroom that led off from the drawing room. The hairy wooden walls had been painted cobalt; and, below a picture of Christ, I went to sleep.

It was night when Udit awakened me. Mrs Jagan had gone back to Georgetown; Dr Jagan was in New Amsterdam. I was to spend the night in Port Mourant. Udit, a grave, kindly man, offered me a pitcher of water to refresh myself, and then took me for a long walk along the main road, bright with shops and new cafés and busy with the Sunday evening cinema crowd. We talked about the diversification of agriculture in the region; Udit told me that cocoa was being introduced. About the contrast between Udit and his brother there was nothing startling; it can be duplicated in many West Indian families who, with an imperfect understanding of the concept, comically described themselves as 'middle class'.

After dinner Dr Jagan's mother showed me the photograph album. It had been extensively rifled. The only photograph of interest was one Dr Jagan had sent back from America while he was a student: a studio portrait by an unimaginative photographer of a dazzlingly handsome young man looking over his shoulder, not unaware of his looks: not the face of a politician or a man who was to go to jail for plotting to burn down Georgetown. If she was proud of her son Mrs Jagan didn't show it. She scarcely spoke of him; and when we closed the photograph album she became much more concerned about my family and about me. I smoked too much; I was damaging my health; wouldn't I like to try to stop? And drinking: that was another bad thing: she hoped I didn't do much of that. While we spoke, Udit's children brought out their school books and worked at the dining table by the light of the Petromax pressure lamp. The house was wired and had bulbs; but the electricity supply was in the hands of various entrepreneurs in the settlement who ran small generating plants; and it seemed there was some trouble about the arrangements. Earlier, someone else had told me about a field clerk who was too 'stuck up' to extend the services of his plant.

Dr Jagan was to return to Port Mourant in the morning, to address a public meeting in the Roopmahal Cinema on the working of the land resettlement scheme. When I left for the cinema Udit's wife asked me to get Cheddi to 'come and take some tea'. The request had to be deferred, for Dr Jagan was already on the cinema stage, with a whole row of government officials, Negro, Portuguese and coloured, seated behind him on folding chairs. The administrators wore suits; the engineers khaki shorts and white shirts.

Questioners were being invited to speak from the stage, and over and over Dr Jagan explained to people who had applied unsuccessfully for land that applications had been carefully considered and preference given to the neediest. At last the landed started climbing up to the stage. They stood correctly, their shirt sleeves buttoned at the wrist, holding their hats behind their backs, and spoke softly, as though sensing the hostility of the landless, who made up most of the large audience. Some objected to government interference; some didn't like being told where to pasture their cattle; some objected to the proposed limitation of holdings.

Dr Jagan: How much land you have?

The Questioner mumbles. Whispers in the audience of 'You see him? You see him? You see how quiet he playing now?'

Dr Jagan: You have a *hundred* acres?

Gasps from the audience, of astonishment, genuine and simulated, mixed with delight at the uncovering in public of a secret long known. The questioner flicks his hat against the back of his thighs and stares straight at Dr Jagan.

Dr Jagan: And how much of this hundred acres you planting?

The Questioner mumbles.

Dr Jagan: Twelve acres. You have a hundred acres and you and your sons planting twelve. But I alone, man, with a cutlass, could do better than that. (Dr Jagan's tone now changes from the conversational to the oratorical.) This is the curse of this country. So many people without land. And so much good land not being used, just going to waste. This is one of the things this government is going to put a stop to.

The Audience hums with approval, which turns slightly to derision as the questioner, squeezing his hat, makes his way down from the stage, looking at the steps. Another questioner goes up and speaks for some time. The audience is still derisive and Dr Jagan holds up his hand for silence.

Dr Jagan: Good. You plant your fifteen acres. You work hard on your land, you been keeping your wife and five children now and you don't see why the government or anybody else should come and tell you what to do or where to tie out your cow. Good. We know you work hard. But tell me. Who rice-land your cows does mash down? And where you does pump your water out? In the next man land, not so? So what about him?

The roar is one of approval for *Dr Jagan's* cleverness in demolishing an argument which had at first seemed fair and unassailable.

And so it went on, until the climax. This had been gigglingly prepared in the back seats by some of the landless who were perhaps also party-workers. A 'character', barefooted, in khaki trousers and shirt, his manner suggesting a slight drunkenness and also a comical hesitation, walked up to the stage, humorously applauded all the way. And once on the stage he delivered an impassioned and controlled oration on behalf of the landless. It was a performance of high finish, from the opening – 'A uneducated man like me don't know how to talk good' – to the well-known local jokes and the devastating denunciation of selfishness and greed which was at the root of the troubles of Guiana. After he had finished there was nothing more to say. The engineer in white shorts had only to hold up maps and explain some technical details.

Even so, Dr Jagan was surrounded after the meeting and made to go over points that had already been explained. One man had a special complaint: the authorities were making him pay an omnibus licence for his taxi, and he wanted Dr Jagan to correct this. The taxi was in the yard of the cinema: it was a van, capable of seating ten.

It was now past midday. We didn't have time to go and take tea with Udit's wife. Dr Jagan had to open a cassava factory in Georgetown at five; his son, waiting for us in New Amsterdam, wanted to get back in time for the matinée of a cowboy film. We started for New Amsterdam with some of the government officials, driving fast along the road, which was here asphalted and smooth. We heard a knocking. It persisted, increased; and the sound was familiar to me from an experience I had had just before leaving Trinidad. We stopped and examined the wheels. The front wheels were firm; those at the rear rocked at the push of a hand. Removing the left hub cap, we found all the nuts unscrewed, projecting evenly beyond the bolts with only a thread or so to go. It was very puzzling.

'You've been seeing politics in the raw this week-end,' Dr Jagan said to me over lunch at New Amsterdam Government House. 'If you want to think at all, you have to go abroad.'

Dr Jagan is all things to all men. For some he is to be distrusted because he is a communist; for others he is to be distrusted because he has ceased to be a communist and is just another colonial politician attracted by power. For some he is a racial leader. For some he is failing to be a racial leader. ('I hate Cheddi,' a well-placed Indian said to me. 'The more I see him the more I hate him. One morning the Indians of this country are going to wake up and find that Cheddi has sold them down the river.') And for others, as a Negro reminded me (it was a point one tended to forget), Dr Jagan represents a radical racial change: he is not white. The colonial system being what it is, many browns and blacks, brown and black but 'respectable', find this hard to forgive.

The West Indian colonial situation is unique because the West Indies, in all their racial and social complexity, are so completely a creation of Empire that the withdrawal of Empire is almost without meaning. In such a situation nationalism is the only revitalizing force. I believe that, below the ebullience and bravado, a positive nationalism existed in British Guiana in 1953. This was the achievement of the Jagans and Mr Burnham and their colleagues, and it was destroyed by the suspension of the constitution in that year and – gratuitous humiliation – by the dispatch of troops. Colonial attitudes, so recently overcome, easily reasserted themselves. Under pressure, like the West Indians in London during the Notting Hill riots, the country split into its component parts; and the energy which, already gathered, ought to have gone towards an ordered and overdue social revolution was dissipated in racial rivalry, factional strife and simple fear, creating the confusion which is today more dangerous to Guiana than the alleged plot of 1953.

It is the waste, the futility which is depressing. For when one thinks of Guiana one thinks of a country whose inadequate resources are strained in every way, a country whose geography imposes on it an administration and a programme of public works out of all proportion to its revenue and population. One thinks of the sea-wall, for ever being breached and repaired; the dikes made of mud for want of money; the dirt roads and their occasional experimental surfacing; the roads that are necessary but not yet made; the decadent railways ('Three-fourths of the passenger rolling stock,' says a matter-of-fact little note in the government paper on the Development Programme, 'is old and nearing the point beyond which further repairs will be impossible'); the three overworked Dakotas and two Grumman seaplanes of British Guiana Airways. And one thinks of the streets of Albouystown, as crowded with children as a schoolyard during recess.

* * *

The middle-aged American with the surly rustic face was leaning against one of the gallery pillars of the ramshackle British Guiana Airways building at Atkinson Field. I guessed he was American because of his clothes. The straw hat and tight khaki trousers were distinctive; so were the spectacles. He also carried a camera and was chewing. His baggage lay around him in polythene sacks; whenever he moved he took the sacks with him. The precaution seemed excessive, for there were few people about, and we were all passengers for the Interior: half a dozen diamond prospectors, Doctor Talbot and myself. Dr Talbot was an old Interior 'hand' who was never so happy as when he was in the bush, drawing Amerindian teeth. His two or three pieces of baggage were tied with rope; he carried an umbrella – odd with his white panama hat – and a parcel of books which were mainly about doctors.

We were going to Kamarang, in the south-west, near Mount Roraima, where the boundaries of British Guiana, Brazil and Venezuela meet. Kamarang was an Amerindian reservation which had recently been opened up. You still needed government permission to go there, though; and the prospectors were being allowed only to pass through on their way to the diamond fields.

The Dakota flew in from the Rupununi, unloaded its cargo of sacked beef, and we went aboard. The American, refusing all assistance from the loader, strung and hung his various parcels and bags about himself and made his way shakily to the aircraft. Then with slow care he unstrung and unhung his parcels, stowed them at the back of the plane, chose a seat, dusted it with a handkerchief, sat down and concentrated on fastening his safety belt, chewing all the while, his deliberateness interrupted by abrupt little pouncing actions, like a man trying to swat a fly after eyeing it for some time.

Within minutes we had cleared the coastal strip. We flew over Bartica and had a glimpse of the red road to the Potaro goldfields. We saw the innumerable forested islands which choked the Mazaruni River. And then it was forest, and forest. We ceased to look through the small oblong windows and just listened to the noise of the aircraft. The Negro prospector beside me was reading the Georgetown *Chronicle*. He caught me looking over his shoulder and passed the paper to me. The headline story on the front page was about the chaotic conditions in the Cuyuni mining area. The prospectors there were apparently without a doctor or an administrator and had to depend on the Venezuelan authorities. The story had been given to the *Chronicle* by a prospector called Agrippa, who was quoted as saying, 'When a man gets chopped in a fight there is no doctor or police to look for him.'

As abruptly as on the ride to the Rupununi, the mountains began. But here they were flat-topped, suggesting a plateau that had in parts subsided and crumbled, leaving sheer walls of grey stone like those of a giant's castle, with neat excisions and neat towers, one quite square, many perfectly round; and down these walls ran thin lines of white water dissolving to spray. 'Wondrous is this wall-stone; broken by fate, the castles have decayed; the work of giants is crumbling.' The academic text returned, unsummoned, after many years; but the Anglo-Saxon poet was speaking of the abandoned city of Bath, and this was the lost world of Conan Doyle.

We prepared to land. I returned the *Chronicle* to its owner, who said, 'So you read it, eh? I am Agrippa. Give the papers the story, man. Don't play with these things.'

Bill Seggar, the district commissioner, met us when we got off the plane. Dr Talbot was to spend the night in his house. The American and myself were to share a room in the rest house. Some Amerindian boys took our baggage there, and the American dutifully tipped each of them. While I arranged my parcels the

American went out to the veranda; when I left the room he went in. We did not speak.

The settlement at Kamarang Mouth lies about the airstrip, which is at the confluence of the Kamarang and Mazaruni rivers. From the rest-house veranda the view was of the black glassy Mazaruni just at the foot of the cliff, still water between walls of trees, reflected clearly on one side, darkly on the other, with blue flat-topped Mount Roraima far away at the end of the river. I walked down the cliff to the water's edge. Three Amerindian girls sat whispering and giggling on a rock, the first smiling Amerindians I saw. Two giggling boys paddled past in a woodskin, which seemed to skid over the smooth dark water. It was like an illustration in a child's book about children with difficult skills in remote lands.

Below one of the unfinished wooden houses of the settlement I came upon three of the prospectors who had travelled with us on the plane. One was Indian; the other two were Negroes, one brown, one black. The Indian – I spotted a bottle of yellow peppersauce among his few belongings – was instantly loquacious; the brown Negro also spoke; but the black Negro remained silent and scarcely looked at me. Everyone knows about the prospectors or 'pork-knockers' of Guiana, and these men, recognizing me as an informed tourist, behaved like men with a reputation to live up to. The Indian told me he was a diver. I expressed the awe which I felt was expected. 'Best way for a poor man to make a living,' the speaking Negro said. The Indian talked about diving. Sometimes, he said, you could stay below water for half a day. 'It depends on your consecution,' the speaking Negro said. 'A man with no consecution will have to come up after half an hour.' I asked the speaking Negro whether he came from Georgetown. He became embarrassed; he said he came from 'another territory'. This meant he was a small islander; I did not inquire further. Something flew to one of the rough wooden pillars and rested above my hand: it was a spider, carrying its large white disc of eggs below its abdomen. I said goodbye to the prospectors, while they settled down in their hammocks for the evening, the Mazaruni black below them, Roraima faint in the distance.

Bill Seggar had invited me to dinner. He had invited the American as well, but the American, muttering something about not using up other people's rations, had declined; and when I passed the rest house I had a glimpse of him in the kitchen veranda carefully opening tins from one of his polythene sacks. In Bill Seggar's plain wooden house, well-stocked with books and magazines, and with Amerindian artifacts on the unpainted walls, Dr Talbot was reading. He had already drawn a number of teeth. Seggar called to me from the shower to have a drink. I took a lager from the refrigerator – everything, I reminded myself guiltily, flown in from the coast – and Dr Talbot explained the Amerindian blow-pipe, the black-tipped arrows and the bead-pouches, 'worn today, alas, *under* their clothes'. Dr Talbot was a romantic. He distrusted mechanical progress of every sort and regretted the days when a journey to the Interior was indeed a journey to the Interior and not a joy-ride on a Dakota. He didn't even care for outboard motors; we were going up the Kamarang next morning to the mission station at Paruima, on the Venezuelan border, in the mission launch, and he would have preferred to make the journey on horseback.

We were joined by the tall, slim Portuguese pilot who on the next day was to fly out the prospectors to the diamond fields, in the cerise-coloured single-engined plane I had seen on the landing strip. The pilot didn't like the prospectors staying in an Amerindian settlement longer than was necessary, and he told me that Dionysus, the Indian who had spoken to me about diving, had no chance of being taken to the diamond area. The very Dakota that had brought Dionysus from Georgetown had brought a message that he was not to be employed.

Bill Seggar came out of the shower, and our dinner party was complete when Mr Europe, the Negro dispenser, came over from his dispensary across the landing strip. (Agrippa, Dionysus, Mr Europe: I didn't believe these Kamarang names.) At Seggar's large plain wooden table we talked, the bats squawking in the roof, of the problems of Guiana. Mr Europe spoke of race and slavery; he reminded us without rancour, that Amerindians hunted down runaway slaves; and we spoke of Amerindians.

They told me of the effect of alcohol on the Amerindian: he vividly remembers insults and injustices many years old, which he had forgotten, and becomes homicidal. And I heard of the *kanaima*, the hired killer, the dread of all Amerindians. The *kanaima* is a dedicated person; he lives apart; he fasts before a murder, which is carried out in a horrible manner and involves a knotting of the victim's intestines. The *kanaima* loses his power if he is ever known. He reveals himself therefore only to his victim. This is why in lonely places Amerindians prefer not to be alone, though even this is not safe, since – who knows? – your companion might be the *kanaima*. For the Amerindian, however, there is no escape from the *kanaima*, because *kanaima* is more than a killer: he is Death. Amerindians never die naturally: they are always killed by *kanaima*.

There was a dog at the station, a powerful, beautiful animal that lived in constant terror. It was afraid of the dark, of insects and of every sudden movement. When the pilot and myself left Seggar's house and made our way by the light of an electric torch to the rest house, the dog walked ahead, always keeping within the wavering light-ray, like an actor edging into an unsteady spotlight. In the rest house the dog rubbed against our legs for reassurance. The lights blinked three times – Seggar's warning that he was turning off the current – and soon darkness fell over the station, and, with the running down of the motor, silence. Reluctantly, I left the dog; he had been frightened by a beetle and was lying between my feet.

My American was sleeping under a mosquito net, which he had hung up on hoops and brackets brought in one of his polythene sacks. My bed had no mosquito net and I had only Seggar's word that there were no mosquitoes. I was about to get into bed when I remembered that during the afternoon the American had opened his bed and examined it thoroughly. This memory of American caution now alarmed me. With unnecessary violence I pulled the bed open; and, creeping about as silently as I could, examined it with my torch.

At seven in the morning the Paruima boatmen clomped up in their gumboots. The American, dressed, packed, his mosquito net dismantled, was still tying one of his polythene sacks, and he apologized to the boatmen for not being ready: he had got up only at half past six. I too was going on the boat. 'If I hadda known you was going,' the American said, speaking to me for the first time, 'I woulda woke you up.' I jumped out of bed, threw some water over myself in the wash-room, had a cup of Nescafé, lukewarm because of my haste, and ran over to Seggar's to get Dr Talbot. He was just sitting down to an elaborate breakfast, appeared to be in no hurry, and expressed strong disapproval of the American. I idled down to the river. The American was in the launch, quite alone, surrounded by his polythene sacks. I went back to the rest house and had a cup of cocoa, and then wandered over to the dispensary, where Mr Europe, who was also the postmaster, was dispensing Kamarang postmarks. Agrippa was with him and another prospector, elderly, bespectacled, schoolmasterly, who took out a glass vial and showed me the diamonds a lucky man might get: they were like bits of stone and glass and broken pencil points, and of the size of pencil points.

At last we were ready. But the boat was leaving from the Kamarang side, and the American had to get out of the launch, where he had steadfastly remained all the while, and, without his parcels, make his way up the hill, across the landing strip and down to the Kamarang bank.

We started. An Amerindian stood in the bow: later he sat on a paddle across the bow, and never moved. His stillness fascinated me and the fascination was made almost unendurable by the tedium of the boat journey: unchanging noise, unchanging river. For hour after hour I was to see that broad blue-jerseyed back directly in front of me, those unmoving gumboots, those hands pressing on the paddle. I took photographs of him; I sketched him; and I took more photographs. His duty was to warn of obstacles, particularly submerged tree trunks with which the river banks were littered. Either he or we were lucky: for the whole of the day he uttered not a single warning cry.

The smooth water was black with warm brown undertones; the narrow river, with forest on either side, felt enclosed. Sometimes we passed Amerindians in their boats, fairer and more handsome than the Amerindians of the Rupununi. A moored woodskin or dug-out, and a rough path up the bank worn into brown dirt steps, indicated a home. A low goalpost-like structure made of tree branches marked a camping site. Birds, always in pairs, played about our boat: large grey birds and small ones with blue-black wings and white breasts. Dr Talbot said that when he first went up the Kamarang the grey birds stayed with the boat all the way. Now they flew a hundred yards or more ahead because the Amerindians shot them for sport. And, indeed, an Amerindian came from the stern with a rifle, his friends sighing and chattering with expectation, and the boat slowed down for him to take his position in the bow, in front of the unmoving lookout. He turned and smiled at us. 'Pay no attention to him,' Dr Talbot said irritably, turning away. 'He is only doing it to show off.'

So I paid no attention and tried instead to make some cocoa, using river water, which Dr Talbot said with almost proprietorial pride was quite pure. The American, who sat behind us, declined briefly: he didn't want to use other people's rations. Dr Talbot lost his cup while trying to scoop up some water from the river. However, cold cocoa was made – the river water was, one might say, *vin arrosé* in colour – and I was lifting my cup to my mouth when I heard the report of the rifle and spilled the cocoa down my shirt and trousers. The Amerindians sighed with disappointment: the bird had not been hit. Attempting to rinse out my cup afterwards, I lost it. At my back I heard the American blowing and sucking at a cup of hot coffee, from the Thermos he had prepared that morning. He was also eating dainty sandwiches from airsealed cellophane packets.

At midday we stopped at a village which, deflating to one's pretensions as a traveller, had neat houses of wood and corrugated iron. It was a branch of the Paruima Mission. The American took photographs, and with elaborate deviousness, which attracted a good deal of puzzled interest, attended to certain natural functions. The Amerindians bought cassava bread, white curling discs about two feet wide and half an inch thick, which they handled with extreme casualness, folding it and stuffing it into the corners of baskets. Dr Talbot bought a disc himself; it was brought down to the boat by a very small boy whom it half concealed. I tried a piece. It was hard and coarse, with a sour smell and almost no taste. The blue-jerseyed lookout had some meat between two of these bread boards. Delight was all over his face. He settled down on the paddle; someone passed him an enamel plate of red-spotted rice, and with every mouthful of rice he ate a shard of cassava bread.

Great brown and grey rocks, great broken boulders, rounded and carved, appeared now on the river banks. Sometimes they were square and huge and cracked: ruins, they seemed, of the fortifi-cations of giants. And on these rocks, on soil just inches deep, the great trees of the forest grew, their roots spreading laterally, so that the soil seemed made of roots and the trees appeared to be growing out of nothing. Many trees had toppled into the river, their green and white and black trunks forming perfect Vs with their reflections, reflections which also created intricate patterns out of broken branches and the occasional isolated bare white stump. Lianas hung on the forest wall like a tangle of white cables, sometimes falling straight and continuing in their reflection. This was not the land-scape for the camera: the tropical forest cannot be better suggested than by the steel engravings in the travel books of the last century.

Presently we were lulled, Dr Talbot read a paperback novel I had never heard of. I took out my book, the Penguin edition of *The Immoralist* – it served me right, reading out of a sense of duty –

and was immediately concerned about the possible impropriety of the title. For Dr Talbot had told me earlier of the prohibitions at the mission, in whose boat we were travelling: no cigarettes, no alcohol, no coffee, no tea, no pepper, no meat, no skin-fish, no singing or whistling of anything except hymns. We had already broken a few rules. The American had been taking coffee and I had steadily been taking whisky to offset the discomfort of my cocoa-damp clothes. I had also been smoking.

Moving always now between rocks, messages being shouted out from the boat to Amerindians on the banks, we came to the portage. We heard the roar of the falls. The sun lit up one bank and the water, which in shadow was black, was like red wine held up to the light, with dancing luminous webs. The launch was unloaded. Dr Talbot and myself entrusted all our baggage to the Amerindians and with difficulty made our way through the mud between tall straight white trees of varying girths. Once or twice we slipped. The American didn't allow anyone to touch his polythene sacks; he strung them all on himself and slowly, very slowly, and more shakily than when approaching the Dakota at Atkinson Field, he picked his way through the thick squelching mud. We waited for him at the other side; and when, many minutes later, he appeared, there was no sign of achievement or sacrifice on his crumpled, fatigued face.

Our journey was nearly over. Within minutes we were at Paruima. The village lay on our left; on the other bank a landing field had been cleared. Palmer, the English agricultural officer, a slightly-built man in his early twenties, wearing khaki trousers, canvas shoes and a large straw hat, was at the river bank to welcome us. He especially welcomed Dr Talbot: there had been much sickness in the mission and even the pastor and his family had been affected. Dr Talbot got out with his books and umbrella; he was staying at the house of the village captain. We went on a few hundred yards to the mission proper. And there on the bank, in bathing trunks, were two children, white and blond and freckled, altogether startling after a day of river and forest and Amerindian faces.

'Who are you?' the bigger boy asked, taking the words out of my mouth. His American accent added to the unreality of the encounter, and gave a touch of impertinence to a simple and legitimate inquiry.

His father, the pastor, youngish, tall, slim and with spectacles, came down the high bank to the edge of the black water.

'The name's Winter,' my American said, holding out a blotched and surprisingly large hand. Hearing his accent against the pastor's, I realized how exaggeratedly southern Mr Winter's was.

We climbed up the bank. The mission, a complex of wooden buildings set in a circle, stood on a slope, at the end of a large clearing still spiky with tree stumps which suggested devastation rather than development. Large rocks, such as one had seen on the river, were embedded in the earth. In two or three places tree roots were burning: flameless, with thick white smoke.

The Americans appeared to be having an effect on one another. Mr Winter, no longer so solicitous about his parcels, was drawling on steadily and indistinctly as though getting rid of the talk he had bottled up for the last two days. The pastor's manner became heartier and his accent more pungent. He invited us to dinner and said he wished he could do more for us.

'If my wife wasn't sick,' he said, 'we would have welcomed you in our home.'

Abruptly Mr Winter's droning ceased. When the pastor, explaining, spoke casually of yellow fever, Mr Winter looked around as if for his polythene sacks. His face went surly again, and he said he didn't like using other people's rations.

We were to share a room in a rough unfinished wooden house that still smelled acridly of new tropical cedar. The pastor strung up my hammock. It gave me a little pleasure to find that for all his polythene sacks Mr Winter had no hammock. He had a palliasse and the only thing on which he could spread this was a low work-bench which was a foot or so shorter than himself. Stowing away his sacks, self-reliant once more, he dismissed the pastor's regrets, and it was like an urgent dismissal of the pastor.

I wanted to go for a swim before the sun set. The pastor said the water was too cold for the saw-toothed perai, and in guarantee of this offered to walk down to the river with me. I was interested by the huge rocks in the ground. They were neatly runnelled, as though turned out from a mould – the effects of water, I supposed – and these runnels were set in similar but vaster excisions which indicated a previous grandeur and wildness. I asked the pastor about the age of the rocks. He said that the Adventists had dispensed with the 'rigmarole of geologists'; the world was six thousand years old. The water was brown-black; and it was terrifying at dusk, in the forest silence, to dive into this liquid blackness. You didn't see the blackness. You felt your eyes were closed; you were in a void.

Lights burned here and there in the houses at the foot of the black forest wall. The burning tree stumps glowed; their crackles carried. Our unfinished room was in darkness. Mr Winter had made his bed – it looked the size of a crib – and tented it with his mosquito net. He was having some coffee and sandwiches by the light of his electric torch. I took a sip of whisky, went over to the house of one of the Negro teachers – bookcases with religious books and schoolbooks, the family (including grandmother) eating silently at an oilcloth-covered table – and borrowed a lantern. Remembering my whisky breath, I asked the teacher whether smoking was forbidden. Grandmother looked at me. The teacher said the pastor was tolerant, but wondered whether I wouldn't like to take this opportunity to stop. I promised to try, and hurried away with the lantern.

'Why, *thenk* you,' Mr Winter said. He was sitting on the edge of his bed, in complete darkness, fiddling with a transistor radio.

The pastor's house, painted and grand from the outside, with a low white wooden fence, was pioneer-rough inside. It smelled comfortingly of fresh paint: comfortingly, because Mr Winter had mumbled about the contagiousness of yellow fever. The pastor's family – pretty daughter, freckle-faced blond boys, and even little Deborah Sue, who brought out her doll, her doll's pram and her teddy bear – was what, from books, films and American tourists, one expected an American family to be. Only their vegetarianism was unexpected. We had a nut meal out of a tin, biscuits, soursop; and we drank milk.

'You haven't given me enough,' the younger boy said, when the nut was being served.

'Hey,' said the pastor rallyingly, 'you are supposed not to like this stuff, remember?'

The pastor told me the mission had been started twenty-five years before at the foot of Mount Roraima on the Venezuelan side of the border. When the authorities, under Roman Catholic pressure, asked them to leave, they came over the border to British Guiana, and the Amerindians followed.

We were in the region of the world's greatest waterfalls – the highest, in Venezuela, was some 3,000 feet – and the pastor thought I might like to go to the Utshi falls. At seven hundred feet Utshi was unimportant, no higher than Kaieteur, but it was only six hours away.

On the way back from the pastor's I stopped at the Negro teacher's. He had a Chinese boy with him, one of my neighbours in the unfinished house. Neither of them liked the idea of the walk to Utshi. They spoke of snakes, tigers and wild hogs. Wild hogs hunted in packs and the only way to escape was to race up a tree, and the straight branchless trees of the forest weren't easy to climb. I remembered a vivid story by a Guianese writer in which a boy had been attacked by wild hogs and eaten from the feet up, eaten so swiftly that he didn't collapse and appeared only to be growing shorter.

Earlier that day, in the Kamarang dispensary, I had asked Dr Talbot about conditions at Paruima. 'City life,' he said disapprovingly.

'With juke boxes playing only hymns,' I said. Agrippa had laughed, but Dr Talbot said, '*No llames bocazas al cocodrilo hasta que cruzes el río.* Don't call the crocodile big-mouth until you cross the river.' But I wasn't far wrong, for I was awakened in the morning by the raucous hymn-singing of the Chinese boy in the next room. So it went on all day: people humming only hymns, and the Chinese boy bursting into loud devotional song at all moments.

After so much talk about contagious diseases I woke up feeling slightly unwell, aching all over, besides, from my night-long struggle with the hammock. Mr Winter had also spent an uncomfortable night in his tented crib, trying to sleep with his knees drawn up.

'Why, good morning,' he said miserably, sitting on the edge of his bed in his underclothes. 'How – did – you – make – out – in – your – hammock?' He spoke so slowly that I strained for the words, always expecting the next one to be very important. 'I remember,' he went on, 'the first time *I* slept in a hammock.'

I stopped tying my shoelaces and listened.

'It was—'

I waited.

'—pretty difficult.'

I didn't feel easier when the Chinese boy said he too had had yellow fever, or when Palmer came over from the village and said Dr Talbot wasn't very well. Mr Winter and I drew closer together. I became as fanatical a water-boiler as he, and even this was not wholly reassuring, for we had to use the mission kettle and the communal mission range. I abandoned my good resolutions and throughout the day took prophylactic sips of whisky. Mr Winter didn't accept my whisky; instead, he took certain pills and secretly and constantly drank hot coffee. 'I sure do like a cup of coffee,' he said, when he was on his tenth or twelfth cup.

In the mission they were preparing for the Saturday sabbath, cooking and baking in advance. The mission store was full of Amerindians, among them the boatmen, waiting to be paid and to spend their pay. Downstairs, among the mammoth banana bunches that grew in this part of the world, a man was strumming the guitar. He was a Spanish-speaking Amerindian from Santa Helena in Venezuela. We talked a little and then he followed me wherever I went, speaking only when spoken to and at other times simply enjoying our silent communion.

Mr Winter had spent the morning collecting samples of earth, which he had laid out on squares of white paper on the narrow carpenter's work-shelf in our room. This, I learned, was the purpose of his visit. 'This soil is mighty interesting,' he said, his voice touched with what was almost glee. 'Mighty interesting.'

When, for want of a chair, I was lying in my hammock in the afternoon, the Negro woman from the adjoining room called out to me to look at the monkeys in the trees at the edge of the clearing. And there, indeed, they were, squeaking and jumping about. 'They always come out at this time,' the woman said. She wasn't Guianese; she came from one of the islands; her husband was studying to be a minister. After I had confessed I was not a Christian, we talked about religion. She had once met a Hindu and had noted the great difference between Hindu views and Adventist views: the Adventists, for example, believed that the world was made in six literal days. They didn't use tea or coffee because these drinks contained caffeine. Someone on the mission had tried using 'Postum', saying it had no caffeine, but the pastor had put a stop to that. She boiled some water for me, and I also asked for a little sugar. Then, remembering what she had said about the sickness at the mission ('You got to be careful. Only those who mix have been ill' – a remark which had unexpected racial undertones) I didn't use the sugar, though I played with it to suggest that I had used a little. Instead, I opened my tin of condensed milk.

Later that afternoon I took a dip in the river. Mr Winter came down, in shorts, with his bucket, and threw water over himself. Some Amerindian women were washing clothes on one of the river rocks. I thought them picturesque, but they left Mr Winter more worried than ever. He said he thought the whole river was polluted. We walked back gloomily through the darkness to our room. There was no escape from Paruima except by the mission launch, and that was leaving in four days. For dinner I had processed cheese and a cup of coffee, the boiling water provided by Mr Winter. The Chinese boy was singing hymns loudly. Our lantern had no oil, and when I went over to the Negro teacher's to get some, I found the whole family singing hymns. Lightless lantern in hand, I waited on the steps, watching the night fall over the clearing, the tree stumps glowing, gaining colour, the pastor's house brilliant with light.

By eight, in the lantern's glim, we had settled down, I in my hammock, Mr Winter in his crib, and we talked about the walk to Utshi, which I was starting on Sunday, after the Saturday sabbath. I had spoken to Palmer about the wild hogs. He said he had once run into a herd; the Guianese with him had fled in terror and damaged themselves trying to scale unscaleable trees, while he, who hadn't heard the horror stories, had taken out his camera and photographed the herd as it ran past on either side of him: his mother lived in the home counties and liked to receive photographs of tropical forest and wild life.

'I sure wish I was coming with you,' Mr Winter said, at intervals. 'Sure wish I was. But I'm too old. I would keep you back. I always fool around for the first hour or two. Let everybody else go ahead. I just go *foo*-lin' around till I get my second wind. Say, do you know what's good for energy on these walks? Parched corn. In Ecuador I always carried around some of that parched corn. Fool around. Eat a handful of parched corn. Fool around. Eat another handful of parched corn. Until I got my second wind. That was how I did it in Ecuador. I would keep you back, though. Sure wish I was coming. Seems a pity to come so far and not see those falls. Say, would you do me a favour? Could you send me a photograph of those falls?'

Saturday at the mission did feel like Sunday, with everyone in his sabbath clothes and very little going on. The Chinese boy remained in his room and sang lustily. Mr Winter offered me some ham for breakfast, and it was at last my turn to decline. He wanted to know why. I explained my semi-vegetarian upbringing, and he said that he himself didn't drink for religious reasons.

'We sure have made life complicated,' he said. 'You think they'd mind if I cooked some of this ham on their range? These people sure do mind if you do things they don't approve of.'

'I believe they do,' I said. 'And when I think of all my smoking—'

'And all my coffee.' His mouth opened slightly and a smile of pure mischief spread over his cracked face. 'But I sure do like a cup of coffee. Want some now?'

Afterwards we walked over to the village and to our relief found Dr Talbot drawing teeth. His own teeth were off and he was in excellent spirits; he had only had a cold. Most of the Amerindians were at Sabbath School. Many of the men were in serge trousers and one or two wore suits. In an unfinished, still skeletal wooden house two youths were playing Sparrow calypsos on a gramophone.

At the mission in the evening the pastor's sister put on an open-air show of colour slides and the Amerindians came over from the village, white figures strung along the forest road and mission grounds, everyone with his electric torch, so that when dusk turned to night the procession became one of bobbing lights. The early slides were of Holland. The audience gasped to see houses choked together, and there were exclamations of incredulity and pity when the pastor's sister explained through an interpreter, proud retailer of marvels, that the tiny front garden was all the land most Dutch people had. Then came slides of Paruima itself. The audience laughed at every scene or face they knew. When the Negro teachers appeared on the screen, their features indistinct, the Amerindians played their torches on the faces as if to light them up. The intent was derisory, and disquieting.

The walk to Utshi was made awkward only by the mud and by the single logs over gullies that were sometimes rocky and steep. The

Amerindian boys with me ran lightly over the logs; I straddled them. Wild life was regrettably scarce. We saw only the tracks of wild hogs, and Lucio and Nicolas, grinning, made noises to attract them. 'Snake!' Lucio cried once, when I had seen nothing. He cut a sapling, trimmed it, used it to beat the snake three or four times, without malice, and then threw the snake out of the way. The track was at times visible only to the boys and towards the end led over a chaos of fallen tree trunks. We heard the falls, had a glimpse of them through the tops of the tall trees and then, abruptly, we were out of the forest and in the open: Nature, already grand, grown grander, the falls set in the middle of a vast curving stone wall, a single, small tree at the top, fine spray over everything, the grass thick and springy and waist-deep, the spray billowing out of the booming gorge like smoke. Lucio went down to the rapids, and when I saw him again he was in blue bathing trunks, climbing up the side of the rocky gorge, getting as close as he could to the falls. At its upper levels the gorge, though knobbed and torred, was covered with grass and looked as lush as pasture land. Nicolas went down after Lucio. They gave scale to the boulders of the scree and the sheer stone wall.

Later, beside the Utshi River, they half-built a leaf hut. They did this only at my insistence (it was getting late, but they were after all costing me three dollars a day each). I went swimming naked in the river, having undressed before them. They, more modestly, dressed and undressed away from me. Then we ate. They took all that I offered, without delight or displeasure, without comment; and then they took out their cassava bread and opened tins of sardines and made what they clearly regarded as a real meal. They showed more interest in my whisky bottle. 'Is that rum, sir?' 'No.' 'Whisky?' 'No. It's something I use for insect bites.' Lucio passed his tongue over his top lip.

Around the fire, the river noise at our backs, we talked. Lucio was seventeen; he wanted to learn French. I gave him a few words and he spoke them with a good accent. But general conversation wasn't easy. It seemed they had a limited conception of time: they could grasp the immediate but could neither look far back nor look ahead. If what I had heard at Kamarang was true, it is only alcohol – and alcohol to which he is unaccustomed – that stimulates the Amerindian's time sense. Lucio could tell me little of himself or of his family, except that his father was dead.

'How did he die?' And I instantly regretted the question, because I knew the answer and didn't want to hear it.

'*Kanaima* kill him,' Lucio said, and threw a stick on the fire.

He didn't think of the future. Of course he would like to get married, but he didn't want an Amerindian girl, and who else would marry him? 'Indian girls not good. They don't know anything.'

The missionary must first teach self-contempt. It is the basis of the faith of the heathen convert. And in these West Indian territories, where the spiritual problem is largely that of self-contempt, Christianity must be regarded as part of the colonial conditioning. It was the religion of the slave-owners and at first an exclusive racial faith. It bestowed righteousness on its possessors. It enabled the Dutch in Guiana to divide their population into Christians and Negroes: the Berbice slave rebellion of 1762 was a war between Christians and rebels. The captured rebels were tried for 'Christian murder', and it is instructive to read of the death of Atta, the rebel chief:

> Five of them were afterwards burnt with small fire, or rather, roasted, and continually nipped with pincers; and another stood on the wood-heap and died at once. After this the fire was slowly lighted around Atta so that his agonies should last longer; through which it happened then, that notwithstanding they kindled the fire at eleven o'clock; he still remained alive half-an-hour later. It was a matter of surprise that they all let themselves be burnt, broken on the wheel, hanged, etc., without shrieking or moaning. The only thing that Atta said was to the Governor, frequently calling out in his negro language, 'My

God, what have I done? The Governor is right. I suffer what I have deserved. I thank him!' This was the end of that renowned monster whose blood-thirstiness and cruelty brought about the death of so many Christians and the almost irreparable destruction of this Colony.

Even while I was in Georgetown reading this account by Hartsinck of the Berbice slave-rebellion, Christians in British Guiana were protesting at the government's plan to take over control of aided schools. Christianity was in danger in British Guiana. Mass meetings of the descendants of Atta's rebels were held; a missionary wrote to *Time* magazine. So quickly have the postures been adopted, the cries of the *jehad;* so quickly has recent history been forgotten. And this history remains important. Although since emancipation Christianity has asserted itself and has in many ways rescued the colonial society from utter corruption, it has not lost its racial associations, its association with power and prestige and progress. The ministers of God, like the senior administrators of the civil service, were expected to be white; it is only of late that the white collars of church and civil service have begun to set off a certain nigrescence. The striving towards the now accommodating faith of an unaccommodating race has inevitably created deep psychological disturbances. It has confirmed the colonial in his role as imitator, the traveller who never arrives. 'Indian girls not good. They don't know anything.' In his attitude to his people, Lucio spoke not only for the Amerindian convert but also for the East Indian. As for the descendants of Atta's rebels, it is the cardinal article of their faith.

I was glad I had insisted about the hut, for it began to rain during the night: a pleasant noise on the sheltering leaves. 'Excuse me, sir,' I heard Lucio say. 'Can Nicolas and I move our hammocks here?' They had been sleeping in the open; and it was astonishing to see them in pyjamas as in the morning to find them pulling out toothbrushes and tubes of Colgate.

On the way back we came upon an old Amerindian bowed down under an enormous load in his *warishi* carrier. Frustratingly, the packing cases were Heineken beer cartons; and the whole load was topped with a brand-new panama hat. Quite half an hour later we met the rest of his family crossing a rocky riverbed: two very old women and two girls, all barefooted, all carrying loads. One of the women held a rum bottle containing a white liquid labelled 'The Mixture'. The forest appeared to be full of Amerindians that morning. A little later, at a cool shallow stream that ran over rocks as large and flat as paving stones, we found the guitar-player from Santa Helena resting with his family and dog on the high dry rocks beside the bank. They were going back to Santa Helena: the walk would take a week. They had built a fire on one rock, and the guitar-player, who wore a knife-chain, shoes and socks, was using his knife to make a sort of *warishi* for his two cardboard suitcases. He asked for a cigarette. Then, suddenly in the Amerindian way, he left, the dog tremulously following through the shallow but swift stream and frantically wagging his tail when after two failures he managed to climb up to the other bank.

Nearing Paruima, we came out of the forest into a clearing, where a low crumbling mud hut was set in a small cultivation of giant plantain trees and clumps of giant sugarcane. A family was sitting in the sun in the yellow dirty yard. The young girl and the women, in dirty sack-like cotton dresses, fled to the darkness of the hut. Two tiny pink rubber dolls were left on the ground among bits of chewed sugarcane. The man, relaxed in the dirt, was eating sugarcane: he bit, chewed, sucked, swallowed, spat out. We exchanged greetings and walked on. When the hut was about fifty yards behind, Lucio said, 'Would you wait for me here?' They had been invited to a meal. We walked back. The boys took off their *warishis* and sat down on low benches in the yard. The women put a grater on the ground, a straw mat on the grater, and cassava bread

on the mat. They brought out various enamel pots: one with vegetables in an oily stew, one with dasheen, one with black-eye peas.
Lucio and Nicolas used pieces of cassava bread as dippers and ate
from the pots. Then from another pot and with great contentment
they drank a thick white liquid. Their hosts looked on approvingly,
the man laughing and chattering in the yard, the women standing
silent in the hut. I was given bananas and sugarcane.*

'Why, hello there!' Mr Winter called, as I came up the hillside.
And he was at once full of questions. What about the wild hogs?
The logs over the gullies? (The Chinese boy had spoken of these
logs and I believe had frightened Mr Winter as much as he had
frightened me.) Were the boys all right? Did they ever leave me
behind? Was I tired when I got there? How long did it take me to
get my second wind?

'It took you two hours, did it? That's the way I woulda done it.
Just *foo*-lin' along for those two hours. Say, what was the water like
up there? White or black? I sure have had enough of this black
water. With all this washing that's been going on, the whole river's
polluted for sure.' He gave me a little of his news. He had rowed
some distance up the river and found a white-water stream. So he
had at last had a proper bathe. 'Say, do you know this yellow fever
they've been going on about? I don't think it's yellow fever at all.
It's hepatitis.'

I didn't know the word.

'You're lucky. I once knew a man who had hepatitis. They've
had twelve cases. And that's enough for a fair-sized town. I know
it's bad not eating their food and things like that. But if I ask you to
my home in the U-nited States – and I would love to have you –

---

* 'Whilst there is no proof that the sugarcane is indigenous in America, it
nevertheless can be found in the remotest Amerindian settlements, and of
types never now seen on the plantations. These canes probably developed
from cuttings obtained from the early settlers.' Vincent Roth: 'Amerindian
Influence on Settlers'. Columbus took cane-cuttings to the West Indies on his
second voyage.

and if I had hepatitis, I wouldn't ask you to my home. I would take you out to a restaurant or something.' The pastor's dinner invitation still rankled. 'Do you know,' he added conspiratorially, 'I boil the water even in my hotel in Georgetown? Boil it and put it in the fridge. To cool.'

In the next room the Negro teacher and the Chinese boy were talking about boiled eggs. Food seemed to be on everybody's mind.

When I got out of my hammock in the morning Mr Winter was dressed and packed. His mosquito net had been taken down and was doubtless in one of his polythene sacks. We had coffee; and, waiting for the launch, we talked about the water problem and the sanitation problem.

'They're gonna have one hell of a sanitation problem. Right now that latrine smells and has so many flies. I don't know what it's going to be like when they get those twenty-five boys they've been talking about. Twenty-five boys in full spate. Boy, they're gonna have a problem.'

By eleven o'clock there was no sign of the launch. We made more coffee. Sipping it, tasting the black river water, we spoke of the deliciousness of pure, tasteless water. I offered the pawpaw the pastor had given me from one of his own trees.

'No, *thenk* you! Never touch soft fruit.'

But he took one of the Amerindian's bananas. We ate slowly, without speaking. The banana didn't help thirst or the craving for fresh water.

'You know,' he said after some time, 'you know – I sure don't like to mention it now – but you know those cans of Trinidad orange juice? Those large cans with the black-and-orange label? I sure would like to have one now. The next time I come on one of these trips I'm gonna stock up with those cans. They're heavy, but they're really worth it.'

It was while I was negotiating for one of the mission's over-large, over-ripe coconuts that the launch was announced. We ran down to the river, got into the open launch, and sat. There were delays. The sun was hot, the water dazzling and there was no breeze.

'I suppose,' Mr Winter said – and now I admired him for his control – 'I suppose now they'll go on to the village and *fool* around there a little.'

So indeed they did, and after a while we joined them. There we saw the reason for the delay: a new single-engined aeroplane on the landing field across the river from the village. It belonged to the mission and had just arrived, piloted by an American in green trousers and a green shirt, with the Portuguese pilot from Kamarang Mouth as passenger. It was now half past one and extremely hot. I spoke to Palmer about crops, but without enthusiasm. Even if we started right away it was now too late for us to get to Kamarang Mouth that day. We could travel on the river only by daylight and would have to spend the night at the Amerindian village half-way down. Then the pastor suggested that we should go back to Kamarang Mouth on the plane.

Half an hour later, after a view of the perverse windings and loops of the Kamarang over which we would have spent a day, the Portuguese and American talking all the way of planes and routes just as other men talk of cars and bypasses, we were at Kamarang Mouth.

I loaded an Amerindian boy with my bags and almost ran to Seggar's refrigerator. I had two beers, the first quickly, the second slowly. Feeling the cold wet bottle in my hand, I luxuriated in the heat. For the first time for days tobacco had a taste. I inhaled deeply and swallowed and gazed down the Mazaruni to where Roraima was hidden by haze. When I went over to the rest house I found Mr Winter lying on his back across the bed, his feet dangling, his hat unhinged without being off, a fulfilled, beatific expression on his face. He raised a languid hand and pointed to the table.

On it I saw a tin of Trinidad orange juice.

'There it is,' he said. 'Left some for you.'

I didn't tell him about the beer. But the orange juice he had left scarcely came to an inch in a tumbler.

'Oh, by the way,' he said, when I had emptied the tin, 'drink as much of that as you can. Drink it all. I've had my share.'

An hour or so later, when calm had returned to both of us and we were preparing once more to leave – a Dakota was coming in unexpectedly and would take us that very afternoon to the coast – Mr Winter said, 'That orange juice sure was good.' A smile broke and spread slowly over his face. 'Drunk more than my fair share.' He started to laugh. 'Drunk more than half. Nearly drunk out the whole can. Did you get much?'

I showed him how much.

'Gee, I sure am sorry about that.' But he was smiling. 'It just looks like I drunk more than my fair share.'

I confessed about my beer.

'It sure did taste good. Boy! I am sure looking forward to getting back to Georgetown. I've got two bottles in the fridge. Boiled. Keeping in the fridge for one whole week. Two bottles. As soon as I get back I'm gonna drink an awful lot of water.'

'No beer?'

'Never touch alcohol. But I sure love water.'

4. Surinam

– The language in which we are speaking is his before it
is mine. How different are the words *home*, *Christ*, *ale*,
master, on his lips and mine! I cannot speak or write these
words without unrest of spirit. His language, so familiar
and so foreign, will always be for me an acquired speech. I
have not made or accepted its words. My voice holds them
at bay. My soul frets in the shadow of his language.

James Joyce: *A Portrait of the Artist as a Young Man*

In 1669 a citizen of the island of Barbados (166 square miles) wrote
in a letter of 'a place much cried up of late, taken from the Dutch,
called New York'. The contempt was justified, for even fifty years
later Barbados was exporting to England nearly as much as all the
American colonies put together. What had happened was that in
1667, by the treaty of Breda, the Dutch had surrendered New York
to the British and taken Surinam in exchange. The Dutch thought
then they had got the better bargain, and think so still, because, as
Dutch school children are taught, the British have lost New York
while the Dutch still have Surinam.

Surinam, former Dutch Guiana, lies next door to British Guiana
on the north-eastern coast of South America; and although the
Corentyne, British Guiana's easternmost region, and Nickerie, Surinam's westernmost, have much more in common with one another

than with their respective capitals, to fly in one hour from George-
town to Paramaribo is more unsettling than to fly from London to
Amsterdam. For suddenly Holland, almost unknown in Trinidad
and British Guiana except as the exporter of beer and powdered
milk, becomes important, far more important than England is to
Trinidad or British Guiana. It isn't only the surprise at hearing
Negroes and East Indians, to all appearances just like those of
British Guiana and Trinidad, speaking Dutch; nor seeing, in a
West Indian setting, the *Ingang* and *Uitgang* and *Niet Rooken* and
Verboden Toegang signs one had before seen only in Holland;
nor the sedate Dutch buildings of the administration in Dr J. C.
de Mirandastraat. The talk everywhere is of 'Hol-lond' and 'Oms-
terdom'. In Surinam Holland is Europe; Holland is the centre of the
world. Even America recedes. 'The first thing you've got to get out
of your head,' an American official said to me, 'is that you're in
Latin America. Why, no shutters even went up over the windows at
election time. The most that happened was that some members of
the opposition who lost left the country. And they went to Holland.'
Notwithstanding that since 1955 Surinam has been virtually independent, an equal partner in the Netherlands kingdom with the
Netherlands Antilles, New Guinea and Holland itself, Surinam
feels only like a tropical, tulip-less extension of Holland; some
Surinamers call it Holland's twelfth province.

Nearly every educated person has been to Holland, and the
affection for Holland is genuine. There is none of the racial resentment which the British West Indian brings back from England. The
atmosphere is relaxing. With Negroes, East Indians, Dutch, Chinese
and Javanese, Surinam has a population more mixed than that of
British Guiana and Trinidad. Yet it does not have the racial problems of these territories, though there is inevitably a growing rivalry
between the Negroes and the East Indians, the two largest groups.
With Dutch realism the Surinamers have avoided racial collision not
by ignoring group differences but by openly acknowledging them.
The political parties are racial, but the government is a coalition of

these parties. Every group is therefore committed to the development of the country. The Dutch complain of Negro hostility, but the complaints, like the demonstrations of hostility, are muted; and in spite of all that has happened in Indonesia and Holland relations between the Dutch and Javanese are cordial.

With no inflammatory political issues, no acute racial problem, and with the Dutch Government contributing two-thirds of the money (one-third gift, one-third loan) for the development of the country, nationalism would seem an unlikely and perverse growth. But a nationalism has arisen which is unsettling the established order, proving that the objection to colonialism in the West Indies is not only economic or political or, as many believe, simply racial. Colonialism distorts the identity of the subject people, and the Negro in particular is bewildered and irritable. Racial equality and assimilation are attractive but only underline the loss, since to accept assimilation is in a way to accept a permanent inferiority. Nationalism in Surinam, feeding on no racial or economic resentments, is the profoundest anti-colonial movement in the West Indies. It is an idealist movement, and a rather sad one, for it shows how imprisoning for the West Indian his colonial culture is. Europe, the Surinam Nationalist says, is to be rejected as the sole source of enlightenment; Africa and Asia are to be brought in as well. But Europe is in the Nationalist's bones and he feels that Africa and Asia are contemptible and ridiculous. The Dutch language is to be rejected — since 'my soul frets in the shadow of his language' — and its place taken by — what? A limited local dialect which used to be called *talkie-talkie*.

Corly met me off the plane and welcomed me formally on behalf of the Surinam Information Office.

'You are a writer and a poet,' he said.

'Not a poet.'

'I knew at once it was you. I felt a sort of trembling.'

Corly himself was a poet. He had just that day published — at his own expense and in a limited edition of four hundred copies – his second book of poems. He had a parcel of them in his office and promised to give me one as soon as we got to Paramaribo. With Corly at the airport was Theresia, a tall pretty girl of mixed race with beautiful hands and ankles. She, somewhat to my surprise, spoke little English; and as we drove in the moonlight along the straight, smooth American road (built during the war) Corly explained the language problem in Surinam and the general cultural struggle, about which the rest of the world knew nothing. Corly loved Holland, Dutch literature and the Dutch people and was in trouble with the Nationalists for writing in Dutch, and not in the local dialect, on themes that were not specifically of Surinam. Matters had not been made easier for him by the Dutch newspaper *Elseviers*, which had described his work as 'an enriching of Dutch poetry'.

It wasn't late when we got to Paramaribo but the town seemed asleep. We found a *pension* – the Negro proprietress looked a little startled – and then went on to Corly's office. On one desk I saw a miniature Surinam flag: five stars, black, brown, yellow, white and red, to represent the various races, linked by an elliptical black line, on a white field. I asked Theresia which star was hers. She pointed uncertainly to the brown star; and, indeed, in one of the handouts which Corly gave me I read: 'In a way perhaps the brown star is the star too with a hidden meaning because its colour could represent also a successful experiment, the harmonious blending of many races into a people; the mainstay of the population of Surinam.' At last Corly undid a brown paper parcel and pulled out his book. An uncomprehending glance showed that the criticisms of the Nationalists must have had some effect. Surinam was frequently mentioned in the poems. Corly also told me that he had invented a name for the ideal Surinam woman. It was 'Surinette', and was the title of one of the poems.

Meeting the Press. Perhaps because of his work, Corly believed in the value of publicity and wanted me to have my fair share of it in Surinam. He thought my arrival was news, important enough to make the morning papers; and after we had taken Theresia home he took me to a newspaper office in a quiet palm-lined street. The office stood, I believe, next to a bakery. We went through a side gate and along a passage to a small brightly-lit room, where a tall pipe-smoking Dutchman in shirtsleeves, holding proofs and a red pencil, shook my hand with an air of surprise. Corly spoke; the Dutchman replied. We were too late. The paper had gone to press. And true enough, at the end of the cluttered room, beyond some bits of machinery, the paper was printing, a gate-like grill flapping back and forth, printing one side of a sheet at a time. So I didn't make the morning papers.

It was unfortunate for the British West Indies that British imperialism coincided with a period of poor British architecture. Trollope was appalled by Kingston, but commented: 'We have no right perhaps to expect good taste so far away from any school in which good taste is taught; and it may, perhaps, be said by some that we have sins enough of our own at home to induce us to be silent on this head.' The Dutch colonies have been luckier in the Dutch; and though Paramaribo is not as handsome as Georgetown, it has a run-down provincial elegance, with its palm-lined streets and dusty side-walks, its close-set wooden houses and their verandaed top floors, its calm main square overlooked by official buildings, *the* hotel and *the* club.

In architecture as in so many things these West Indian territories have a mother country fixation, and – compare Rotterdam with any new British town – the results continue to be as disastrous for the British territories as they are happy for the Dutch. Federation Park in Port of Spain is an example of tastelessness which is almost like cynicism; so too are the buildings of the University College of the West Indies in Jamaica. Paramaribo, on the other hand, has half a dozen modern public buildings of which any European city might be proud. But these buildings suggesting the metropolis are incongruous in the heat and dust and afternoon stillness. For Paramaribo is provincial. Paramaribo is dull.

I had a little provincial excitement on my first morning, when I was awakened by a military band. The small procession of white and black soldiers in white, and black policemen in chocolate, passed three times in the street below. The streets never offered anything like that again. In fact, very little happens in the streets of Paramaribo after midday. Because of the heat offices and shops open at seven in the morning and close for the day at half past one. As a result, everyone goes to bed early, and throughout the morning people are to be seen eating in offices.

A roof garden had been opened on the new Radio Apintie building. It was a club, Corly said; but as a foreigner I would be admitted without any trouble. There was no trouble. We were welcomed by the barman, who had no other customers and was glad of our company. We looked over the silent city. At the back of most private houses, grand and not so grand, there were whole ranges of ancillary buildings: the big house and tenants, in one yard: a relic of slavery, which was abolished here only in 1863.

'What,' Corly asked, 'do the Surinamers do when they are doing nothing?'

In Georgetown I had longed for the liveliness of Port of Spain. Now I longed for Georgetown, and the people of Paramaribo told me I didn't know what dullness was: I should go across the border to French Guiana.

The C.I.D. Man. I had met the Inspector of the C.I.D. Special Branch in one of the fine new banks where I was disadvantageously changing my British West Indian dollars for guilders. He invited me to visit him at headquarters, and when I did so I found him in a small white office which was full of newspapers from various West Indian territories. The Inspector read these newspapers diligently. His concern was the security of Surinam and it was his duty to study political trends in neighbouring territories. He was going to British Guiana to 'observe' the elections.

Below the shuttered afternoon calm, however, passions were engaged. A fortnight before, an 'advisory council for cultural co-operation between the countries of the Netherlands Kingdom', had been set up with the aim, in Surinam, of promoting 'interest in and a knowledge of Western culture, especially in its Dutch mani-festations'. The Nationalists had responded vigorously; and their four-page manifesto, issued while I was there, contained their denunciations and resolutions, together with the text of a radio talk by Dr Jan Voorhoeve. It is typical of the fairness and urbanity of the Dutch-inspired administration (which has produced the only incorruptible police force in the Western Hemisphere) that the Nationalists should have access to a radio station; and not surprising that Dr Voorhoeve is himself a Dutchman, a member, moreover, of the Netherlands Bible Society. Voorhoeve's intelligent, temperate talk was especially interesting for its analysis of the colonial society.

> A colony is a strange sort of society, a society without an élite . . . The leaders come from the motherland, are people with another culture . . . The colonial cultural ideal has pro-nounced bad consequences for the individual. It is in fact an unattainable ideal . . . A few exceptional people . . . come to great achievements, but thereby lose their nationality . . . And what goes for them does not go for ten thousand others who must remain stuck in a soulless imitation, never achieving any-thing of their own. They learn to despise their own, but get nothing in its place. So, after the war there were many in Surinam who thought themselves far above the ordinary people because they had been able to assimilate the Dutch language and the Dutch culture. Sometimes they wrote a pretty little poem à la Kloos, or painted a pretty little picture, or played a Mozart sonata not without skill; but they were not capable of any true cultural achievement. When this new generation was

able after the war to go to Holland in greater numbers . . . they
discovered their cultural emptiness with a shock. They came
into contact with the great world, the community of nations,
and stood there with empty hands. They did not have their
own songs; they hardly had Mozart. They did not have their
own literature; they only had Kloos. They had nothing and
were worthless elements in the life of nations. What once was
reason for pride – 'Surinam is the twelfth province of Holland'
– was now reason for shame and disgrace.

Controversy at this level could scarcely become public in the British
West Indies. True, there is talk about West Indian culture, but this is
ingenuous where it is not political, and is rooted in the colonial
attitude which rejects as barbarous all that does not issue from the
white mother country. That a colonial society might be one without
an élite is too frightening even to be perceived. One reason for this
British West Indian passivity is that the British have never attempted
to turn their colonials into Englishmen. They have in fact been
irritated by the assumption, made so easily by the Dutch or French
West Indian, that equal opportunities existed in the mother country.
In their empire the British were 'Europeans', and the West Indian
conception of the mother country has caused amusement, dismay
and alarm in England. The Dutch have latterly encouraged Surinamers to think that they could become Dutchmen; and I was told of
a club in Amsterdam where, over their *genever*, these Surinamer
Dutch speak with regret of the loss of Indonesia. The paradox is
that Dutch idealism is leading to rejection, while out of British cynicism has grown a reasonably easy relationship between colonials
and metropolitans.

The Dutch have offered assimilation but not made it obligatory.
Their tolerance and understanding of alien cultures is greater than
the British, and the very reverse of the French arrogance which
makes the French West Indian islands insupportable for all but the
francophile. And one cannot help feeling it unfair that the Dutch

should have their own cultural offerings spurned by their former colony. Surinam has come out of Dutch rule as the only truly cosmopolitan territory in the West Indian region. The cosmopolitanism of Trinidad is now fundamentally no more than a matter of race; in Surinam diverse cultures, modified but still distinct, exist side by side. The Indians speak Hindi still; the Javanese live, a little bemused, in their own world, longing in this flat unlovely land for the mountains of Java; the Dutch exist in their self-sufficient Dutchness, the Creoles in their urban Surinam Dutchness; in the forest, along the rivers, the bush-Negroes have re-created Africa.

Despite all the talk of culture, however, Surinamers have little idea of the diversity and richness of their own country. My recurring exclamations at the Javanese costume made my Creole friends laugh. The Creoles know only Europe; they have made no attempt to get to know the Javanese or the Indians and it is only recently, under the Nationalist stimulus, that they have tried to understand the bush-Negroes. One Nationalist even suggested that the existence of Javanese and Indian culture in Surinam was a barrier to the development of a national culture! This pointed to the confusion and the unexpected racial emotions that lie at the back of the Nationalist agitation. The cultural problem in Surinam is mainly a problem for the Negro; it is only he who has rejected his past, all that attaches him to Africa.

For the Negro of the islands Africa is no more than a word, an emotion. For the Surinamer Africa is almost in his backyard. Beside the rivers the bush-Negroes have maintained their racial purity, their African arts of carving, singing and dancing, and, above all, their pride. Rediscovery was not hard.

At Home. The minister, big and black and bluff, played bush-Negro songs on the record-player in the greenheart-floored drawing room of his fine new minister's house. 'You wouldn't have heard these songs in a drawing room a few years ago,' he said. Afterwards, as if emphasizing the new era, he told jokes in the local language, which is *talkie-talkie* for the irreverent, *negerengels* – Negro English – for the correct, and *Surinam* for the nationalist. Later he took the two other ministers, of different races, to the bar in the corner of the room for a political confabulation. While this was going on the three wives made little jokes about politics and the ways of politicians.

The Nationalists hope to replace the Dutch language by Negro English; and Mr Eersel, who has done much work on the language, explained the possibilities to me in his *Volkslecturing* office. I put Mr Eersel in his forties; he was grave and very gentle, with one of those sculptured Negro faces in which every feature appears to have been separately cast, so that one studies the face feature by feature. He said that Dutch was not properly understood or spoken by the majority of Surinamers, while everyone understood Negro English. They had already compiled a dictionary of Negro English; and the language was growing: they made up new words in conversation every day. I said that the adoption of this language would mean that every important book in the world would have to be translated: did they have the resources? They would manage. But what about the writers? Was it fair to ask them to write in a language spoken by only a quarter million people? That was no problem, Mr Eersel said; if they were good they would be translated. Was this language capable of subtlety? Was it capable of poetry? Mr Eersel asked me to test him. From a faulty memory I wrote:

> They flee from me that some time did me seek
> With naked foot stalking in my chamber
> I have seen them gentle, mild and meek
> That now do scorn to remember
> That they have taken bread from my hand.

He at once translated:

> *Den fre gwe f'mi, d'e mek' mi soekoe so,*
> *Nanga soso foetoe waka n'in' mi kamra.*

Mi si den gendri, safri,
Di kosi now, f 'no sabi
Fa den ben nian na mi anoe.

My memory had mutilated and simplified Wyatt's simple lines and
Mr Eersel had simplified them further, but there was no denying
the sweetness and rhythm of the language. I would have liked to
see how it would handle something more abstract, but my memory
failed me altogether.

I know no Dutch and relish it for its improbability, its air of
recent and arbitrary manufacture. *Oost woost thoos boost*, you utter,
or sounds like that, and you've said, 'East west, home's best'. While
English breeds dialects that are recognizably English and scarcely
modify the standard language, Dutch, because of its difficulty or
improbability, breeds new and separate languages which very soon
destroy Dutch. There is the kitchen Dutch of South Africa, the
Papiamento of the Netherlands Antilles, the *negerengels* of Surinam.
A passion for bad grammar is one of the singular features of
regional pride in Dutch territories. The Surinam district of Nickerie, which is noted for its independent spirit, has a cyclostyled
newspaper called *Wie for Wie*. The paper is written, no doubt
impeccably, in Dutch; but its name, which is simply ungrammatical
dialect English – 'we for we' – proclaims the dialect as an exclusive
possession.

The importance of English in Surinam dialect is puzzling until
one remembers that British Guiana is next door – in Nickerie they
even play cricket – and that Surinam was British until 1667. It is in
fact the English left behind three hundred years ago, in the minds
of the slaves, which is the basis of Surinam Negro English. And
this is the true wonder. Though Trinidad was Spanish until 1797
and thereafter, with immigration from the French islands, French-
speaking for three-quarters of a century, Spanish in Trinidad is dead
and French survives only in a few phrases and constructions. In
Surinam, however, after three hundred years, a form of English

survives. At first the English element in Mr Eersel's translation seems negligible; but this is largely the effect of corrupt pronunciation.

Ah dee day day we. This, improbably, is nearly all English, and from English-speaking, sophisticated Trinidad. Unscrambled: I did there there, oui: I did find myself there (to there, to find oneself, to be), yes: I *was* there. Considering the English the Surinam slaves must have spoken in 1667, and considering the pronunciation of the time in England, it is remarkable that so many words are still recognizable. We can tell how the language had developed a hundred years later, in the 1770s, from Stedman's *Narrative of a Five Years' Expedition against the Revolted Negroes of Surinam.*

In one of the minor actions of the war a military detachment was cut to pieces in the forest by the rebellious slaves, who, following the custom of the time, began cutting off the heads of the dead soldiers. One soldier was only pretending to be dead, however; and before his turn came, the head-cutter put away his cutlass, saying, '*Sonde go sleeby, caba mekewe liby den tara dogo lay tamara.* – The sun is going to sleep. We must leave these other dogs till tomorrow.' During the night the soldier escaped. Though the sentence has been twice reported, first by the Dutch soldier and then by Stedman, it needs only to be spoken quickly to be recognized as English, English in the mouth of a West African.

You no sabi waar she iss? Dutch sounds so made up that at times it brings on a light-headedness in which you feel that anything said in a Dutch accent would be understood. In a restaurant in Arnhem I once found myself, with perfect seriousness, speaking pure gibberish to a waitress who continued misleadingly to smile. And something like this happened when I went to call on Theresia one afternoon. A woman from one of the tenements in the backyard (relic of slavery, I remembered) told me Theresia was out. Improvising an accent, the words coming from I know not where, I asked, 'You no sabi waar she iss?' '*Ik weet niet waar ʒe is,*' the woman replied in careful Dutch, and tossed her head. '*Ik spreek geen talkie-talkie, mijnheer.* I do not speak talkie-talkie, sir.' So I hadn't spoken gibberish; I had spoken *negerengels*.

It may be smart for ministers and others to speak *negerengels*, but for the proletariat, to whom it comes naturally, it remains a degradation. Until recently, according to Dr Voorhoeve, children whose mothers caught them speaking *negerengels* were made to wash out their mouths.

Sixty miles south of Paramaribo, at a place called Brokopondo, an American aluminium company is building a hydro-electric station for an aluminium smelting plant. There is more in the project for the company than for Surinam, but it is regarded as part of the country's development, and the Information Office laid on a tour in a large American motor-car of the 'estate' type.

At an important hotel we picked up an important Negro official from Aruba, and his photographer. In a dusty palm-lined street, at a *pension* less imposing than mine, we picked up Alberto. Alberto was an Italian magazine photographer who was making a whirlwind tour of South America. I had read in the Georgetown newspapers of his arrival in British Guiana a few days before I left that country; and his departure, I believe, preceded mine. Now he was in Surinam for a few days, on his way to French Guiana; he was hoping to reach Rio in time for the Carnival. Alberto was slender, of medium height, and his movements were of Italian 'elegance'. He had thick wavy brown hair, which he combed continually, a thick moustache in a plump reddish face, and busy eyebrows over large bright eyes. He was in his early twenties but – the moustache perhaps, and his journalist's self-possession – he looked at least thirty-five. His voice was hoarse.

We were settling down for the long journey when we stopped at a middle-class suburban housing development and three women ran happily out of a house towards the car. They were coming with us; and Alberto, the Aruban photographer and I were made to leave

our comfortable middle seats and sit cramped in the back, facing
the road. There were no compensations. One of the women was
Brazilian, fat, with ugly white tights and an ugly white-and-yellow
straw hat fastened with innumerable hairgrips to untidy brown hair.
One was Dutch and young and ponderously girlish. One was tall
and grave, married, older than the other two and slightly motherly
towards them; she too was Dutch.

As soon as we started off the women burst into some incomprehensible song. We stared resentfully at the road. Asphalt gave way
to dirt, and soon we were on the red road through the forest. We
didn't see the forest; we saw only red dust. It blew into our faces
and we turned up the glass. Red dust slid down the window, staining
it, and presently little view-obstructing dust-drifts and dust-banks
had formed, which we all three tried to clear by continually banging
on the window with our palms, a discordant accompaniment to the
songs at our backs. Fine dust had been coming through the rubber-
insulated crevices and settling on us so gently that we didn't feel it.
We didn't look powdered; we looked dyed, and the dye was getting
deeper. The two younger women were now attempting close
harmony. Whenever they failed they broke into girlish giggles.

In spite of all our pleas the women had their windows turned up
to protect themselves from the dust created by the occasional
passing car. We stifled. Alberto lost his fresh, brushed look of the
morning. Dust reddened his neglected hair. He ceased to talk of
his travels ("Aiti was something disgusting') and sat hunched in his
corner. 'I am suffering,' he said, his hoarse voice fruity with
anguish. I thought he wanted the car stopped and was too embarrassed to ask. But at that moment the fat woman in the straw hat
started on a Portuguese song; and Alberto, turning his eyes slowly
to one side and frowning, the dust flaking off his forehead, cried out,
'Goodness, I'm suffering!'

A drink at the Brokopondo guest house refreshed us. Alberto
recovered his journalist's energy and ruthlessness. He was full of
questions and requests. Could he cross the river? Were there bush-

Negroes in the neighbourhood? Could he be taken to a bush-Negro village? And while the man from the Information Office broke off a few needles from the Honduras pine in the garden of the guest house and offered them to the Aruban official — the Aruban photographer snapping away — and myself, to smell, Alberto was scrambling here, there and everywhere, taking photographs. Once I saw him far below on one of the rocks in the wide shallow river.

When he came back to us we drove on to the dam. On the river bank the fat woman stepped into some mud and lost her shoe. She uttered girlish cries of discomfiture. Alberto gave her a look of annoyed contempt and was off, up the steep mound, moving briskly and well for all his Italian elegance and hair-combing. 'No photographs!' the man from the Information Office cried. 'It is forbidden.' Alberto didn't hear; he had disappeared. When we saw him again he was at the far end of the site, squatting, rising, a tiny figure moving rapidly in short steps, knees close together, legs working from the knees down.

Two bush-Negroes, purple-black and shining and naked except for red loincloths, came up in a canoe and tried to sell us a watermelon. I hadn't seen any bush-Negroes before, but these were familiar: I had seen them on innumerable postcards in Paramaribo.

We waited in the shade of the huge new bridge for Alberto. At last he came, and was told of the bush-Negroes. 'But *I* want to see bush-Negroes,' he said, peeved. And the words became a refrain: 'Can't you take me to see bush-Negroes? I want to see bush-Negroes. Is that a bush-Negro?'

Back at the guest house, we both had showers before lunch, which was eaten rapidly. The fat woman with the straw hat ate mounds of potatoes. Conversation became general. Introductions were made — the Aruban photographer clicking away — and professions revealed.

The Dutch girl, still energetically girlish, said she had twelve children.

'Twelve children,' Alberto said sympathetically, refusing to see the joke. 'That's something dreadful.'

The girl tried again. 'I know a writer,' she said. 'In Rio.'

She scored. Alberto, passionate for helpful South American names and addresses, softened. He took out his notebook. 'Is he nice?'

'He is fifty.'

Alberto lost his temper. 'I cannot understand you,' he said, putting away his notebook. 'I ask you whether 'e is nice and you tell me 'e is fifty.'

The Aruban photographer photographed the Aruban official, who was now relaxed and picking his teeth, his dark glasses reflecting the wild landscape of forest, rivers and rocks.

After lunch Alberto had his wish. We went to a bush-Negro village. It was in a clearing off the main road, a short dusty street with neat weatherboard boxes on either side, not at all what we had expected: no carved doors, no sign of the African-style handicrafts we had read about, only glimpses of radios in dim interiors, sewing-machines and one or two well-kept bicycles. The man from the Information Office reminded us that the village was near a modern project; the men worked on this project and wore proper clothes. But there were naked children rolling in the dust and the women had their breasts uncovered, pendulous things like squashed pawpaws. Alberto started clicking away. The women fled, smiling, into their boxes. The Aruban official looked about him with bene-volence and was luckier. He had no camera, and a guilder persuaded a woman to do a dance with a dog behind her house. At the approach of Alberto and myself, non-paying visitors, she stopped.

'I must get a picture of these bush-Negroes,' Alberto said. But he was unable or unwilling to pay. We walked between the houses, women scattering before us, naked breasts swinging and flapping. 'That girl is completely idiot. Is he nice? 'E is fifty. Is completely idiot. Shh!'

Carefully he approached a woman at a sewing-machine. She took up her sewing and disappeared.

He rejoined me. Then he was off again, camera at the ready, his high fluffy hair bobbing with his quick little steps. This time he was more successful. I saw him enter a hut. Just then the girls bounded up. The Dutch girl gave a shriek, ran into the hut after Alberto, and Alberto instantly emerged, intensely irritated.

'God, I am suffering! But 'ow I am suffering!'

We started back, Alberto disconsolate. 'Goodness, I wanted a picture of these bush-Negroes.' And all the way to Paramaribo he worked off his irritation in talk. 'Did you 'ear that man at the dam? No photographs. But why? It is a completely idiot rule, and when something is so completely idiot the Italian says all right, but let me try to come to some arrangement to enable me to take photographs. I thank goodness I am Italian. Why are we going so slow? The road is empty. Why are we going so slow?'

'The speed limit,' the Aruban photographer said. 'And this is a government car.'

'Is an idiot reason. In Italy we would say *because* it is a government car—' He broke off and commanded, 'Stop!' He jumped out and photographed a bauxite crusher. 'I wish I 'ad more time,' he said, returning. 'Then I would take good photographs. 'Ello!'

A slip of paper had been put into his hand by the Dutch girl, who was staring ahead and smiling. The paper carried a schoolgirl's drawing of a woman's profile.

'What do I do with this?' he asked. 'I was just 'olding the 'and here and in comes this letter. What do I do?' He stuck it in his red-striped sock and whispered, 'Is this an insult?'

'God,' he said later, ' 'Ow I 'ave suffered today!'

Little boy lost. The West African calls himself a black man. For some West Indians, continually striving to make black white, this is too blunt: it suggests that evolution is impossible. Euphemisms vary from territory to territory, and in Surinam I was told of the description of a Negro boy which appeared in the Lost and Found column of a newspaper: *een donkerkleurige jongen met kroes haar*, a dark-complexioned boy with curly hair.

The leader of the Nationalists and possible the most discussed person in Surinam is Eduard Bruma, a Negro lawyer in his middle thirties. He is dark-brown, of medium height and build, with an unusually striking face: his brow puckers easily above the nose-bridge and he has high eyebrows that slope steeply outwards over deep-set intense eyes. When he drives around Paramaribo in his monster green Chevrolet boys and men wave, and there is a hint of conspiracy in their greeting. For though the Nationalist agitation is carried on openly, the Nationalists have as yet no official positions and the movement has a touch of the underground. I once saw a middle-aged woman pluck Eersel's sleeve in the street and whisper congratulations.

It was in Amsterdam, a city known to every educated Surin-amer, that the Nationalist movement started. Bruma himself spent seven years there. He enjoyed his stay and claims that the move-ment has no basis in racial resentment and is not directed against any racial group. Not all of Bruma's supporters, who are mainly Negro, would agree; nor would the Dutch in Surinam. And it is hard to see how racial feeling can be avoided, for the cultural problem that exercises Bruma and his followers is essentially a problem for the Negro in the New World. In Trinidad and British Guiana there is no widespread realization that such a problem exists, and it is to the credit of the Nationalists in Surinam that they have made it a public issue without going to the extremes of the back-to-Africa Ras Tafarians in Jamaica or the Black Muslims of the United States. There is much in their thought, however, to frighten the respectable and excite the cry for the *jehad*. Their view of Chris-tianity is historical: they see it as much a part of European culture as the Dutch language.

But how can Christianity — for the West Indian more than a

faith: an achievement – be replaced? By the adoption of the sur-
vivals of African religion found among the bush-Negroes? By the
adoption of Islam? Religions cannot be replaced by decree any more
than languages can. Negro English is no substitute for a developed
language. The bush-Negroes are interesting and in some respects
admirable, but between these forest-dwellers and the sophisticated
Continental Surinamer there can be no deep sympathy. It would
appear then either that the solution to this problem has to be violent
and extreme, or that there is no solution at all. And perhaps no
solution is necessary, and all that is required is a profound awareness
that countries and cultures exist beyond the white mother country,
beyond Europe and America. To create this awareness is not easy.
For just as Christianity is more fervently adhered to in Jamaica, say,
than in London, so the provincialism of the mother country finds a
more extreme expression in the West Indian colony: to the respectable black West Indian Italy is as foreign and ridiculous as Japan or
Nigeria.

Whether the Nationalists can create this awareness in Surinam
without slipping into a futile black racism is problematical. That
they have seen the problem so sharply is due, I feel, however
paradoxically, to their Dutch inheritance and above all to their
possession of the Dutch language. English belongs to all who speak
it. Dutch belongs so clearly to the Dutch that the colonial who
speaks it as his mother tongue cannot fail to be struck by the oddity
of a situation which for the British West Indian is natural and
proper. Speaking a language little understood by the outside world,
the Dutch have become great linguists. So have the Surinamers.
English, Dutch, French, *negerengels*: these are the languages spoken
by the educated Surinamer; and to this list the Indian adds Hindi,
the Javanese Javanese. Having access to so many worlds, the Surinamer is not as colonial-provincial as the British West Indian and is
able to have a more objective view of his own situation.

A growing language. I showed Corly Eersel's translation of the lines by Wyatt and I could see that in spite of his differences with the Nationalists he was impressed. He read the translation again. '*Gendri*,' he said at last. 'What is that word? I don't know what that word means. It has been in existence for only twenty-four hours.'

Not far from the international airport at Zanderij there is a bush-Negro village called Berlin. Corly, Theresia and I drove there one Saturday afternoon. Not to see the bush-Negroes, who, living so close to the capital, are citified and corrupted and not genuine forest-dwellers. We went there for the black-water creek, these forest creeks, black water in snow-white sand, being the Surinamer's substitute for the bathing beaches which the muddy South American coast does not provide. We paddled in the lily-spotted creek, sunlight striking through the trees, turning the Coca-Cola water (the Surinamer's description) into wine. Theresia, more beautiful than Rembrandt's model, completed the Rembrandt picture.

Later we walked through the village, which had nothing to mark it as a bush-Negro village. Wooden houses in the Dutch style lined the dirt road, here and there were hedges; and there was even a refreshment shack with one or two advertisements. Two children rolled about in the dusty road, naked; but everyone else was clothed. Towards the end of the street we heard drums. Theresia was at once aroused. She ran into a yard and made inquiries in *negerengels*; she got offended replies in Dutch and came back to us, saying what sounded like '*Hit iss in de bos*.' So we made for the *bos*.

The bush began just at the end of the street. And there, beyond a short wavering path through high grass, were the dancers, in a small shed roofed with corrugated iron. Corly was nervous; he said he heard people saying, 'Who are these *bakra* (whites, foreigners) coming to see? What do they want?' But the men and women who were not dancing were friendly enough, and we sat on a bench outside the shed and watched. Whisky was passed around from spectators to dancers and back; beer, too, in glasses. The drummers, stick-beaters and tin-beaters sat at one end of the shed and before them, as before an altar, the dancers performed, each person absorbed in his individual dance: one man doing something like a cossack dance, another squatting and dancing only on his toes, an old woman, her eyes closed, going through stylized sexual motions. The dancers' dusty feet were continually brushed with wet twigs by the spectators.

So far each dancer had been keeping to his corner of the shed, but now one thick-set man began throwing himself to the ground, rolling and groaning. I thought this was done for our benefit, but the sweat that broke out on his face was real enough. He rolled to where an old woman in a blue frock was sitting. She got up to give him room, and gave us a friendly smile. 'I don't like this,' Corly said, his face blank with distaste and alarm. Two men shammed a fight with nothing of play in their expression or manner. Corly wanted us to leave, but Theresia, tapping her feet to the drumming, was unwilling.

And then two striking figures appeared, a woman and a man, their faces and bodies chalked white. The woman wore a blue sari-like garment which left her shoulders bare, the man a red sarong and a red cap. They scarcely danced. In the midst of vigour they proclaimed their feebleness, and from time to time the man had to be supported by one of the dancers. His chalked face held no emotion; and he constantly chalked himself, sometimes passing the chalk to the woman. The dance had become intimate, and I began to feel as anxious as Corly. I remembered that we were close to the city, that the airport was near ('Surinam is a member of the jet age,' the government handout said), but I was glad when, to Theresia's annoyance, Corly insisted that we should leave. As we stepped out of the bush a drunk old woman embraced Corly and a man embraced Theresia. And Corly, who throughout had been worried that he might be offered drinks, was made to drink a small glass of whisky.

'If I had stayed half an hour longer,' Corly said, 'I would have got heart failure.'

Corly was born in Paramaribo, just forty minutes away, but he could tell me nothing of the dance we had just seen; nor could Theresia. To both of them it was as new as it was to me. I had not thought Corly's agitation absurd, in spite of the nearness of the airport and the city, and the authority I consulted* did not offer complete reassurance. If my observation was just and if I read right, the dance was 'spiritualist':

> Messages to the living may also be conveyed through a person who has become possessed in the course of dancing to the drums. The possessed conveys the message by singing. Apparently a person may feel that his god wishes him to convey some message to the living and in consequence feels a restlessness. This prompts him first to wash and then daub himself with white clay, white being the colour of the ancestors . . . On the auspicious day the person bedaubs himself with more white clay, and perhaps some of the participants in the ceremony too, and then prepares to go into a trance so that the god can speak through him. The rhythm of the drum helps to bring on possession.

*   *   *

Slavery was abolished in Surinam in 1863; so someone might still be alive who was born a slave. It was hard not to think of slavery, and not only because of the reminders on every side of big house and slave quarters. So many things in these West Indian territories, I now began to see, speak of slavery. There is slavery in the vegetation. In the sugarcane, brought by Columbus on that second voyage when, to Queen Isabella's fury, he proposed the enslavement of the Amerindians. In the breadfruit, cheap slave food, three hundred trees of which were taken to St Vincent by Captain Bligh in

* *Bush Negro Art: an African Art in the Americas* by Philip J. C. Dark (London, 1954).

1793 and sold for a thousand pounds, four years after a similar venture had been frustrated by the *Bounty* mutiny. And just as in the barren British Guiana savannah lands a clump of cashew trees marks the site of an Amerindian village, so in Jamaica a clump of star-apple trees marks the site of a slave provision ground. (Trinidad, with only forty years of slavery, has proportionately far fewer star-apple trees than Jamaica.) There is slavery in the food, in the saltfish still beloved by the islanders. Slavery in the absence of family life, in the laughter in the cinema at films of German concentration camps, in the fondness for terms of racial abuse, in the physical brutality of strong to weak: nowhere in the world are children beaten as savagely as in the West Indies.

West Indians are frightened and ashamed of the past. They know about Christophe and L'Ouverture in Haiti and the Maroons in Jamaica; but they believe that elsewhere slavery was a settled condition, passively accepted through more than two centuries. It is not widely known that in the eighteenth century slave revolts in the Caribbean were as frequent and violent as hurricanes, and that many were defeated only by the treachery of 'faithful' slaves. In Trinidad almost nothing is known of the bush-Negroes of Surinam, though their story might promote a recovery of racial pride.

Negro slaves had always been escaping into the bush in Surinam – in the smaller islands there was no such possibility – but the movement did not become general until 1667, in the interval between the British withdrawal and the Dutch occupation. The movement continued throughout the next hundred years, brutality leading to escape, massacres, reprisals, increased brutality. 'It is felt as a terror', an English traveller wrote as late as 1807, 'to menace a Negro with selling him to a Dutchman', and Stedman's *Narrative* shows why. 'The colony of Surinam', Stedman wrote, 'is reeking and dyed with the blood of African negroes', and this was no figure of speech. The first object Stedman saw on landing (and sketched for his book) 'damped' his pleasure at being in the tropics. It was:

... a young female slave whose only covering was a rag tied round her loins, which, like her skin, was lacerated in several places by the stroke of the whip. The crime which had been committed by this miserable victim of tyranny, was the non-performance of a task to which she was apparently unequal, for which she was sentenced to receive 200 lashes, and to drag, during some months, a chain several yards in length, one end of which was locked round her ankle, and to the other was affixed a weight of at least 100 pounds . . . I took a draft of the unhappy sufferer.

The lacerated slave with the chain, the artist with his pad: it is a curious scene. One wonders whether there was any local comment. Stedman reports none, and perhaps there was only that amused surprise which the native feels at the exclamations of the tourist. Torture was a commonplace in Surinam and never concealed. Stedman later spoke and gave a few coins to a slave who was chained for life in a furnace room; he sketched a slave who was hung alive by the ribs from an iron hook and left to die.

In the early nineteenth century the book of 'dear old Stedman' – the phrase is Kingsley's – was popular in England for its natural history and for the story of Stedman's romance with the mulatto slave-girl Joanna, which Kingsley thought 'one of the sweetest idylls in the English tongue'. And this popularity, this talk of idylls, is a puzzle; not only because eighteenth-century refinement falls flat today, particularly in someone like Stedman, to whom it does not come easily; but because Stedman's story is terrifying and in its nauseous catalogue of atrocities resembles accounts of German concentration camps during the last war. Stedman was no abolitionist – he went out to Surinam to help put down the slave rebellion of 1773 – and his work cannot be dismissed as propaganda. He tried hard to display the fine sensibility which was admired at the time – he apologizes, for instance, to his 'delicate readers' for speaking of lice – and he cannot be accused of sensationalism. Yet one needs a strong stomach to read Stedman today. The Surinam he describes is like one vast concentration camp, with the difference that visitors were welcome to look round and make notes and sketches. The slave-owner had less on his conscience than the conentration camp commandant: the world was divided into black and white, Christian and heathen. White might conceivably be expected to show some scruples in his relations with black; but the Christian had no such inhibition in his relations with the heathen. In fairness to the Dutch, however, the earlier quotation should be given whole: 'It is felt as a terror to menace a Negro with selling him to a Dutchman. The Dutchman, however, has a like terror in reserve, and threatens to sell his slave to a free negro.'

The runaway slaves fought with a spirit which could not be matched by the Dutch mercenaries or the 'faithful' slaves (in Stedman's regiment there were the Negroes Okera and Gowsary, who ten years before had betrayed Atta, the leader of the Berbice slave rebellion) and they were never defeated. Towards the end of the eighteenth century hostilities ceased, and the independence of the bush-Negroes was tacitly recognized. In the forest the bush-Negro reorganized his life on the African pattern; tribes were formed, tribal territories demarcated. The bush-Negro never married outside his tribe or race and was proud of his pure African descent: it marked him as a descendant of free men. Settled along the rivers, he developed his outstanding river skills. Isolated from the world, he remembered his African skills of carving, song and dance; he remembered his African religions. He developed his language; in the far interior it became Africanized. And fifty years ago he developed a script.

In 1916 Dr C. Bonne, a physician at the Government Hospital at Paramaribo, saw one of his patients, a Bush Negro by the name of Abena, of the Aucaner or Djuka tribe, writing strange characters. Abena was quite willing to explain their significance and said that they were originated by another member of his tribe, called Afaka. Bonne came to know this Afaka, who repeatedly explained to him and to Father Morssink (a Catholic missionary) how at the time of Halley's Comet he had a dream in which a Person appeared with a sheet of paper in his hand, ordering him to devise a script for his people. The first should bring the second, the second the third; and so on. Following this vision, he devised a sign every two or three days until in the end he had about 56 characters by which he could write down his thoughts. In 1917 Bonne made a trip to the Djuka country, and by means of the new script could send messages, which were understood and acted upon.*

Though Afaka was disowned by the Granman (the etymology is obvious) of his tribe for daring to produce a script without permission, and damned as '*na wissi-wassi man*' – that wishy-washy man – his script survived; in 1958 Mr Gonggrijp sent and received messages in it. Afaka Atumisi died in July 1918. On his grave was found a cross with an epitaph in his script: '*Masa Atumisi fu da Santa Katoliki Kerki*', Atumisi was one of the Holy Catholic Church. This was not strictly true; but it was his Christian leanings which had made him suspect to the bush-Negro chiefs. Now here is the mystery: thirty-four of Afaka's signs are found in the script of the Vai tribe of Liberia. Is this an example of racial memory? Or did Afaka have a touch of the Moses of Thomas Mann's mischievous tale, *The Tables of the Law*?

An invitation to coffee. I telephoned Corly and invited him to have coffee with me at my *pension*. 'Yes,' he said, 'I will come to have some coffee with you. I will come at 7.30. We shall drink coffee until eight. But what shall we talk about after eight? The minister? Did you like your talk with the minister? Was it intellectually profitable? No? That is not the way I like it. We must fill our

---

* J. W. Gonggrijp: 'The Evolution of a Djuka Script in Surinam': *Nieuwe West-Indische Gids*, 1960, p. 40.

evening substantially. Let me see. Yes. Bruma. We shall talk about Bruma.' But at this stage I thought it better to withdraw the invitation.

I could not leave Surinam without going to the district of Coronie, whose inhabitants had endeared themselves to me by their reputation as the idlest people in Surinam and their universal description as *de luie neger van Coronie*, the lazy Negroes of Coronie.* When slavery was abolished the coconut-planters abandoned their plantations to their former slaves, who settled down to an idyllic, isolated existence (communication between Coronie and Paramaribo was by sea), chasing out all newcomers of other races, including one hundred Indians, whose energy threatened to disturb Coronie calm: to this day the Negroes of Coronie will not sell land except to Negroes, and Negroes like themselves. From time to time they need money; then they gather some coconuts and sell them to the oil factory. The factory is regarded only as a convenience and its full capacity is seldom engaged. The planners despair, but the Negroes of Coronie, who are now in possession of the vote and know their own power, refuse to be rushed. They permit Chinese to do the shopkeeping for the district; and for some reason they have allowed one Indian farming family to settle.

* From the article on Surinam in the *1958 Yearbook of Jehovah's Witnesses*:

'In spite of rough travelling conditions, crossing two rivers by ferry and finally loading all the brothers into trucks for the last stretch, 175 tired but happy witnesses reached the assembly destination, a coconut plantation called Coronie. One of the highlights of the assembly was the unexpected attendance of 408 at the public talk given across the street from the Protestant church. The sight of some 300 persons watching the baptism of twelve new brothers in a nearby canal made one think of how it must have been in the days of the apostles.

'We are proud of one of our isolated brothers, who, besides his daily fishing work on the rivers, also takes time to fish for men of good will. Although being the only witness there, he never becomes discouraged, but is known for his preaching activity.'

This at any rate is the legend in Paramaribo. Johnny, the barman at the Palace Hotel, who knew Coronie and knew its one Indian family, offered to come with me; and early one morning we started on the hundred-mile ride. Outside the town the road was unsurfaced and worn into corrugations such as might have been caused by the passage of a tank. Cyclists were masked against the dust and many of the innumerable roadmenders wore goggles.

The land was flat, always flat. The forest lay immediately behind the huts that were strung along the road. Surinam is an underpopulated country. Here it felt neglected and abandoned and, oddly, related to nothing else, with the inhabitants, mainly Javanese, lost in an unfamiliar landscape, whose monotony invited no exploration. But each hut had its provision garden; here were not the helots of the British Guiana coastland.

Cool coconut groves, spotted with soft white blurs of sunshine, announced Coronie. We stopped under the eaves of a Chinese shop and I looked for *de luie neger*. Three old men were gossiping across the road in the scant shade of a tree. Surreptitiously, because of the reported hostility to foreigners, I made ready to photograph them. I caught them posing, with fixed smiles. One man was filling a water-barrel on an ox-cart; he too posed and made his son smile. Another man was wheeling a bag of coconuts on the handlebar of a bicycle, doubtless on the way to that celebrated oil factory. No one else was around. I put away my camera. I suppose I had expected something more Arcadian, something less familiar than a run-down West Indian village with its concrete government buildings and wood-and-corrugated-iron food-shops.

Below a high hot sky the flat fields spread north to the sea, intersected by long straight canals in which one or two Van Gogh-like masted boats rested askew in the mud. We walked to the coconut fields, where the grass was thick, the ditches choked, and the mosquitoes large and vicious, injecting their stings through my khaki trousers and terylene socks. Small grey-black wooden houses on low stilts were set in clean dirt yards baked by the sun; and in these yards pomegranate trees grew, three or four to a house. Each yard had a small heap of coconuts, and in each yard there was a little wooden stand with a modest display of fruit: two or three oranges, a melon perhaps, two or three pomegranates, nothing more: stall facing petty stall across the grassy footpath and the deep ditches. Dangerously narrow lengths of board, and sometimes only a trimmed coconut tree trunk, bridged the ditches.

Johnny the barman had seven children and wanted to take back some fruit to Paramaribo. He crossed a ditch into a yard, climbed up the front steps of the house and knocked on the closed door, the lintel of which was marked in blue paint: *God is boven alles*. A window was opened; Johnny explained. Presently the door was opened and a Negro, adjusting his clothes, came down barefooted into the yard, picked some pomegranates from the low trees, tip-toeing once or twice, gave the fruit to Johnny, received some coins, politely bade us good day, went up the steps and closed the door once more.

We had some trouble locating the Indian family: the paths and ditches and houses and fields looked so alike. The house stood on a rectangular plot of land, and, with ditches on all sides, appeared moated. Rusting junk in a rusting corrugated-iron shed; a bicycle wheel against a pillar; chickens in the dust and drying mud below the two or three dwarf coconut trees; a bad-tempered barking mongrel; and the mosquitoes thick in the damp heat. A young spastic Indian woman in a slack cotton dress held the dog. We crossed the moat and made our way to the back of the house where, unprotected from the sun, a very old man with white hair and a bristle of white beard sat on the ground rubbing oil on himself. The mosquitoes left him alone; they left Johnny alone. But they fastened on to me, to my hair, my shirt, my trousers, and even the eyelets of my shoes. Movement didn't disturb them; they had to be brushed off.*

---

* Stedman once killed thirty-two mosquitoes at a single stroke.

The old man was pleased to have visitors. He had just had a nasty accident: he had fallen from the top window of his house to the ground. 'It cost him thirty guilders,' Johnny said. But the old man told the story as though it were the purest comedy. He was amused at his own decrepitude – it was, after all, so very absurd – and he invited us to share the joke. His face, though shrunken, was still handsome; his eyes were the liveliest part of him. He was born in India and had come out to British Guiana as an indentured labourer. He had served his indenture and gone back to India; then he had indentured himself again. He spoke English of a sort and Hindi, no Dutch. How did he come to Surinam? That was the sweetest part of the whole joke. He had married in British Guiana and then – he had run away from his wife! He said this more than once. That act of roguishness of forty or fifty years ago was the biggest thing in his life and had never ceased to amuse him. He had run away from his first wife!

While he spoke the woman sat with the angry dog in the shade some distance away and looked at us, playing with her loose dental plate.

And what about me, the old man wanted to know. I had been abroad? What was it like? Did people have to work? What sort of work did they do abroad? What did abroad look like? He wanted me to give him concrete details. I tried. And so I really knew this abroad? He was amused and incredulous but reverential: he called me *babu*. He could scarcely conceive a world outside British Guiana and Coronie – even India had faded, except for a memory of a certain railway station – but he felt that the outside world was the true, magical one, without mud, mosquitoes, dust and heat. He was going to die soon, on that moated plot in Coronie; and he spoke of death as a chore. In the meantime he spent his days sitting in the sun, sometimes lying down in what looked like a fowlcoop; it was only at night that he went indoors. But he was forgetting: we were visitors: would we take something? A coconut?

He rose, the woman rose, the dog growled. He took a cutlass from the dust below the house and cut a few coconuts for us.

My back itched. It was bumpy with mosquito bites. So was my scalp. Neither Italian cotton nor thick hair was protection against the mosquitoes of Coronie.

A derelict man in a derelict land; a man discovering himself, with surprise and resignation, lost in a landscape which had never ceased to be unreal because the scene of an enforced and always temporary residence; the slaves kidnapped from one continent and abandoned on the unprofitable plantations of another, from which there could never more be escape: I was glad to leave Coronie, for, more than lazy Negroes, it held the full desolation that came to those who made the middle passage.

5. MARTINIQUE

I HAVE NEVER cared for dressing up or 'jumping up' in the streets, and Carnival in Trinidad has always depressed me. This year, too, the 'military' bands were not so funny: they vividly recalled the photographs of the tragic absurdities in the Congo. With this Carnival depression I flew north over the Caribbean. The sea was turquoise, with blurred white banks and blue deeps; out of it rose brown islets frilled with white.

In the society page of the *Trinidad Guardian* I read that yet another American had bought a piece of the island of Tobago, following those who had bought pieces of Barbados, Antigua, Dominica, Montserrat (the Montserrat Government had been running a campaign to attract American buyers). These islands were small, poor and overpopulated. Once, because of their wealth, a people had been enslaved; now, because of their beauty, a people were being dispossessed. Land values had risen steeply; in some islands peasant farmers could no longer afford to buy land; and emigration to the unwelcoming slums of London, Birmingham and half a dozen other English cities was increasing. Every poor country accepts tourism as an unavoidable degradation. None has gone as far as some of these West Indian islands, which, in the name of tourism, are selling themselves into a new slavery. The élite of the islands, whose pleasures, revealingly, are tourist's pleasures, ask no more than to be permitted to mix with the white tourists, and the governments make feeble stipulations about the colour bar.

'And so she went down to the ladies' room,' a taxi-driver in one of these islands told me. 'And – you know these people – they thought she was just another black 'oman. And they tell she no, sorry, no black 'oman could use the ladies' room.' The taxi-driver cackled. 'They didn't know she was the minister wife, man. They had to apologize like hell. We don't stand for that sort of thing here.' For the taxi-driver it was a personal triumph that the minister's wife, if no one else, was permitted to 'mix' with the tourists.

We stopped for a few minutes at St Lucia. The landing field was next to the sea and the airport buildings were like those of a railway halt. 'Reminds me of dear old Tobago,' one bermuda-shorted tourist said. And my depression was complete.*

Martinique is France. Arriving from Trinidad, you feel you have crossed not the Caribbean but the English Channel. The policemen are French; the street name-plates in blue-and-white enamel are French; the cafés are French; the menus are French and are written in a French hand. The landscape, in the south, is not stridently tropical. Rolling pasture land, worn smooth and unfruitful by cultivation, with dark blobs of scattered trees, and little claws and tongues of land sticking out into the clear sea, suggest a gentler Cornwall. Unlike the other islands, which have one main town to which everything gravitates, Martinique is full of little French villages, each with its church, *mairie* and war memorial (*Aux Enfants de —— Morts pour la France*), each with its history and its illustrious, for whose descendants pews are reserved in the church. The radio station announces itself as 'Radiodiffusion Française'. The political posters – *Voter Oui à de Gaulle* (the referendum

---

* 'On the quiet and picturesque island of Tobago, twenty minutes' flying time to the north-east of Trinidad, the district servant said the humble inhabitants would easily take first place in the West Indies for politeness and friendly reception. There are many sheep-like persons in Tobago, and by Jehovah's undeserved kindness they will be gathered before Armageddon.' From the *1958 Yearbook of Jehovah's Witnesses*.

had taken place not long before) and *Meeting de Protestation: Les Colonialistes Ont Assassiné Lumumba* – are of metropolitan France and unlike anything else in the Caribbean. The tobacco kiosks stock Gauloises; and the advertisements are for Cinzano and St Raphael and *Paris-Soir*. Only, most of the people are black.

They are black, but they are Frenchmen. For Martinique is France, a legally constituted department of France, so assimilated and integrated that France, or what is widely supposed to be that country, is officially seldom mentioned by name. '*M. Césaire est en métropole*,' the *chef-de-cabinet* said to me, as though M. Césaire had simply motored down to the country for a long week-end and hadn't flown 3,000 miles to Paris. The myth of non-separation is carried to the extent that *routes nationales*, which presumably lead to Paris, wind through the Martiniquan countryside.

Even thirty years ago, according to Geoffrey Gorer in *Africa Dances*, a Martiniquan in the French Army in West Africa was officially a Frenchman, a cut above the native African, who was segregated from him. Times have changed; in Martinique I met a Martiniquan Negro woman who had left her home in Senegal because of African racism, to her an incomprehensible phenomenon, a sign of primitive perversity; she spoke with some bitterness and referred to herself as *une française*. In a restaurant during a tourist invasion I saw a white woman turn to a sun-glassed black Martiniquan and say, '*Nous sommes les seuls français ici*.' 'You are English?' a white Martiniquan asked me. No, I said; I came from Trinidad. 'Ah!' he said, smiling. '*Vous faites des nuances!*' Alexandre Bertrand, the Martiniquan painter, who is not altogether satisfied with conditions in Martinique and is something of a nationalist, wanted to know about the race riots in England. What had caused them? He couldn't understand how colour prejudice could exist in a country like England. His pipe almost fell out of his mouth when I told him about discrimination in housing and employment; it was like explaining the Earth to someone from another planet. 'I am glad I am a Frenchman,' he said. The word had slipped out. 'Well, a Martiniquan with French affiliations.' More than England to the British West Indian or even Holland to the Surinamer, France is the mother country to the Martiniquan. The highest positions are open to him in France; it is a cause for pride, and not surprise, that a French West Indian represents an important French town in the National Assembly and was for some time the constitutional successor to President de Gaulle.

Dr Saint-Cyr, who comes from one of Martinique's distinguished coloured families, invited me to lunch one Sunday at his in-laws' country house at Sainte Anne. Saint-Cyr was a tall, well-fleshed mulatto; but after a minute you forgot his race and were aware only of his Frenchness, in speech, manner, gestures. On the way south we stopped to meet and guide more guests, two metropolitan Frenchmen and a Frenchwoman, who were waiting in their car at the roadside. We were late for this rendezvous, and Saint-Cyr's profuse apologies were adroitly brushed aside by one of the Frenchmen: '*Mais c'est ma faute. On m'a dit qu'aux Antilles il est impoli d'arriver à l'heure.*' After this exchange of courtesies we started off, stopping at two or three places to admire, for a few calculated minutes, certain approved views. Past the smooth brown slopes of La Monnerot, we came to Vauclin, where, the fishing boats arriving as if to Saint-Cyr's order, we made a further stop to admire the picturesque haggling scenes. And so at last to Sainte Anne.

We were introduced to Madame Saint-Cyr, her father, and her two brothers who in appearance and charm were indistinguishable from Frenchmen. Guests arrived continually in new cars, up the concrete drive between the slender-trunked trees, through the old gateway, to the spacious grounds of the spacious house, which was one hundred and fifty years old, ancient by the standards of Trinidad. We sat in the low-walled veranda, drinking apéritifs of milk and rum and nutmeg, nibbling savouries of fish-fries; and we looked down past a rusting rum-factory to the sea, Diamond Rock in the distance, the light changing continuously and with it the colours of the sea and sky, Diamond Rock disappearing whenever it drizzled.*

The Prefect, a short, blunt-featured Corsican, arrived. Everyone rose to greet him and his handsome white-haired wife.

Dr Saint-Cyr announced a short swim before lunch for all who cared. I changed in one of the bedrooms upstairs. The bed was high and wide and massive. On a shelf there was a small collection of old books, among them an old edition of *La Cathédrale*, as brown and as sharply musty as only old French books can be: reflecting a once alert French taste and now suggesting, not a West Indian house, but a French house from which, with the ageing of its old and the growing-up and departure of its children, a tradition of reading had disappeared.

We drove down to the beach in two cars; and after exclamations at the beauty and warmth of the water, the whiteness of the sand, the perfection of the brain-coral found on the beach – every pleasure noted and acknowledged, it seemed, for the benefit of the host, who appeared to instruct and regulate our delight – after the briefest of dips, we went back to the house and dressed and had a further drink before sitting down at the long table, where covers had been laid for twenty or more.

Dr Saint-Cyr sat at one end of the table; the Prefect, I believe, sat at the other. First we had sea-eggs. Then lobster. Then a third fish course, the large fish appearing whole, but sliced. Then came the meat. Rice and minced meat, first of all. Then, to sighs and exclamations, a servant entered, bearing a whole roasted pig on an enormous platter. The pig was displayed to each guest, the servant

* In January 1804, during the war against Napoleon, this isolated bare rock, as faceted as a diamond, was garrisoned by the crew – one hundred and twenty men and boys – of a British cruiser, and commissioned as a sloop-of-war. H.M.S. *Diamond Rock* harassed French shipping for eighteen months and surrendered only after a fortnight's blockade by 'two seventy-fours, a frigate, a corvette, a schooner, and eleven gunboats'.

walking round the table, fighting back a smile; there were continual exclamations and even some slight applause. The pig was then taken away, to reappear presently, dismembered, on several small platters. Between courses we were refreshed with salads; and from sea-eggs to the blancmange of various flavours champagne never ceased to be poured. When coffee and brandy came it was half past four. Madame Saint-Cyr's father was telling stories about his youth and early manhood. The Prefect, who during the lunch had startled the table with the semi-official disclosure that unexpected economic development awaited Martinique, told stories about President de Gaulle's recent visit. (I had heard earlier that the President had received a welcome so rapturous that he kept asking those nearest him, '*Mais sont-ils sincères? Sont-ils sincères?*' The island was Vichy during the war.) '*Vous m'avez trompé,*' the President had told the Prefect. 'You told me it was just three steps to the Hôtel de Ville. I find it's only two.' There was laughter around the table; eyes moistened.

The Prefect left first; and two by two the other guests followed. As long as anyone stayed refreshments were passed around: coffee, brandy, ice-cream, and even tea. When most of the guests had gone. Madame Saint-Cyr read aloud a letter from her son, a student in Paris. It was full of criticisms of students and professors; its iconoclasm was greeted with laughter.

That Martinique is France, and more than in appearance, that France has here succeeded, as she has perhaps nowhere else, in her '*mission civilisatrice*', there can be no doubt. This is the aspect of French colonialism in the West Indies which has impressed English travellers from Trollope to Patrick Leigh Fermor. 'It is a significant tribute to France's management of her Empire,' Leigh Fermor wrote in 1959, 'that her distant territories should consider this (assimilation as departments into the *métropole*) to be the highest compliment and benefit they could receive.'

Yet eight years after this was written there were race riots in

Martinique in which three people were killed; and these disturbances were repeated in 1961, just a fortnight after I had left the island. The Martiniquans may all be Frenchmen, but most of them can be simple Frenchmen only outside Martinique. In Martinique they are black Frenchmen or brown Frenchmen or white Frenchmen.

In spite of all that has been said about French colour-blindness, race has always been important in Martinique. In the days of slavery the free coloured were forbidden by law to wear clothes similar to those worn by the whites; and pedigrees are so carefully watched that there is no possibility whatsoever of anyone with the least tincture of Negro blood, however unapparent, passing as white. One of the futile skills unconsciously acquired by anyone who has grown up in the West Indies is the ability to distinguish persons of Negro ancestry. I thought I possessed this skill to a reasonable degree until I went to Martinique. Time and time again I was told that a white-skinned, light-eyed, straight-haired person I had just met was really 'coloured'. Such information constantly circulates; so, in this Martinique oral tradition, family sagas are preserved.

Trinidad is more humane and allows people who look reasonably white to pass as white. Humane is perhaps not the right word, for this generosity can occasionally impose on the Trinidadian a burden of deception which the Martiniquan, who openly calls himself 'coloured' because the whole island knows he is only fifteen-sixteenths white, never has to bear. Trollope became skilled at spotting persons who were made neurotic by their incomplete whiteness; his tips hold good today.* Nevertheless there is in Trinidad an intention of tolerance and a general laxity which would

---

* ' "A nice fellow, Jones; eh? very intelligent, and well mannered," some stranger says, who knows nothing of Jones's antecedents. "Yes, indeed," answers Smith, of Jamaica; "a very decent sort of fellow. They do say that he's coloured; of course you know that." The next time you see Jones, you observe him closely, and can find no trace of the Ethiop. But should he presently descant on purity of blood, and the insupportable impudence of the coloured, then, and not till then, you would begin to doubt.'

appal the Martiniquan. And though shade distinctions exist in Trinidad, they are never as oppressive as in Martinique. This comes out clearly if one compares Lloyd Braithwaite's *Social Stratification in Trinidad* with Michel Leiris's *Contacts de Civilisation en Martinique et en Guadeloupe*. Braithwaite is a Trinidadian and a Negro; in his admirable study comedy keeps breaking in. Leiris, a Frenchman of liberal views, conducts his survey with a sustained seriousness which at times erupts into indignation.

If the French have exported their civilization to Martinique, they have also exported their social structure. The hard social prejudices of the metropolitan bourgeoisie have coalesced with the racial distinctions derived from slavery to produce the most organized society in the West Indies. In this society education and money and cultured Frenchness matter, but Negro blood is like an ineradicable commonness, a mark of slave ancestry; and in this society, with its single standard of bourgeois Frenchness, social prejudices (which might be racial prejudices) are of importance. No social prejudice, no social sanction really matters in Trinidad: standards are too diverse and society is split into too many cliques. Living in Trinidad and then as an outsider in England, I had never before experienced the organized, single-standard society where sanctions could cripple; and in Martinique I felt choked. Prejudices have been imported wholesale from the *métropole*. I could never get used to hearing coloured Martiniquans say, just like Frenchmen of a certain type, 'That damned Jew's place is in the ghetto.'

The dinner-table gossip was the most sanctimonious and the most assassinating I have ever heard – the French flavour of the last adjective is appropriate. This, combined with what an American official described to me as 'the French Antillean morality', whereby every self-respecting man has a mistress and every self-respecting woman a lover, all the island knowing exactly who sleeps with whom – this made me long for the good humour, tolerance, amorality and general social chaos of Trinidad.

The division of Martinique society into white (of certifiable purity), mulatto and black is accepted as valid and unalterable by all sections. No other territory in the West Indies could produce a popular Negro song like this:

> *Béké ka crié femme-li chérie,*
> *Mulâtre ka crié femme-li dou-dou,*
> *Neg-la ka crié femme-il i-salope.*
> *En vérité neg ni mauvais manière.*

The white man does call his woman *chérie*; the mulatto does call his woman *dou-dou*; the nigger does call his woman a stinking bitch. Nigger ain't have manners, for truth.

> *Béké ka mangé dans porcelain,*
> *Mulâtre ka mangé dans faience,*
> *Neg-la mangé dans coui.*
> *En vérité neg ni mauvais manière.*

White man eating out of ware-plate; mulatto eating out of earthenware; nigger eating out of calabash. Nigger ain't have manners, for truth.

At a higher level, it might be said that in his poems about his childhood in the nearby French island of Guadeloupe St John Perse is not forgetful of his whiteness; while the subject of Aimé Césaire's *Cahier d'un Retour au Pays Natal* is blackness. At all levels in Martinique race is important and inescapable. This is one reason perhaps why Martiniquans are all Frenchmen. All cannot be white, but all can aspire to Frenchness, and in Frenchness all are equal.

The prejudices of Martinique lose their validity in metropolitan France, and in Martinique metropolitan Frenchmen are exempt from the racial regulations of the society. But one of the paradoxes of the Martiniquan situation is that it is against metropolitan Frenchmen that animosity is directed. The policy of assimilation, which in its intention was idealistic and generous, has had unhappy consequences. It has not, as Patrick Leigh Fermor wrote, given to Martinique 'the same privileges, status and representation as the Bouches du Rhône or the Seine Inférieure'. The social benefits of metropolitan France have not been extended to Martinique: the island's economy would have been disrupted, it is said, and the expense would have been too great anyway. Investments have not come to Martinique. With the fierce jealousy characteristic of petty, tight, self-important communities, every Martiniquan capitalist ridicules and does his best to block every project in which he does not himself have a hand. Little is therefore done, and Martiniquan capital is invested instead in France and elsewhere. Martinique is poor, the middle-class Martiniquans say. Scarcely any development is possible, for no Martiniquan industry could compete with a French one; and without her connexion with France Martinique would be lost.

So Martinique produces nothing apart from sugar, rum and bananas. Couldn't they even make their own coconut oil for the margarine factory that employs seven people? Surely coconuts can grow in Martinique? 'Impossible,' says one. 'The man is mad. Pay no attention,' says another. And so the bickering goes on and coconut oil is imported, and milk is flown in from France, from the Vosges, by the Air France milk plane. And because Martinique is part of France, her unique rum cannot be exported direct to North or South America, but must first cross the Atlantic to Paris and be redirected from there, enriching middle-men all the way. Assimilation has not made Martinique an integral part of prosperous France, but has reduced the island to a helpless colony where now more than ever the commission agent is king.

For the metropolitan civil servant Martinique is a relaxing but not important post which he hopes presently to leave for higher things in the *métropole*. For the metropolitan or the Algerian *colon* with even a little money Martinique, with its unlimited cheap labour, is inviting. Unpleasantnesses continually occures; and to the coloured population the presence of French police (the Martiniquan policemen serve in France) is an added provocation.

It was the cane-cutting season, and armed French police continually patrolled the trash-littered country roads in jeeps. It was an unusual sight in the West Indies; but I attributed it to the French flair for melodrama.

In one restaurant one day a strapping young mulatto leaned across my table and said in English, with teeth-grinding passion, that he was going to start a revolution. He objected to the service that had been given to a sad little prostitute with her over-dressed baby. It irritated him, he said, to see black people being offensive to black people. He wasn't a politician; but he was going to start this revolution, kick every white out, and then hand the island over to the politicians. He had already started in a small way: he had just slapped a metropolitan in the rue Victor Hugo.

And then early one morning a young Negro called on me at the hotel. He waited patiently in the restaurant downstairs. He must have thought me a newspaperman: he said he wanted me to know certain facts about Martinique. He told me little I hadn't already learned – race, poverty, over-population – but I remembered him for his despair. He promised to call again, but never did.

The blue-suited French *chef-de-cabinet* said with wild French gestures and an official smile that there were no serious problems in Martinique. Industries were being encouraged and so on. At his back there was a large bright painting of a Martiniquan scene. The chair on which I sat, one of three for visitors, was so far from his massive desk that I had to lean forward while he leaned back and made continuous circular gestures with both hands. At the end of every long sentence the movement of his hands was arrested and I was fixed with a brief, wide smile.

It was from M. Gratian, the communist mayor of the small airport town of Lamentin, that I learned there was a strike of labourers in the country districts. The communists had been regaining strength in Martinique, and their cause had been helped by M. Gratian's administration of Lamentin. This was admitted by all to be efficient and honest and was proving an embarrassment to Gratian's opponents, who had somehow to put over the view that honesty was the worst policy. Dandling his grandchild on his knee, M. Gratian (he had been chief speaker at the *meeting de protestation: 'Les colonialistes ont assassiné Lumumba'*) said that the strike was the most important happening in Martinique. It certainly led, a few weeks later, to Martinique's most serious disturbances.

I did not know about the strike because Martinique had no daily newspaper. Surinam has six, and several weeklies besides; but in Martinique the newspapers come from Paris, with the milk. One result is that there is an acute shortage of wrapping paper; and old newspapers have to be imported in bulk from France, particularly by the banana-growers. Bananas are delicate, and before they are shipped have to be carefully wrapped. The wrapping consists of an outer sheet of stiff brown paper and an inner quilt of straw in old newspaper. Straw, brown paper and old newspapers have all to be imported from France.* And to France they presently return. The Compagnie Générale Transatlantique alone is permitted to carry cargo between Martinique and France; it is a lucky shipping line which carries the same cargo back and forth, continually making work for itself.

Martinique in the interior is prettily feudal, with a white or coloured gentry and a respectful mass of straw-hatted black people who

---

* From the article on Martinique in the *1959 Yearbook of Jehovah's Witnesses*: 'There is the opportunity of witnessing to drivers of trucks bringing bunches of bananas from the thirty-two communes of the island to load special boats. At times fifty or more of these trucks are waiting in line at the gates of entrance to the docks. The alert publisher will use the *Awake!* magazine and offer it to the driver of the first truck and work from one to the other through the whole line. A pioneer reported: "I placed more than thirty magazines within an hour's time." '

can only be described as 'peasants', the twentieth-century literary discovery, whose soft manners, acquiescence in their status and general lack of ambition or spirit can be interpreted as 'dignity'. The peasant doffs his broad-brimmed straw hat to the master, but a man is a man and the peasant will be offended if the master does not shake his hand. This fisherman-peasant was carrying live and frenzied lobsters in both hands; and, on being introduced, I only bowed. For this I was later rebuked by my host. I had wounded the peasant; and I felt I had also damaged the dignity of the host himself. I should have offered my hand; the peasant would have turned away the lobsters and offered me his forearm, his biceps or even his shoulder. So later, when I was introduced to this other peasant whose hands were thick with mud, I confidently stuck out my hand; and he, sure enough, offered me a sweating forearm.

In this village Monday was a big day for the peasants, with cock-fighting in the afternoon and folk-dancing in the evening. On the stony, rutted, pot-holed road that ran between the dripping sugar-cane – it had been raining – we passed a peasant riding erect on a ribby horse. The cockpit was in somebody's damp bare yard, on the flattened top of a low incline that rose directly from the road. It was a small pit, a wooden O, hedged with staves over which hung barefooted peasants in straw hats and topees, shouting, 'Tor! Tor!' Above the pit and around it were two tiers of seating roughly made from trimmed tree-branches; but no one sat there, apart from two or three children absorbed in their own affairs. The cock-coops stood at one side of the pit.

The heads of the fighting cocks were pecked and bloody and disfigured; so were their necks and rumps, which had been shaved and looked obscene. The cocks were tired and I felt they didn't want to fight; a Martiniquan in our party said they were of poor quality. Sometimes the cocks only rubbed their bloody necks together. Sometimes they wandered away from one another; then the shouts of the peasants brought them together again, and they leapt and pecked for a moment or so, their wings outspread. When a cock collapsed there was a roar as at a knockout, and the fight temporarily ceased, the owners climbing over the staves into the pit and holding their cocks until the bell (I believe) went.

Somehow the fight ended — I was told, though I did not see, that the spectators had been gambling heavily — and the battered cocks were taken away, their heads erect, their eyes bright and staring. Their owners caressed them and whispered endearments to them. It was an abrupt moment of solicitude and hurt and calm, both bird and owner withdrawn in the midst of the shouting that had broken out over the new fight. Blood was wiped off with fingers from rump and neck and beak. Then the owner, whispering as with pure love, put the cock's head in his mouth, sucked away the dark thickening blood and spat it out. This was done four or five times. A lemon was peeled and rubbed gently, sacrificially over the bird's torn shaved skin.

In the evening the yard was lit by flambeaux. The cockpit was occupied by gamblers, and the sloping patch of damp black earth between pit and hut by barefooted dancers. The dancers pretended to wrestle; the drummers drummed; and everyone sang '*Votez oui, pas votez non*' — the Gaullist referendum slogan already turned into a folksong. When the master joined the dance the peasants applauded, and even the gamblers in the cockpit stood up to watch and clap.

The Americans came ashore in uniform, the sailors in theirs, the tourists in theirs: the men in bermuda shorts, gay hats, short-sleeved shirts, and both men and women carrying blue overnight bags lettered 'Caribbean Luxury Cruise' or something like that. 'Where do we have lunch?' one called. 'Restaurant dee Europe,' said another, reading the sign. The French gendarmes, in their very short khaki shorts, noticeably stiffened. The taxi-drivers were feverishly on the prowl, sniffing up streets, peering through café windows, accosting everyone who looked foreign, even those who had settled down in the Restaurant de l'Europe. Very soon the tourists had disappeared from the main square. In less than half an hour they were drifting contentedly back, each carrying a bag from the Roger Albert duty-free shop, each bearing a slip of the *balisier* wild flower like a standard. An American sailor was drinking white rum straight from the bottle and shouting from one end of the rue Victor Hugo to the other. The tourists regarded him with distaste. In the bar the tall North American with the humorous face, who had been drinking steadily since the evening before and buying drinks for all who spoke to him, chanted, 'I'm not a Yank. I'm a Canadian.'

The Caribbean has been described as Europe's other sea, the Mediterranean of the New World. It was a Mediterranean which summoned up every dark human instinct without the complementary impulses towards nobility and beauty of older lands, a Mediterranean where civilization turned satanic, perverting those it attracted. And if one considers this sea, which the tourist now enlivens with his fantastic uniform, as a wasteful consumer of men through more than three centuries – the aboriginal population of some millions wiped out; the insatiable plantations: 300,000 slaves taken to Surinam, which today has a Negro population of 90,000; the interminable wars: 40,000 British soldiers dead between 1794 and 1796 alone, and another 40,000 discharged as unfit – it would seem that simply to have survived in the West Indies is to have triumphed.

There are degrees of survival. And here and there in the West Indies are little groups of 'poor whites', English, Irish, French and even German, whose poverty is their least sad attribute. Their loss is greater: they have forgotten who they are. A history book I used at school said that the Amerindians 'sickened and died'; these Europeans, during a period of unchallenged European authority, only sickened, and are like people still stunned by their transportation to the islands of this satanic sea.

It had been my intention to go to the Isles of the Saints, south of the island of Guadeloupe, to visit the Breton poor whites whom Patrick Leigh Fermor described in *The Traveller's Tree*:

The remarkable thing about them is that they have turned themselves into Negroes in all but colour, and if all the races of the Caribbean sea were to be repatriated to their countries of origin, the Saintois would now feel more at home in the African jungle than in Brittany. They have long ago forgotten the French language, and speak nothing but the Afro-Gaulish patois of the Negroes, and are more inexpert in correct French and more illiterate than the humblest black inhabitants of the Guadeloupean savannahs.

After my discovery of the Indians of Martinique, however, there was no need to visit the Saintois.

I had never known there were Indians in Martinique beyond the usual businessmen from Trinidad. I had never known that in the French islands, as in the British, indentured Indian immigrants and some Chinese had replaced slave labour after emancipation, and that seventy thousand or more Indians had come to Martinique. Unlike the Indians in British Guiana, Trinidad and Surinam, they came from South India, many from the French Indian colonies. They did not flourish. As one Martiniquan said to me, with disgust and pride, 'They died like flies.' Some of the survivors emigrated to Trinidad and settled in west Port-of-Spain. Only four or five thousand remained in Martinique, labourers on the sugar estates of the north, sweepers in the city, and they made no mark on the society; no Indian even opened a shop. It might be that their numbers were too small. Or it might be that, unlike the Indians of British Guiana and Trinidad, who came in such balanced proportions that they were able to re-create an India in miniature, with the basic Hindu–Muslim antagonism, Shia and Sunni divisions among the Muslims and a complex if rapidly disintegrating caste system among the Hindus – it might be that unlike these Indians, the Martinique Indians came from a single depressed Hindu caste. There is evidence for this in their physical similarity and their religious practices. There is the remarkable fact that just as in India the sweepers' settlement is separated, perhaps by a river, from the town, so in Fort de France the Indian sweepers are separated from the rest of the town by a canal. It is also to be noted that among those who emigrated to Port-of-Spain there was a tradition, now lost, of road-sweeping; and they have proved the most assimilable of Trinidad Indians. It is easy to see how such people, without the traditions, aptitudes and drive of other castes, would be helpless; or how any small, alien, impoverished group would remain submerged in Martinique, where society was as rigidly organized as Indian society but where standards were incomprehensible and beyond attainment. The white-mulatto-black world presented a common front of unac-commodating Frenchness; the Indian remained an outsider.

I didn't know of the existence of Martinique Indians until Alexandre Bertrand showed me his drawings of Martiniquan Hindu dancers and told me of their 'Hinduism', nothing more than an occasional sacrificial slaughter of sheep, a degraded form of the degrading *kali puja*, which, though Catholic converts, they still practise. And one Saturday Anca Bertrand drove me north to the Hindu 'chapels'. We drove through well-kept hills in all the gradations of green, through land that appeared to have been land-scaped by cultivation, with little of the tropical disorder of Trinidad; we had a glimpse of cloud-topped Mont Pélé.

The first chapel we came to was a small rectangular concrete shed with a corrugated-iron roof and walls painted in stripes of chocolate and ochre. A number of people, Negro and Indian, came out of a dingy barrack-like building in the same scuffed yard and stared: an elderly, coarse-featured, kinky-haired Indian woman, a baby on her hip, and her equally coarse-featured daughter, a very small and very old woman in spectacular rags, a tall Negress, a mulatto in a big loose cotton dress, an Indian woman in a Martini-quan turban, and a young Indian man, small and thin, with his hair in a fringe below an old felt hat, tattered khaki shorts, a torn and dirty shirt, and black mud on his bare feet. We spoke to the young man. His features were fine, as though worn away by undernourishment and underprivilege, his eyes bright and unreliable; he was even handsome, if you forgot the weakness of his face and the debility of his attenuated limbs. His head rocked like a bird's on his stick-like neck, and he continually scratched one muddy foot with the big toe of the other. He didn't speak French; Anca Bertrand had to translate his patois.

The sacrifice, he said, took place on the stone outside the chapel. The stone was below a frangipani tree, now almost bare of leaves and in full flower; delicate pink blooms were crushed into the black, chicken-trampled mud. He went off to get the keys, and the women, all silent and staring, drew closer to us. The young man came back and opened the chapel door (an arch painted in chocolate directly above) and calmly, without flourish, revealed the hideous, tallow-smelling childishness inside: one large figure on horseback to the right, one to the left, both crudely sculptured and painted in strident yellow and red, the mustachios black, the features – pathetic in this setting – aristocratic and serene. Long carved cutlasses rested on their hafts between the forelegs of the horses; the ground in front of them was dark with candle-grease. On the low concrete platform at the back there were many smaller red-and-yellow statues, the minia-ture form betraying more clearly the crudity of the hand that had fashioned the larger statues. This was the king, the young man said; and that was the queen; and those were their children.

All places of worship have a distinctive stale smell; this dark little hole smelled warmly of stale, nauseous oil and tallow. Even while we gazed, the woman with the turban – an exhibitionist, I felt – went in, loudly sucking her teeth, and lit candles before the statues. The young man, his explanation given, leaned against the wall, looking away from us and down at the mud; his face was almost hairless. There were no sacred books, he said; he didn't know whether there were any sacred songs; the 'priest' knew every-thing. How was the priest chosen? He couldn't say. Sacrifices took place when they wanted to ask a favour of the king and the queen.

What sort of favours? He didn't know; the priest knew everything, and the priest was working in the sugar-factory that afternoon.

We drove on to a small town where the sugar workers lived in hovels beside the large trailers of neatly packed canes. We went into an estate barrack-yard which contained an *épicerie* offering *huil* (comforting to see such misspellings in a French territory) and were introduced to Indian women who were quite negroid. Then into a choked little room adorned with Catholic pictures and some photographs. Here we met the estate 'driver'. He was small, black, fine-featured, though with a bulbous nose. He wore a khaki jacket and a white topee (in Martinique this appears to be a symbol of a sort of servile authority: it is worn by drivers of official cars).

He sat us down on benches and chairs and announced with peasant pride that he had worked on the sugar estate for thirty-six years and what he didn't know about sugarcane wasn't worth knowing. He didn't speak French and couldn't even understand it; he spoke the Creole patois and said he knew 'Indian'. What was the name of this Indian language? 'Tamul,' he said. And he could sing the sacred Tamul song all night. What was this song? He behaved like a man who wasn't going to reveal a secret.

His brother came in and sat on a bench against the oilcloth-covered table and said nothing. A very small boy, the driver's son, very black and handsome, drifted into the room and was introduced; he was shy and shook hands with his left hand. The driver, who was also the priest of the Hindu 'chapel', said he was born in the district and had lived there all his life. Was I an Indian? Were there Indians in Trinidad? He looked incredulous. He said he would have been able to keep up his 'Indian' if only he had someone he could practise it with. He spoke a few individual words; not knowing a word of Tamil, I didn't understand them. He allowed himself a small smile.

We were offered drinks. I accepted a green-coloured soft drink but was unable to finish it. The driver brought out photographs of his daughter's wedding and passed them around. In the photographs he was wearing a bow-tie. In one of the photographs the blindfolded bride was surrounded by unmarried girls and playing the wedding game, people pretending to be normal, to have important lives of their own. The passport-size photographs on the wall, the glasses on the table, the drinks: it was like any other hovel in the island. Only, it wasn't. Slumped on his bench, shuffling his precious photographs and quite suddenly lost in their contemplation, the driver reminded me of those Amerindians whose huts I had entered in British Guiana and Surinam. You enter a filthy Amerindian hut; your attitude is one of curiosity and recoil; the owner sits content, bemused, indifferent to your intrusion. Ask him a question and he will answer; say nothing and he will remain silent.

We roused the driver, and he took us to his chapel. The barrack-dwellers, Indian and Negro, followed us with their gaze, proud to be the object of a visitor's interest. This chapel was much smaller; it was almost like a closet. There was an eroded, indistinct carving on the sacrificial stone outside, and the statues inside were if anything cruder than those we had seen before. There were no riders on horseback, only a shelf of images. That, said the driver, pointing to one statue, was *la sainte vierge*. Was Joseph there as well? Of course, of course, the driver said, affronted that I should ask. People from all over the world came to see this chapel. Did I know that? His eldest son had done the carvings. It was a sacred art, and he had handed it down to his son. Did the Indians in Trinidad – in whose existence he made it clear he did not believe – have chapels as fine as this? They didn't? Did they have a statue of *la sainte vierge* with a bracelet? He was beginning to regard me as an impostor. There were little dark bowls of stinking oil before the statues; this oil was brought by the faithful. We walked back to the car, past a trailer packed high with canes. Did they have lorries as big as that in Trinidad? In England? I said no. He looked pleased, though not surprised.

Anca Bertrand, who is a folklorist as well as an original and accomplished photographer, had a folk-dance rehearsal that evening. It took place in a seaside settlement, in a low *case* of naked corrugated-iron, which on the inside was papered over with sheets of *France Soir*. The oil lamp had a long slender glass chimney; it threw theatrical shadows. The drummers sat on their drums on a table; there were also stick-beaters and an accordionist. After much chatter space was cleared for the dancers, and they started. The dance was the *bel-air*. The ladies were old and wore large straw hats; one man wore a white topee. And in the dark *case* full of badly dressed people whose features for the most part remained purely African, in the long yellow-lit room where, by listening beyond the drums to the accordion, one could perceive the stringed instruments of two centuries ago, and see the dances which even now were only slightly negrofied, the atmosphere became thick and repellent with slavery, making one think of long hot days on the plantation, music at night from the bright windows of the estate house, the acrid, flambeau-lit interiors of negro-houses which were like this *case*. It was hot and the air was heavy. The dancers sweated. The old ladies, their faces hidden by their straw hats, looked down as if studying their steps. Despite their age and size they moved lightly, even daintily. The music and motions of privilege, forgotten elsewhere, still lived here in a ghostly, beggared elegance: to this mincing mimicry the violence and improvisation and awesome skill of African dancing had been reduced.

To the people of Trinidad, Wilberforce is a name in a history book. In Martinique the name of Schoelcher, the emancipator who came a decade after Wilberforce, cannot be avoided. He is commemorated in a grotesquely ornate building in the centre of Fort de France, in the names of streets and schools throughout the island. There is no need to ask why.

When I was making my way back late that night to the hotel, a Negro youth shouted contemptuously: 'Ey! You! You are an Englishman!' It must have been my purpleheart walking-stick – I had been limping about on one. Whatever it was, I was getting tired of the French colonial monkey-game.

6. On to Jamaica

ANTIGUA, AND AN APOLOGUE

As soon as we were seated in the British West Indian Airways plane it was no longer of importance to be French, and it was chastening to see how within minutes some of the Martiniquan passengers declined from privileged mulattoes, Frenchmen, the cream of *café-au-lait* society, into fairly ordinary Negroes, the very word 'mulatto', with its precise and proud racial connotation, being used less frequently outside the French islands.

Glad as I was to leave Martinique, I was inexpressibly saddened to land in Antigua. They have sold portions of the tiny island to tourists; they have built a nice new airport to receive the tourists; and tourists were as thick on the ground as West Indians in Victoria or Waterloo Station when the immigrant boat-trains arrive. I hadn't planned to go to Antigua – I was only there because there were no direct flights to Jamaica – and had made no arrangements. A hotel list, with prices in American dollars as well, showed that I couldn't afford a hotel. I could barely afford a boarding-house; and the four-mile taxi-ride to the city would cost seventeen shillings. There was some competition among the uniformed Negro taxi-drivers to take this sum off me. I chose one driver, and we scooted away before the disapprobation of the others.

'They don't like me here, you know,' my taxi-driver said, quickly getting in his taxi-driver's chatter (we didn't, after all, have far to go). 'I am not a native of this place, you know. I know these Antiguans well, man. Is only when you live here as long as me that you know the sort of animal it is.'

We stopped outside a pinkish wooden house, at the downstairs window of which I saw two patriarchal Negroes. My bag was passed up to them from the street, and I entered a shabby room furnished in the dark crowded style of Negro petty bourgeois houses. There were calendars and holy pictures on the walls. A side door opened on to a garden where chipped metal tables and chairs rusted below trees. The bulky radio was turned up loud: the Antigua Broadcasting Service, just a few days old, playing records. The announcer had a soft voice that was charged with delight and became reverential during his frequent breaks for station identification. When, at two o'clock, he had to close the transmission, I could feel his grief.

I went out to explore the town of St John's. It was dead and empty and lay bleaching in the sun. The houses were white and low, the streets wide and straight and black. Doors and windows were closed everywhere. *Jaycees say slow down and keep alive*, one sign said. And: *e.e.moore*, said another. I made my way back to the boarding-house. The window overlooking the street was closed; there was no sign of the patriarchal Negroes. The door was closed; I had no key. No one answered my call. I went for another walk down the empty white-hot street; came back and banged on the closed door; took another, longer stroll down to the *e.e.moore* sign; came back and, convinced now that I had no audience, banged in long hysterical bursts until, abruptly, the door yielded, and a servant, very calm, let me in without a word. I walked quietly up to my tiny room, where curtains and bedspread and linoleum were in small flowered patterns.

I couldn't sleep. If four miles cost seventeen shillings I clearly didn't have the money for a taxi to Nelson's derelict dockyard (regarded in its time as one of the Royal Navy's most insalubrious stations). My suitcases were at the airport. I had no books, no paper, and my pen had been emptied for the aeroplane flight. I began tiptoeing through the house, looking. I fiddled timorously with the radio. No sound came out of it. In a passageway off the drawing room I saw a bookcase with some tattered magazines and a few bound books. The magazines were religious and warned of the coming end of the world. The books were all 'Yearbooks'. Opening the *1959 Yearbook of Jehovah's Witnesses* at random, I read: 'Guatemala. There was a hectic five months of provincial rule following the shooting of the Guatemalan president, but the preaching word had to go on.' I turned a few pages and read: 'Bequia. Investigation reveals that the good efforts of two pioneer sisters are largely nullified by loose morals of those professing interest in the truth.' I took the book up to my room.

Just before four it occurred to me that there might be a telephone service in Antigua. I prowled through the empty house and was overjoyed to find a telephone and a toy telephone directory. I began telephoning government departments. Sometimes I put the telephone down when a voice answered; sometimes I got no reply; sometimes I made an appeal for help. At last, to my surprise, I drew a positive response, from a kind voice which I had heard before: it belonged to the announcer of the Antigua Broadcasting Service.

Fifteen minutes later he came, and drove me to the two-roomed radio station which stood closed and deserted in a sun-scorched field. He had the keys to the building; we went in. While he made ready for the evening transmission, I looked through the station's records and tapes. I came across a tape of one of my own broadcasts and played it over twice.

A brisk young woman arrived. She sat before the microphone, looked at her watch and asked, 'Start off now?' My announcer nodded. The woman threw some switches and began to speak. The evening transmission had begun. I went outside and sat on the concrete steps. A horse galloped past, a Negro boy riding bareback and barefooted. The sun was going down. The low hills were growing faint and for a few moments a golden light touched the brown field.

The boarding-house was alive when I went back. The two patriarchal Negroes were at the window and a trio of young English hearties – the only other guests, and on excellent terms with management – filled the shaky old house with their rompings and laughter. The servant was muttering to herself in the kitchen, and when I passed she muttered more loudly. 'I don't know what she feel she is. Ordering me about this how and that how. Don't do this. Do that. Hm! Like she feel I bound and 'bliged to stay here, nuh. Hm! Well, you have a shock coming to you, missis.'

When I came down for dinner the English trio were talking about the race problem in the West Indies. They spoke their liberal views in loud voices; their liberalism had reduced the complex West Indian race situation to the simple and unimportant, though more satisfying, issue of white prejudice.

'Trinidad is the worst place,' one of the men said. 'The whites there are the scum of the earth. Do you know what —— told me?'

I was interested, but the no doubt sensational sentence that followed was whispered.

The girl, who was wearing tights, said loudly, 'Well, *I* have friends of *every* shade.'

The talk turned to hunting and shooting, and I gathered that the accident rate in America was higher than in England.

'In England,' the younger man said, 'you learn never to point a gun at anyone. You learn it in the nursery. If you come from a shooting family.'

The older man came over to me and said, 'Excuse me, sir. Do you know the doctor?' He indicated the lesser Negro patriarch. 'It's his birthday. He's just coming in and we are going to sing Happy Birthday for him.'

I pushed my coffee cup aside and ran upstairs.

The announcer had promised to send a friend of his to help me through the evening; and shortly after the birthday gaiety the friend came and took me on a tour of Antigua by night. Once our headlamps picked out the English trio dancing in an empty street. The lounges and patios of the tourist hotels looked like Hollywood film-sets with well-drilled well-dressed extras and no stars. At one hotel the most noteworthy performer was an energetic little Negro boy. He was dressed up like a member of the band and danced without inhibition; it was generally agreed that he was cute.

The patriarch of my boarding-house had given me three sheets of ruled paper and after much searching had dug up a pencil stump. With this equipment I was working in bed late that night when I heard a knock. It was the patriarch. He was worried that I had fallen asleep and left the light on.

In the morning I discovered that the servant had been sacked.

The proprietress said, 'The young white girl ask she, all inno-cently, whether she liked the work. *And* you shoulda hear how she start up! Saying how I oppress she and work she hard and don't give she enough to eat. Shaming me in front of the poor white girl.'

'She too *lavish*,' the patriarch boomed. 'Too *lavish*.'

* * *

THE REJECTION OF BABYLON

Jamaica was a nice island, but the land has been polluted by centuries of crime. For 304 years, beginning in 1655, the white man and his brown ally have held the black man in slavery. During this period, countless horrible crimes have been com-mitted daily. Jamaica is literally Hell for the black man, just as Ethiopia is literally Heaven.

'The Creed of a Ras Tafari Man'*

* *The Ras Tafari Movement in Kingston, Jamaica* by M. G. Smith, Roy Augier and Rex Nettleford. Institute of Social and Economical Research, University College of the West Indies, 1960. I have drawn extensively from this pamphlet in this section.

Jamaica presents to the outside world two opposed images: the expensive winter resort – turquoise sea, white sands, reverential bowtied black servants, sun-glassed figures below striped umbrellas: *Tourism matters to you* is the theme of a despairing advertising campaign run by the Jamaica Tourist Board to diminish the increasing hostility to tourists – and the immigrant boat-trains arriving at London's gloomy railway stations: *Niggers go home* painted in large red letters in Brixton and *Keep Britain white* chalked everywhere.

It is possible, though, to be in Jamaica for some time without seeing either the Jamaica of the tourists or the Jamaica of the emigrants. The tourists are on the North Coast, which is separate from the rest of the island and almost like another country. And the Jamaican middle-class world, in which the visitor moves, with its spaciousness and graciousness, its tradition of hospitality, its PEN meetings and art exhibitions, its bars expensive or bohemian, its clubs and hotels, its cocktail parties and dinner parties, is physically so disposed – almost by design, it appears – that one can move from suburb to suburb and never cease to be sheltered from offending sights. On drives to the country peasants can of course be seen; but these people have little in common with the desperate and rebarbative immigrant stereotype; their manners are gentle, they have a Welsh feeling for rhetoric, and they speak the purest English of all West Indians.

To see the Jamaica of the emigrants you have to look. And once you start looking, you can see nothing else. The slums of Kingston are beyond description. Even the camera glamorizes them, except in shots taken from the air. Hovels of board and cardboard and canvas and tin lie choked together on damp rubbish dumps behind which the sun sets in mocking splendour. More respectable and on drier ground are the packing-case houses, the tiniest houses ever built, suggesting a vast arrested community given over to playing in grubby doll's houses. Then there are the once real houses packed to bursting point, houses so close in streets so narrow that there is no feeling of openness. Filth and rubbish are disgorged everywhere; everywhere there are puddles; and on the rubbish dumps latrines are forbidden by law. Pigs and goats wander as freely as the people and seem as individual and important. Outside each 'yard' there is a cluster of raised letter boxes – these Jamaicans, I was told, like writing 'little notes' to one another – and these letter boxes are like tiny toy houses which repeat the shape, number and often the positions of the buildings whose correspondence they receive. They emphasize the lilliputian aspect of the Kingston slum settlements, where everything has dwindled beyond what one would have thought possible. And wherever you look you see the surrounding Kingston hills, one of the beauties of the island: freshening now into green after rain, blurred in the evening light, the folds as soft as those on an animal's skin. Against such a view lay a dead mule, its teeth bared, its belly swollen and taut. It had been there for two days; a broomstick had been playfully stuck in its anus.

Neuroses afflict communities as well as individuals, and in these slums the sects known as the Ras Tafarians or 'Rastas' have developed their own psychology of survival. They reply to rejection with rejection. They will not cut their hair or wash; and for this neglect of the body, this expression of profound self-contempt, they find biblical sanction. Many will not work, turning necessity into principle; and many console themselves with marijuana, which God himself smokes. They will vote for no party, because Jamaica is not their country and the Jamaican Government not one they recognize. Their country is Ethiopia, and they worship Ras Tafari, the Emperor Haile Selassie. They no longer wish to be part of that world which has no place for them – Babylon, the world of the white and brown and even yellow man, ruled by the Pope, who is really the head of the Ku-Klux-Klan – and they want only to be repatriated to Africa and Ethiopia. They are not interested in – indeed, some discourage – improvements in Jamaica, for such improvements might only encourage them to remain in slavery in

Babylon. Already the Jamaican Government is compelling black men to go to England, where Queen Elizabeth I – reincarnated as Elizabeth II – and her lover Philip of Spain – reincarnated as Philip, Duke of Edinburgh – rule as the last sovereigns of white, black-enslaving Babylon. But the emancipation and triumph of the black man is at hand. Russia, the bear with three ribs mentioned in Revelations, will soon destroy Babylon. God is, after all, black; and the black race is his chosen race, the true Israelites: the Jews have been punished by Hitler for their imposture.

The Ras Tafari movement is not organized. It is split into various sects, and has no fixed hierarchy, doctrine or ritual. The movement had its origin in the back-to-Africa campaigning of Marcus Garvey (to whom several hundred speakers on the subject of racial harmony are indebted for that metaphor about the white and black piano keys). One of Garvey's statements was that the deliverance of the black race would occur when a black king was crowned in Africa. In 1930 Haile Selassie was crowned Emperor of Ethiopia. The Emperor was a brown man, and in his country there were still Negro slaves. This was unknown or disregarded. Ethiopia was an African country; it was a kingdom; it was independent. Photographs of the Emperor went up in thousands of Negro homes throughout the West Indies. What followed remains a puzzle. Several Jamaican preachers, of a type in which the island abounds, after independent study of the Bible, Garvey and the newspapers, decided that the black race in the New World were Ethiopians, that Ethiopia was the black man's promised land, that Haile Selassie was divine; and at more or less the same time began to spread this last message of hope through the slums of Kingston.

The Italian invasion of Ethiopia in 1935 was seen to fulfil certain prophecies in the Bible, and gave the movement impetus. Italian propaganda did more. Shortly after the invasion was set afoot, an Italian called Frederico Philos wrote an article alerting the white world to the existence of a secret organization of 190 million blacks pledged to exterminate the white race. The organization was headed by Haile Selassie; it was called *Nya-Binghi*, 'death to the whites', had an army of 20 million and unlimited supplies of gold. The article was reprinted in a Jamaican newspaper, and the news was received with considerable satisfaction by some of the Ras Tafari brethren. Niyabinghi groups were formed; their password was 'Death to the whites!'

In Jamaica, burning with the enthusiasms of innumerable revivalist sects, it caused no surprise that one section of the community should have withdrawn into a private world of farcical fantasy, and until the mid-1950s the Ras Tafarians were regarded as harmless vagrant lunatics made more than usually repellent by their indifference to dirt. But the movement was growing; it was attracting, particularly from America, people who were more embittered than resigned; relations with the police deteriorated. And it was only when the movement claimed its first deaths in 1960 that its strength was realized. The attitude of the middle class was one of horror and shame. There were protests when a study team from the University College of the West Indies reported on the movement with sympathetic understanding: this, it was felt, was giving respectability to rabble. While I was in Jamaica one of the convicted Ras Tafarians was due to be hanged. The local evening paper, with its zestful accounts of last hours and last words, generated the atmosphere of the public hanging, almost, it seemed, as a warning to others. So that at last what was farce had turned into grotesque tragedy.

Nationalism in Surinam, a movement of intellectuals, rejects the culture of Europe. Ras Tafarianism in Jamaica is nothing more than a proletarian extension of this attitude, which it carries to its crazy and logical limit. It resembles African nationalism, which asserts the importance of the 'African personality', and is the opposite of middle-class West Indian Negro nationalism, which is concerned only to deny the existence of a specially Negro personality. It is regarded by the largely brown Jamaican middle class as a black lower-class contagion, a sort of backyard Mau-Mau. Your gardener begins to behave strangely; his talk becomes cryptic; he speaks of the promised land of Ethiopia or Saudi Arabia (still a slave country) or even Israel; he starts to grow a beard. The Rastas have got him: you ridicule him or you sack him: henceforth he is unemployable.

The movement awaits organization and exploitation, by communists (Cuba is just to the north) or by politically ambitious racists. It may, however, frustrate or destroy those who attempt to manipulate it; for Ras Tafarianism is like a mass neurosis and can respond positively only to unreason which is on its own level of unreason. This is its greater danger. On the advice of the University College study team the Jamaican Government decided to send a mission to certain African countries to study the possibilities of Jamaican immigration. This was like treating the symptoms of a neurosis: before the mission could leave, one of its Ras Tafarian members went to prison on a marijuana charge. Repatriation, even if it comes, will not magically remove the Ras Tafarian's life-long sense of rejection and will not alter the social and economic conditions in Jamaica in which the movement flourishes.

Jamaica is eighty per cent black; and what cannot be denied is that just as in England the fascists frenziedly proclaim the racial attitudes of the majority, who are scandalized only by the exhibitionism, so in Jamaica the Ras Tafarians express the basic racial attitudes of the majority of the black population. Race – in the sense of black against brown, yellow and white, in that order – is the most important issue in Jamaica today. The hypocrisy which permitted the middle-class brown Jamaican to speak of racial harmony while carefully maintaining the shade distinctions that preserved his privilege is at last provoking anger and creating a thoroughly black racism which could conceivably turn the island into another Haiti.

The business enterprise of the Chinese and Syrian communities has aroused envy and hostility. And the rich white tourists, enjoying the private white sand beaches of hotels where the charges for one day exceed the average earnings of a Jamaican for a month, are a standing provocation; so that the Tourist Board is now equally concerned with attracting tourists and reconciling the natives to their presence. As someone connected with the 'industry' said to me: 'Chappie pays a lot of money to fly out here. He goes into his hotel, slips into his little bermuda shorts and hot shirt, hangs his little camera round his neck, sticks a cigar in his mouth, steps out into this damned expensive Jamaican winter sunshine. And *bonk*! What does he see? A poster begging the natives to be nice to him.'

The *Sunday Gleaner* of 2 April 1961 carried a whole-page article on the race problem by a student at the University College. In its frank, brutal self-analysis it recalled the mood of the Negroes of British Guiana.

THE QUESTION OF BLACK AND WHITE:
WHO HATES WHO – AND WHY
In a letter to the *Sunday Gleaner* from an unknown author

Sometime ago the Hon. R. L. M. Kirkwood made a broadcast in which he condemned the rise of the incidence of hatred of blacks for whites in the island . . .

Another worthy gentleman, Mr Barham, has written two letters to 'The Gleaner' in which he warned that the people who controlled money in this island were whites, Chinese, Syrians and Jews. He threatened that unless Negroes ceased to abuse and vilify these people they would leave the island and, so to speak, leave the Negroes to stew in their own juice – unemployment and economic stagnation.

. . . If the black Jamaican hates other races in the sense that Mr Barnham means then they express their hate differently from other people.

I feel quite sure that if the Creator offered the black Jamaicans the opportunity to be recreated as white men, eight out of every ten black persons in Jamaica would want to become white . . . The Negro as a rule shows preference for people of other races . . . We, the Negroes, love people with fair skins, straight noses, straight hair and blue eyes . . . You would think

education would make a difference but it does not. Right here at
University a black girl becomes a beauty queen only if the girls
of other types stay out . . .

There are comparatively few Negro parents who object
when their children take partners of another race. If there is an
objection, it is usually grounded in fear that the son-in-law or
daughter-in-law of another race will alienate the affection of the
son or daughter from the parents . . .

The black people of Jamaica has served and slaved for
people of other races for many a decade. Our newest masters
are the Chinese who are doing a good job of treating Negroes
the way white people do. In spite of all they have suffered the
black man still likes to serve and honour the white man in
preference to his own brethren . . .

Chinese shops are going up all around us every day all
over Jamaica and good shops they are too. But the Chinese
shopkeeper with the quickness of his race has learned to snob
[*sic*] the Negro customer when there are white or fair people
around . . .

It can't be by accident that in a country in which 75 per cent
of the people are Negroes in almost every bank in Kingston the
staff is composed entirely of people of every other race except
the Negro race. (The coloured girls in the banks would be
offended if you called them Negroes.)

It is an insult to the Negro race . . .

Today the black man, unless he has education, is still a
'black boy'. In the civil service respectable men with families
are called 'Caleb', and 'Williams' just like that because they
happen to be on the subordinate staff. If anybody thinks the
black man is satisfied with the *status quo*, he is mistaken. He
wants a change in this social structure geared to help a few and
hinder the many; he wants respect and recognition for his
status. He may be deciding that if he is not respected he won't
respect anyone. Above all he wants money and economic stab-
ility as a race. The saying 'The black man has no money' which

is true now must not be true in the next thirty years. If a change cannot be effected by social evolution then it will become necessary to use the methods the white man has used so successfully in so many countries. Either way we are going to get what we want.

As for Mr Barham and the sacred, 'divinely' appointed lords and masters of our race, if they cannot tolerate the growing-pains that the black section of society is showing, we wish them god-speed, they may go in peace. Their threats and menaces will not deter us.

Finally let me say to all black people in this island that envy and abuse of the other races is not the answer to our problems. To solve our problem this is what we must do.

   (i) Respect ourselves.

  (ii) Support our own people first – others after. All other races do this.

 (iii) Our men must show a greater sense of responsibility and physical courage.

 (iv) We must develop our capacity for independent action and do not depend on government for everything.

  (v) We must learn the value of 'group-consciousness' and be ready to sacrifice our personal and sectional interests for the good of the race.

 (vi) We have got to wipe out illiteracy and cut illegitimacy among our people.

(vii) Promiscuity of our men and the looseness of our women is sapping the vitality of our race. Our young men need to marry earlier and bring up children in well-ordered homes: as it is our young men spend most of their time philandering, drinking and carousing generally.

(viii) Get into business – scrimp and save and expand.

Not a word, you notice, about the white and black piano keys making harmony together: so far has the nationalism of the twenties and thirties grown more embittered, so close has the intellectual moved to Ras Tafarianism.

I went to the country to talk to one of the communists 'in the field'. He received me in a box-like one-room office which stood on stilts and contained two tables, one chair, one typewriter and nothing else. He stood up and began delivering an oration with so many gestures and in such a loud voice that I begged him to sit down and speak more softly. He announced with a slightly crooked smile that he was a man with 'international connexions'. It had been a long drive, and I was too hot to be frightened or impressed. He said again that he had international connexions. I invited him to have a drink in the Chinese rumshop, where we would at least have more room. He made a speech about the evils of drink. I said if he didn't come I would go alone. He shut up his little office and we drove to the rumshop. He never gave a straight reply to any question and said with a smile that he had learned 'caution'. He spoke in pure metaphor. Were the communists gaining strength in his area? 'The river must flow,' he said. To another question he replied, 'We need petrol for the lamp of revolution.' At one stage he made a long speech about the oppression of the people and the inevitability of revolution. Were they getting help from Cuba? 'I have learned caution. I am a man with international connexions. Do you think you can bell the cat?' I felt they were getting no help from Cuba. I asked him how he started. Here he became more conversational and West Indian and told me of his wartime beginnings as an agitator among Jamaican airmen in the R.A.F. 'I used to be a sort of lawyer for the boys. Whenever they was in hany real trouble I used to tell them, "Boy, your only hope is to start bawling colour prejudice." ' The memory amused him. Then, speaking as of a triumph which was yet an injustice, he said, 'They push me up to a place in Scotland. Not one black man in the place.' At this stage I saw that the move to the rumshop was an error. The two foolish Jamaicans I had brought with me from Kingston for their local knowledge were drunk. They began to speak against communism in ear-splitting shouts, and my communist, absolutely sober, responded gamely with all his distorted Jamaican Welsh rhetoric. I left them and went to the bar and took some Phensic. The shouting went on. Drink, rhetoric, loud repetitive argument: many of the Jamaican gatherings I went to ended like this.

So always in Jamaica one lived in two unrelated worlds, the world of the middle class — the businessman's Jamaican-grand, pseudo-American talk, the women's chatter about the wages of servants and the treachery of servants — and the vaster, frightening world beyond it. You went to Caymanas for the Jamaica Turf Club meeting. You had to take another trip to the Caymanas of the sugar estates: the unemployed labourers in bright jerseys idling below a tree, their faces sullen with resignation, complaining without passion about the destruction of their vegetable gardens by the estate: 'Young, young pumpkins,' they said, and made it sound like murder, though there was clearly another side to the story; the sign on the factory gate: 'Anyone found eating canes in the yard will be dismissed'; the beautiful black peasant woman with seven children by her 'present' and 'twelve in all, including abortions': 'They have no thought for us, down in the dust and the hashes.'

Beyond the world of refrigerators and motor-cars on hire-purchase ('Everybody's car-conscious,' an English girl told me), the hi-fi record players and the talk of Lawrence Durrell, one found the attitudes, little changed from those which infuriated Trollope a hundred years ago, of people who objected to regular work and were content to live from hand to mouth. Like the man in the rumshop outside Mandeville who had given up his job with the bauxite company because it simply went on and on, and he preferred intermittent employment. 'When I left the bauxite people,' he said, 'I rested myself well for a month, taking my two waters (rum and water) every day.' Each world made the other unreal; and the radio services overlaid both with an atmosphere of fantasy. The breathless, opulent gaiety of the commercial jingles of Radio Jamaica; the quality service of the Jamaica Broadcasting Company, its talks, features, well-mannered discussions and news-analyses: they both belonged to a settled, confident society. I could not associate them with the people or the land about me, and they seemed no more than irrelevant words and music in the overheated air.

*   *   *

I had been travelling around for nearly seven months. I was getting tired. In Jamaica my diary entries grew shorter and shorter and then stopped altogether. There was nothing new to record. Every day I saw the same things – unemployment, ugliness, overpopulation, race – and every day I heard the same circular arguments. The young intellectuals, whose gifts had been developed to enrich a developing, stable society, talked and talked and became frenzied in their frustration. They were looking for an enemy, and there was none. The pressures in Jamaica were not simply the pressures of race or those of poverty. They were the accumulated pressures of the slave society, the colonial society, the under-developed, over-populated agricultural country; and they were beyond the control of any one 'leader'. The situation required not a leader but a society which understood itself and had purpose and direction. It was only generating selfishness, cynicism and a self-destructive rage.

FINALE AT FRENCHMAN'S COVE

One evening Dr Lewis, the Principal of the University College, said to me, 'I have an indirect invitation for you. From Grainger Weston. He owns a place on the North Coast called Frenchman's Cove and wants to offer hospitality to someone connected with the arts.'

I had heard about Frenchman's Cove almost as soon as I had got to Jamaica. In a land of expensive hotels – thirteen guineas a day for a cramped double room in Kingston and up to twenty pounds and more on the North Coast – Frenchman's Cove was said to be the most expensive. No one was sure just how expensive. Some said two thousand American dollars for a couple for a fortnight; some said two thousand five hundred. Lunch cost five guineas, dinner nine. And even so, one Jamaican told me with almost proprietorial pride, you were turned away if it was found that you weren't in the New York social register.

It seemed, though, that once you had been accepted and had paid, your every request was granted. You could order exactly what you wanted to eat ('caviare for breakfast'); you could drink as much as you wanted ('champagne every hour'); you could take boat trips and air trips around the island; motor-cars were at your disposal, horses, rafts; you could telephone any part of the world. You could even leave Frenchman's Cove, if you didn't like it, and stay at a hotel of your choice: Frenchman's paid.

For many days after Dr Lewis had spoken to me I heard nothing. A post office strike, one eruption of the prevailing unrest, was followed by a strike of government subordinate workers. I was resignedly preparing to investigate the problems of tourism in Jamaica when the strikes ended and Mr Weston's invitation came.

We took the mountain road to the North Coast and then drove east. This part of the coast is not greatly developed; hotels do not screen the sea. The sand is in places greyish, acceptable by the standards of England and even Trinidad, but disregarded locally. (There are unfounded complaints that hotels have bought up all the white sand beaches, leaving only black sand for Jamaicans: a neat symbol of the racial resentment tourism is exciting.) The road is narrow and winding, not like the tourist road that runs west from Ocho Rios to Montego Bay, which is wide and smooth and reasonably straight and carries hotel signs, real estate signs and signs reminding motorists to drive on the left. We drove past broken-down villages, the unremarkable rural slums of the tropics: decay in lushness: pink-distempered shacks of broken boards and rusting corrugated iron, more ambitious concrete buildings, ugly and stained, dingy cafés stocked with aerated water, cakes and patent medicines, and made bright with enamelled advertisements for soft drinks. We came into Port Antonio, a banana port which is seldom busy and had ceased to grow. Then bush and black sand began once more. It was hard to think of this as a setting for luxury, a hideout for millionaires.

Presently we found ourselves driving beside a long stone wall. Separate letters attached to the wall spelled out FRENCHMAN'S COVE. We turned into the wide drive. The vegetation here was abruptly ordered and open. Beyond the asphalted area gravelled paths led up gentle inclines and disappeared. The grounds were quiet. There were two sports cars, one red, one cream, below the concrete canopy of the lodge, a low stone-and-glass building with clean straight lines. More cars were parked neatly in the sun. I looked with interest and apprehension for millionaires and members of the New York social register. I saw no one. The stillness was unsettling, but the driver behaved as though he drove up to Frenchman's Cove every day. He drove right under the canopy, came to a stop beside the glass entrance to the lodge, jumped out and opened doors and boot with a decisiveness and noise for which I was grateful.

A young Jamaican woman came out of the lodge. She said calmly, 'Welcome to Frenchman's Cove,' and gave me a letter. Thereafter things happened quickly. My driver was sent away. A Jamaican in black trousers, white shirt and a black bowtie put my luggage on a small white electric car; I sat down; and with my luggage and myself quite exposed, we drove out from under the canopy into the sunlight and up the narrow gravelled path, hearing no sound except the whirring of the motor. We followed the path where it branched right, went past a pale-green shadowed pool, then up an incline between trees. I had a glimpse of the beach: a break in the coral cliff, the water blue shading into green and almost colourless where it touched the white sand. Black canvas chairs stood in the shade of almond trees; but the beach was deserted. Climbing higher, we drove at the edge of a lawn planted with young coconut palms. Then up a sharp incline over-arched by more trees, and we came to a house. 'This is your cottage,' the driver said, stopping at the foot of the concrete steps. Throughout the drive I had seen no one.

My cottage was a complex of two grey stone cottages and a stone-and-glass house, set at different levels. The cottages were on either side of the steps, the house at the top. The stone was handcut, the blocks of varying sizes, the mortar deeply recessed. The black door of the house opened and a middle-aged Jamaican woman in spectacles, pink dress and a small white apron, smiled welcomingly.

I went in and found myself in a large high room almost at the edge of a coral cliff. The wall overlooking the sea was of glass. The terrace was set in the coral, which looked like foam rubber.

I looked at the furnishings: the low, plain, inviting chairs and sofa set on three sides of an Indian carpet with an un-Indian design, the tall lamps with pottery bases and large linen shades, the glass table spread with magazines and books (*The Power Elite* among them). It was familiar because ideal; one had known it from the escapist magazines of design; and because ideal it was a little separate from reality. The unexpected setting made the separation complete. Beyond the glass wall and rising, it seemed, out of the grey coral, were the almond trees, most artificial-looking of tropical trees, with round leaves, green and copper, set symmetrically on horizontal branches, and between the leaves one saw the high irregular cliffs, the blue sky, the limpid, dancing blue-and-green sea.

From disordered bush along the winding Jamaican road, to a drive in a comic white car through silent, deserted, landscaped grounds, to a stone-and-glass house with a view of the sea below: it was as though one had driven out of Jamaica, as though, to find the West Indies of the tourist's ideal, one had had to leave the West Indies.

Yielding to the serenity, the feeling of abrupt transference, I had not thought it strange that although moments ago it was warm, it was now cool, and though the sea below was restless, it made no sound. Now I saw that the house was completely enclosed and air-conditioned.

I read the letter the secretary in the lodge had given me. It welcomed me more formally, told me how I could get what I wanted, asked me not to tip, and gave the name of our housekeeper. Then I took up the Visitors' Book. Among its few names I saw those of a Rockefeller and the Diefenbakers.

'You will like it here,' the housekeeper, Mrs Williams, said. 'And that,' she added, 'is the telephone.'

Instantly I knew that this was the instrument, the Aladdin's lamp of Frenchman's Cove, about whose powers ('champagne every hour') all Jamaica knew. 'Anything you want,' Mrs Williams said, 'you just take up the telephone and ask for.'

The telephone was grey, of a design I had never seen: It stood upright on a round base.

'Suppose I wanted champagne?'

'Anything. The people before you, you should see them drink! Ooh! These Americans can drink. You would like the champagne now?'

I needed something stronger. 'A little brandy? Whisky?'

'Just telephone the bar.'

I hesitated.

'You're bashful.' Mrs Williams lifted the grey telephone, dialled briefly and said, 'This is Stokes Hall. My guest would like a bottle of whisky, a bottle of brandy and some sodas.'

The telephone squawked. Mrs Williams handed it to me.

'What sort of brandy, sir?' a male voice asked.

My response was automatic: I spoke the words of a well-known advertisement.

'Dudley is a good boy,' Mrs Williams said.

I was relieved that the man on the telephone had a name.

There was a knock at the door and Mrs Williams let in a European who was dressed like a chef.

'Morning, sir.' I couldn't place his accent. 'And what would you like for lunch?' He pulled out pad and pencil.

He caught me by surprise. Remembering only now that I didn't eat meat, I asked, 'Do you have eggs?'

The chef's disappointment was expressed only in the slight separation of pad from pencil.

I wished I had paid more attention to the stories I had heard ('anything you want', 'caviare for breakfast').

'Or fish?' I could think of nothing else.

Pad came closer to pencil. 'A little salmon, perhaps?'

'Yes, a little salmon.'

I watched the chef go down the hill in his little white car. Then another car came up and a bowtied Jamaican got out with a case.

'Your drinks, sir.' He seemed extraordinarily pleased. With light, swift gestures he set the bottles out; and he was gone.

Glass in hand, I explored. The bedroom extended the width of the house; its glass louvres were shadowed by trees outside. The bathroom had a sunken tiled bath which was like a small pool. And there was a carpeted dressing room. I went back to the main room, slid the glass door open and went out on to the terrace on the coral cliff. At once I was aware of warmth, wind, noises: birds, leaves, the sea below. A rowing-boat bucked in the bay.

I sat down in a low chair, shook my glass to hear the ice tinkle; and, dropping the ash from my cigarette into a dark blue ashtray, began to read *The Power Elite*.

Mr Wright Mills's style becomes almost impenetrable when taken with whisky and soda. I put down *The Power Elite* and picked up a magazine. It was an escapist magazine of design. In it I saw the carpet on which my feet rested.

Someone was at the door. Mrs Williams admitted two handsome waiters carrying a basket which I thought far too large for what I had ordered. Briskly they laid the table. Then, ceremoniously, they invited me to sit. They moved lightly and their gestures – the bows, the extended dish-bearing hand – were a little extravagant. Exaggerating their role, they behaved like benevolent magicians.

The salmon was garnished with caviare.

I heard music.

The taller waiter was standing, with his magician's smile, beside what I now recognized as a stereophonic record-player.

Within twenty-four hours my interest in food and drink had disappeared. Everything was at the end of the telephone, and it was my duty to have exactly what I wanted. But how could I be sure what I wanted *best*? Wouldn't a whisky now spoil my appreciation of the wine later? Wouldn't the wine now send me to sleep for the rest of the precious afternoon? Did I really want a soufflé? No decision couldn't be regretted. I gave up. I left everything to the chef. I never ordered a meal, and the next day I went without dinner.

The struggle between duty, to indulge, and inclination, which was not to bother, was unequal. I fell into a torpor. The whisky remained untouched beyond that first day's sampling; and at the end of my stay I had drunk only half the bottle of brandy. All the stories about Frenchman's were true. But I didn't want to go rafting or boating. I couldn't be a tourist in the West Indies, not after the journey I had made.

'You're very quiet,' Mrs Williams said. 'Just like the Diefen-bakers.'

For seven months I had been travelling through territories which, unimportant except to themselves, and faced with every sort of problem, were exhausting their energies in petty power squabbles and the maintaining of the petty prejudices of petty societies. I had seen how deep in nearly every West Indian, high and low, were the prejudices of race; how often these prejudices were rooted in self-contempt; and how much important action they prompted. Everyone spoke of nation and nationalism but no one was willing to surrender the privileges or even the separateness of his group. Nowhere, except perhaps in British Guiana, was there any binding philosophy: there were only competing sectional interests. With an absence of a feeling of community, there was an absence of pride, and there was even cynicism. There was, for instance, little concern about West Indian emigration to Britain. It was a lower-class thing; it was a black thing; it was a Jamaican thing. At another level, it was regarded with malicious pleasure as a means of embarrassing the British people, a form of revenge; and in this pleasure there was no thought for the emigrants or the dignity of the nation about which so much was being said and which on every side was said to be 'emergent'. And the population was soaring – in thirty years Trinidad has more than doubled its population – and the race conflicts of every territory were growing sharper.

Dr Arthur Lewis has drawn the distinction between 'protest' leaders and 'creative' leaders in colonial societies. It is a distinction of which the West Indies are yet scarcely aware. In the West Indies, with its large middle class and its abundance of talent, the protest leader is an anachronism, and a dangerous anachronism. For the uneducated masses, quick to respond to racial stirrings and childishly pleased with destructive gestures, the protest leader will always be a hero. The West Indies will never have a shortage of such leaders, and the danger of mob rule and authoritarianism will never cease to be real. The paternalism of colonial rule will have been replaced by the jungle politics of rewards and revenge, the text-book conditions for chaos.

In a recent issue of the *Caribbean Quarterly* there is an article called 'A Theory of a Small Society', in which Dr Kenneth Boulding, Professor of Economics at Michigan University, describes the small society's 'road to ruin':

> Population grows unchecked, doubling every twenty-five years. Emigration cannot keep pace and in any case skims off the cream of the people. Farms are sub-divided and sub-divided until the country produces far more people than it can take and the people crowd into huge city slums where there is large-scale unemployment. Education collapses under the strain of poverty and the flood of children. Superstition and ignorance increase, along with pride. Self-government means that every pressure group has to be placated, and there is less and less discrimination between high and low quality products whether bananas or people. This ends in a famine, an insurrection. The regiment shoots down the mob and establishes a military dictatorship. Foreign investments and gifts dry up; the islands are left to stew in their own misery and the world in effect draws a *cordon sanitaire* around them. That the road to ruin is a real road, and a distressingly wide and available one, is shown by the example of some nearby islands which have gone a long way down it.

'If we could,' wrote Trollope, 'we would fain forget Jamaica altogether.' The West Indies, he might have said. With immigration to Britain now controlled, a *cordon sanitaire* of a sort has indeed been drawn around the islands. The process of forgetting has begun. And the West Indies, preoccupied with its internal squabbles, hardly know it.

The day before I left Frenchman's Cove, the telephone, unusually, rang.

'Mr Naipaul? This is Grainger Weston.' The voice was brisk, even hurried. 'We wonder whether you would like to come over this evening after dinner.'

I had my last dinner and, with it, a bottle of Château Lafitte-Rothschild.

The waiter said, 'See you next season.'

The Westons didn't live in Frenchman's Cove but at Turtle Cove, a short distance away. I was not surprised to find that the house was an old-fashioned Jamaican country house, not remarkable in any way, and without air-conditioning.

Grainger Weston turned out to be a slender man with a sharp ascetic face. I thought he was in his thirties. He wore belted khaki shorts and a white T-shirt. I met his wife and his sister-in-law. We sat outside in the dark and talked, mostly about Frenchman's Cove.

Mrs Weston said they were always interested in the reactions of their guests. Some became restless; others just grew very quiet. I recognized the Diefenbakers and myself.

Drinks were brought out: ginger ale.

I offered cigarettes. The Westons didn't smoke.

Hesitantly, I asked exactly what the charges were at Frenchman's.

'I can tell you that,' Grainger Weston said. 'A thousand pounds a month for two."

Two days later I was sitting in a B.O.A.C. Britannia, bound for New York. Beside me was a well-fleshed businessman from the Bahamas. In his lapel he carried a button which marked him as a Gideon, a member of an American Bible-distributing brotherhood. My appearance marks me as a heathen. My expression is benign, my manner gentle; and all the way from Kingston to Nassau I received the Christian message.

September 1960 – December 1961